before happiness

THE 5 HIDDEN KEYS
TO ACHIEVING SUCCESS,
SPREADING HAPPINESS, AND
SUSTAINING POSITIVE
CHANGE

before happiness

SHAWN ACHOR

CROWN
BUSINESS
NEW YORK

Published in the United States by Crown Business,
an imprint of the Crown Publishing Group,
a division of Random House, Inc., New York.

www.crownpublishing.com
CROWN BUSINESS is a trademark and CROWN and the Rising Sun colophon are
registered trademarks of Random House, Inc.

Crown Business books are available at special discounts for bulk purchases
for sales promotions or corporate use. Special editions, including personalized
covers, excerpts of existing books, or books with corporate logos, can be created
in large quantities for special needs. For more information, contact Premium Sales
at (212) 572-2232 or e-mail specialmarkets@randomhouse.com.

Library of Congress Cataloging-in-Publication Data
Achor, Shawn.
Before happiness : the 5 hidden keys to achieving success, spreading happiness, and
sustaining positive change / by Shawn Achor.
p. cm
Includes bibliographical references and index.
1. Happiness. 2. Positive psychology. 3. Change (Psychology) 4. Success. I. Title.
BF575.H27A267 2013
158—dc23
2013022564

ISBN 978-0-7704-3673-5
eISBN 978-0-7704-3674-2

PRINTED IN THE UNITED STATES OF AMERICA

Line art and pyramid graphic by Tam Nguyen
Jacket design by Jess Morphew

1   3   5   7   9   10   8   6   4   2

First Edition

To Michelle Gielan,
who changed everything I knew about happiness.
She is living proof that when we shine brightly,
this world can be transformed.

contents

Acknowledgments   ix

Introduction: Beyond Happiness   xiii

The Power of Positive Genius   1

SKILL 1:   Reality Architecture: Choosing the Most
Valuable Reality   21

SKILL 2:   Mental Cartography: Mapping Your
Success Route   64

SKILL 3:   The X-Spot: Finding Success Accelerants   107

SKILL 4:   Noise Canceling: Boosting Your Positive Signal by
Eliminating the Negative Noise   146

SKILL 5:   Positive Inception: Transferring Your Positive Reality
to Others   182

Positive Inspiration: A Case for Change   226

Notes   233

Index   245

acknowledgments

As I reflect on the wild ride of the past few years—getting to travel around the world researching and speaking about happiness—I am continually humbled by the realization that I began this journey in the depths of depression while at Harvard. I remember during divinity school my first attempt at journaling, in which I wrote, "I don't remember being happy." Some people who read this book will know that place well. And others will never experience that dark night of the soul. But I know this: Change is possible only when we link our lives to others. There are no words that can convey the deep gratitude I have for all the people who make every day, during every shining success and daunting setback, joyful and worth living.

This list is only a small fraction of those people.

Michelle Gielan, my fiancée, business partner, fellow researcher, best friend . . . so pretty much she deserves an entire acknowledgment *book*. I plan on spending my life writing it. She read *The Happiness Advantage* while in the UPenn positive psychology program. She e-mailed me, we met up, started working together, and fell in love all while researching and spreading happiness. If I had only known I'd get to meet her, I would have written the book earlier.

My sister Amy (the unicorn) and my brother Bobo Blankson

for being both my compass and my rock. Their love, support, and wisdom are worth mixing metaphors. Little Ana, Gabri, and Kobi are the living fruits of their generous spirits.

Joe and Sharon Achor, lifelong educators, who taught me how to love. There is no better compliment.

Jordan Brock for his genius in helping grow our company; he believes so strongly that this research needs to be heard because he lives it as a business leader, husband, and father. He and his family are our family now.

Talia Krohn, my editor, who patiently worked with me for two years on this book as I kept trying to cram it with new research or rewrite whole sections as I got excited about something else. She's amazing.

Stuart Johnson and Meridith Simes from *Success* magazine. Stuart is a visionary and Meridith makes it happen. They are not only reinventing *Success*, but they are going to be at the vanguard of how entrepreneurs worldwide use this research. They are also incredibly generous souls and friends. Thank you to their team, including Susan Kane, who has helped spread and advance this mission.

Rafe Sagalyn, my literary agent, who believed in me from the beginning. If you want an agent, Rafe is one of the best in the industry.

Jenny Canzoneri, Holli Catchpole, and the SpeakersOffice team in California, which officially handles all our back-office logistics flawlessly and tirelessly. If you are a speaker, you couldn't find a better partner supporting your efforts.

CorpU for turning our research into an entire online academic and social course for companies worldwide. CorpU is the future of online education, so I'm so grateful that they are so interested in starting with happiness research.

Greg Kaiser, Kevin Karaffa, Greg Ray, and the entire International Thought Leader Network, including Donald Bargy, Marti Kaiser, and Reggie Tyler, for partnering with us to create a sustainable way to cascade the happiness advantage throughout companies. The parable-based train-the-trainer program we launched at Nationwide is fantastic, thanks to their dedication.

Heidi Krupp-Lisiten and Darren Lisiten from Krupp Kommunications (K2), who served as our top-notch PR team. It is great to work with a husband-wife team, as Michelle and I work hand in hand as well. They are fantastic if you want to reach multiple PR verticals and want to have fun doing it.

Crown Business team at Random House for their marketing efforts and investing so much energy in this project.

Ali Crum, a former student turned friend and inspiration. She is the rarest of breeds: a world-famous, brilliant academic with a way of connecting to anyone with her warm heart.

Marty Seligman for not only creating the field of positive psychology but also enabling an entire generation of disciples to bring this message forward.

Jeff Olson and Amber Olson, who dedicated themselves to rallying the troops at Nerium to make this research turn into a movement.

Cory Ludens and Mattress Firm for partnering with us on research and becoming a positive outlier company that thrives on passion.

Adam Grant, a modern-day genius and a new friend. Literally the smartest person I know. His book *Give and Take* is fantastic, and he helped me brainstorm several of the ideas in this book.

Gerry Richman from PBS and Colleen Steward from Tremendous! Entertainment, who partnered with us to create the PBS show for *The Happiness Advantage*. Thanks to them, the show aired in 88 percent of American homes.

Tony Hsieh, Jenn Lim, and James Key Lim at Delivering Happiness for partnering with us to help create culture change at companies based upon their incredible work at Zappos and the Downtown Project.

Christian Long and TEDxBloomington for getting us the TED spot that went viral.

Tal Ben-Shahar, who has inspired not only me but thousands like me to make positive changes, to become a better person, and to be excited about life.

Barbara Teszler, who is a PR bulldog who gets things done. She helped breathe PR life into the Institute for Applied Positive Research and *The Happiness Advantage.*

Alexis Roberts, for keeping her finger on the pulse of the happiness movement and beating a constant drumbeat of positivity.

Brent Furl, my spiritual buddy and lifelong friend, who keeps me focused on what is most important.

Kelci Brock, who is a continual source of light, wisdom, and fun. We could not do what we are doing without her.

Mike Lampert and Laura Babbitt, whose warm friendship has served as a great "Haven."

Writing a book requires massive emotional support. Thank you for my friends who were there to shoulder the burden or be patient or just be fun: Olivia "Sfouf" Shabb, Greg and Cathy McCain, Max Weisbuch, Caleb Merkl, Matt and Jess Glazer, Eric Karpinski, Heidi Hanna, and many others.

I study positive outliers: people who are up above the curve for any given dimension. This whole group of amazing outliers and friends needs to be studied more. I hope you hear their voices on every page.

introduction

BEYOND HAPPINESS

{ *If you want to change your life, you first have to change your reality.*

In my first book, *The Happiness Advantage*, I described the research on how a happy brain reaps a massive advantage in the workplace. I wrote about how, when we find and create happiness in our work, we show increased intelligence, creativity, and energy, improving nearly every single business and educational outcome. In short, that book was about how happiness comes before success. This book is about what comes before *both*. If you want to create positive change in your life, you first have to change your reality.

To be honest, I think I've learned more about happiness over the past five years than I did in a decade sitting in labs and teaching in classrooms at Harvard. During this time, I have had the opportunity to travel to fifty-one countries, speaking at companies and schools and learning more about this connection between success and happiness. But each place I visited pushed me harder. The more I observed, the more I wanted to understand how we can positively change people's view of the world to make them not just happier in the moment but more engaged, more motivated, more alive—permanently. I wanted to learn how we could help people not just succeed at certain tasks, or accomplish certain goals, but reach entirely new levels of success. But over the course of my travels I also found that it wasn't enough to study success and happiness where it was easiest: in a controlled experiment with privileged university students as subjects. I wanted to test my theories where it was hardest.

So to my mother's dismay, I was driven to lectures in Venezuela in bulletproof cars to speak with leaders under threats of "express kidnappings" about the research on resilience. I slept in huts in Tanzania surrounded by the biggest spiders I've ever seen (and I'm from Texas, so that's saying something) to hear from people who had been kicked off their land but who remained optimistic. I spoke about happiness at a public school assembly on the one-year anniversary of a mass shooting at the school. In a shantytown in Kenya I met with illiterate mothers, one of whom was determined that her eight-year-old daughter would go to Harvard someday. I was the positive psychology expert for the Everyday Matters campaign to see if happiness remains a choice for individuals with a chronic neuromuscular disease. I worked with the U.S. Department of Health and Human Services in the midst of an epidemic of depression, and Freddie Mac in the midst of a mortgage crisis. My company began working on an ambitious initiative at Walmart aimed at raising the happiness levels of their

1.5 million associates who are struggling to make ends meet in the face of complicated family and educational issues. And I met with doctors attempting to cure terminal cancer in children at St. Jude and Boston Children's Hospitals to find out why sick four-year-olds are more likely to tell their parents that "everything will be okay" than the reverse.

At the other end of the spectrum, I was invited to work with Google and Facebook as they dealt with the confusing influx of wealth that was, ironically, sapping employees of their engagement and motivation. What did I learn? That for all my research about the connection between success and happiness, I was missing something important.

Happiness led to success, true, but what gave someone—especially someone facing obstacles and hardships—the understanding that happiness was possible in the first place? Why did achievement and happiness seem like a possibility to one person but impossible to someone else in the same position or situation? Why did some illiterate mothers believe their children could get into Harvard, while others couldn't fathom the idea? Why did some of the impoverished children in Indonesia create a happy playtime with only some sticks and string, while others sat bored and sullen? Why could missing out on a bonus inspire one leader at a UK financial services company to work better and harder, while causing another leader at the same company to give up and stop trying? Why did some people diagnosed with MS suddenly start training for marathons, while others remained mired in the belief that they'd lost the ability to participate fully in life?

Soon it became clear. The reason some people were thriving while others—people in the exact same situation—were stuck in hopelessness was that they were literally *living in different realities.* Some were living in a reality in which happiness and success seemed possible, despite the obstacles. Others were living in a "reality" where it was not. After all, how could someone expect to achieve happiness *or* success when stuck in the mindset that neither was possible?

I began to realize that if we wanted to create a real, long-lasting, and sustainable change, we needed to show people how to fundamentally change their reality—the entire lens through which they viewed their world.

Of course, there are certain objective facts we must accept about our lives. Those kids in Tanzania *are* poor. Those UK bankers *did* miss out on those bonuses. Those MS sufferers *are* sick. But how we choose to *look at* those objective facts is in our minds. *And only when we choose to believe that we live in a world where challenges can be overcome, our behavior matters, and change is possible can we summon all our drive, energy, and emotional and intellectual resources to make that change happen.*

My research over the past five years, coupled with other amazing research emerging from positive psychology labs all over the globe, helped me understand what I had been missing: that *before happiness and success comes your perception of your world. So before we can be happy and successful, we need to create a positive reality that allows us to see the possibility for both.*

This book is the culmination of my research showing that there is a simple five-step process for raising our levels of success and happiness by changing our reality to positive.

But to be clear, when I say, "creating a positive reality," I don't mean simply being optimistic. I also don't mean adopting some sort of deluded view of the world in which simply wishing for wealth will suddenly result in a windfall of millions, or simply envisioning your cancer disappearing will cure you forever. This is neither positive nor productive. When I talk about a positive reality, I'm not talking about one in which good things magically happen by the sheer power of positive thinking; I'm talking about one in which *you can summon all your cognitive, intellectual, and emotional resources to create positive change, because you believe that true change is possible.*

The consistent ability to create this kind of reality is called *positive genius*, and it turns out to be the greatest precursor of success, performance, and even happiness. In this book I'll share five practical, research-based steps to help you raise your levels of positive genius and, in turn, your rates of success. The steps are:

1. *Choose the most valuable reality*: How to see multiple realities and select the one that leads to positive growth.

2. *Map your meaning markers*: How to identify and chart the best route to accomplishing your goals.

3. *Find the X-spot*: How to use success accelerants to propel you more quickly toward your goals.

4. *Cancel the noise*: How to boost the signal that points to greater opportunities, possibilities, and resources.

5. *Create positive inception*: How to amplify the effects of a positive mindset by transferring your positive reality to others.

Before potential, there is a motivation. Before motivation, there is an emotion. And before emotion, there is your *reality*.

This reality is the difference between fleeting happiness and a permanent mindset that fosters success in every personal and professional endeavor. The goal of this book is to help you become a positive genius so that you can achieve true greatness in every aspect of your life and career.

the power of positive genius

Before I was born, my father, who was a neuroscientist at UC Irvine at the time, made me an unwilling subject of one of the very first EEG experiments conducted on an unborn child. He and his colleagues hooked up electrodes to the belly of my very pregnant (and clearly very patient) mom to see if they could detect and analyze my brain wave patterns. The tests failed (I'm not sure what that says about my brain), but some influences in our lives run deep. Even before birth, I was wired for a love of psychology and science.

A mere six years later, I willingly volunteered for another neuroscience experiment, which, though of course I had no way of knowing it at the time, would ultimately lead to the writing of this book. By that point my father was a professor at Baylor University. All of my babysitters happened to be students from his introductory psychology classes, and I was in love with all of them. But as I slowly started realizing that my relationships with them weren't going as well as I'd hoped (for instance, my parents had to pay the girls at the end of the date), I decided—after observing the successes of Ariel in *The Little Mermaid*—that I would need to become part of their world. So I asked my dad if I could be part of one his classroom demonstrations. He was so excited that his son might be following in his footsteps that he didn't stop to wonder if I had ulterior motives—as indeed I did.

Regardless, he brought me to Baylor University for one of his famous lectures. I remember sitting in the bulky, brown chair in front of the class as he attached electrode after electrode to my scalp with conductive jelly. I didn't care; I was just happy because all of my girlfriends' eyes were on me.

But in his excitement about having his son in class, my dad made a simple mistake. He forgot to ground the wire and left it lying across a copper strip on the floor. When he turned on the machine, the current passed right through me—it was as though I had stuck my finger in a socket. To this day, I don't blame my dad for shocking me. I do blame him for laughing along with the entire class as I angrily pulled off all my electrodes and strode off with as much indignation as a six-year-old could muster.

Not surprisingly, I never did get to date any of his students. But I am grateful to my dad nonetheless for hooking me up to that torture machine, because his experiments gave me a lifelong fascination with studying how the brain perceives the world. That evil instrument was a primitive *evoked potential* machine, a device that records the electrical activity along the scalp, thus allowing neuroscientists to measure and record levels of activity in the brain as it processes stimuli from the external world.

Look around at the people in your office, on the subway, sitting across from you at the cafe. Have you ever wondered if the world you see is the same one they see? Have you worked with a stressed manager who constantly points out only the flaws and none of the good, or spent time with a relative during the holidays who complains about everything despite being surrounded by love, and thought to yourself: How could they *possibly* see the world that way?

The reason some people see the world so differently from others is that the human brain doesn't just take a picture of the external world like a camera; it is constantly interpreting and processing the information it receives. Every time the world provides us with information, whether the report of a down stock market, a stressful e-mail, or a smiling coworker, our brains expend energy creating our understanding of this information. This energy is called "evoked potential," and EEGs were some of the first instruments that allowed us to peek behind the curtain and better understand this process.

While the human brain receives *eleven million* pieces of information every second from our environment, it can process only forty bits per second, which means it has to *choose* what tiny percentage of this input to process and attend to, and what huge chunk to dismiss or ignore.[1] Thus your reality is a choice; what *you choose* to focus on shapes how you perceive and interpret your world.

Today, using EEGs, fMRIs, and eye-tracking machines, we have the ability to measure and study those energy patterns. And more important, we are now learning how to *change* these energy patterns to help us create a more positive interpretation of the world around us.

This is key, because *the better your brain is at using its energy to focus on the positives, the greater your chances at success.*

This book is all about how to evoke *your* potential, by changing your mindset.

EVOKING POTENTIAL

The goal of science is prediction. If you take vitamin C, doctors want to be able to predict whether it will lower your chances of getting a cold. If you drop a bowling ball at one hundred feet, physicists want to predict how hard it will hit the ground.

The goal of business is to build revenue and create sustainable, growing income. Since a business can only be as successful as the people working in it, companies have long sought a way to use science to predict high performance in individuals. Yet for all the research that has been done on the topic, no theory has ever been able to fully explain the science of human potential—until now.

Back in the nineteenth century, Sir Francis Galton was among the first to study how our brains' energy patterns predicted performance. Without the aid of EEGs, of course, he posited that intelligence could be quantified and predicted by the speed of the brain's processing system.[2] The faster your brain is at discerning sensory stimuli and reacting, he hypothesized, the smarter you are. But of course, reaction time is only one small piece of the complex equation of human intelligence.

From the 1920s through the 1980s, scientists thought potential could be measured by IQ, which was basically just a measure of one's verbal and math skills. So businesses and governments poured money into pumping up math and reading in public schools and shut down the arts and music programs. HR departments designed tests based upon IQ, then hired everyone from salespeople to CEOs using those same yardsticks of intelligence.

Problem was, they had it all wrong. As it turns out, IQ and technical skills combined predict only 20 to 25 percent of job success.[3] That means that over 75 percent of your career outcome has *nothing* to do with your intelligence and training—which is a huge problem because in a down economy companies spend a majority of their training budgets attempting to raise employee intelligence and technical skills. This money, scientifically speaking, is irresponsibly spent.

So how else can we predict professional success? If IQ is a bad predictor, maybe SAT scores, a more modern testing tool, would be better? Not the case. As a matter of fact, they are much worse. SAT scores predict only 8 to 15 percent of college freshmen's GPA, which means that for around 88.5 percent of college students SAT scores are no better at predicting academic success than a pair of dice.[4] (Again, it is a shame that we waste hours and hours preparing for predictive tests that are not actually predictive.)

The next metric businesses tried to use to predict prospective employees' performance was grades. High school grades are twice as predictive of college success as SAT scores. Great, grades must predict potential for future success in the workplace too, right? Thomas J. Stanley, PhD, author of *The Millionaire Mind*, begs to differ. After a decade of research, he found *no* correlation between grades and professional success: a coin flip would be as predictive of greatness as grades.[5] This explains the oft-cited paradox that so many C students in business school end up running companies and so many A students end up working for them.

Enter researchers like Howard Gardner and Peter Salovey. Gardner was the first to argue that the ability to understand one's own feelings as well as the feelings of others was more important than IQ. In 1990, two psychologists, Peter Salovey at Yale (whom you will read more about later) and John D. Mayer at the University of New Hampshire, published an earth-shattering paper arguing that the predictive value of IQ was low and that the ability to understand feelings was a far greater predictor of human potential.[6] They dubbed this *emotional intelligence*.

Most of you are probably familiar with emotional intelligence. It refers to your ability to *regulate* your emotions, and for the past two decades it has been thought to be the key to succeeding in the often stressful and volatile world of business. Spurred on by Daniel Goleman's internationally bestselling book *Emotional Intelligence*, which popularized research like Salovey's, companies all over the world began testing employees' and potential employees' emotional intelligence quotient (EQ) instead of IQ. The big debate among academics and at companies became, Which is more important, IQ or EQ? This is where society and science took a major wrong turn. Now, please do not misunderstand, I think emotional intelligence was one of the best theories to come out of psychology labs in the 1990s. But the question of which kind of intelligence was more important was the wrong one.

Soon, Gardner introduced his second main category of intelligence, the ability to understand and relate to other people. He called it "social intelligence," and again, Goleman introduced it to the business world with his bestselling book *Social Intelligence*. Again, the science was valid, but its value as a predictor of potential was undercut by the misguided "which is most important" debate.

Companies and researchers have been arguing this question ever since. Which is most important: IQ, emotional intelligence, or social intelligence? This is talking in circles. It's like asking which is more important in sports, offense or defense, or who is more important to a business, clients or employees. To be truly successful, instead of thinking about intelligence in isolation, we need to focus on how to *combine all our intelligences*.

Once I immersed myself in the research, it couldn't have been clearer. Yes, all these intelligences matter, but what matters most is how your brain knits them together. Thus the question should not be, which intelligence is most important, but how we can learn to harness and amplify them.

THE PRISM OF SUCCESS

How can you predict or measure greatness?

The question is not merely a preoccupation of today's leaders seeking to take their teams or companies from good to great; it's been around since the dawn of civilization. In fact, it was addressed by the very first ancient Greek philosopher.

Thales of Miletus had a problem: he wanted to figure out how great the Great Pyramid was. But as it was the tallest building created (and would be for another *thousand* years!), he could hardly measure its height with a tape measure. And sadly, he had no Internet service, so Wikipedia was out.

So how do you figure out how tall the Great Pyramid is without the ability to measure it?

Any ideas? I didn't figure it out at first, which might explain my geometry grade in high school. Fortunately, Thales did. He thought, *What if I measure the length of the pyramid's shadow? If I could do that, then perhaps I could calculate the missing leg of the pyramid.*

But as the sun moved, the shadow of the Great Pyramid would shorten or lengthen, so he soon realized he needed another piece of information: when the sun was in perfect position where the height of the pyramid and its shadow would be equal (an isosceles triangle, for those of you who like geometry). Thus he merely stuck a stick in the ground, measured the height of the stick, then waited all day until the sun made a shadow exactly equal to the height of the stick. At that precise moment, the pyramid's shadow would be equal to the height of the pyramid.[7]

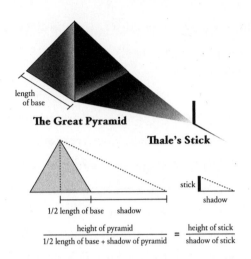

The Great Pyramid

Thale's Stick

$$\frac{\text{height of pyramid}}{\text{1/2 length of base + shadow of pyramid}} = \frac{\text{height of stick}}{\text{shadow of stick}}$$

Thales had figured out how to measure the height of the pyramid by *triangulation* when there was no other way to figure out how great it truly was.

Over the last hundred years, academic giants similarly attempted to triangulate human potential. For the last twenty years we knew that the three sides of the triangle were IQ, emotional intelligence, and social intelligence. Yet something was still missing.

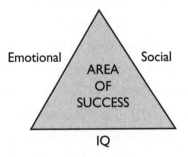

While each of these intelligences on its own had some impact, the shadow of greatness kept shifting. Like scientists studying dark matter in the universe, we knew a hidden dimension must exist, but we didn't know how to measure it. Like Thales, we still didn't know all the dimensions of the triangle.

I started working with companies in the midst of the Great Recession to find the missing dimension. At first my goal was to help companies stop making the mistake of arguing about which side of the triangle was most valuable. But I couldn't stop there, because I was still left with some really important questions: What are emotions based upon? Where does a person's perception of the world, which is not an emotion, fit in? And most important, what predicts how a person will *use* all three of the intelligences to create greatness?

After five years of extensive research, it all finally clicked: the hidden leg of the triangle—the one that allows us to summon, combine, and amplify these three existing intelligences—is the ability to *see a reality in which success is possible.*

There's no question that emotional intelligence, social intelligence, and IQ have an impact on our success rates. But these all arise from one place: our underlying reality. Because before you feel an emotion about the world, before you connect to another person, before you begin solving a problem, your brain has already created a reality about whether success can be achieved. That reality is the key to everything. It is what lets you see opportunities instead of obstacles, new roads instead of dead ends, paths to success instead of failure.

While I was consulting out in California, one of the senior innovation leaders at Google told me he felt that "some people just saw a different reality at work, which changed how much they could lead or innovate." He was right. Everything we do in business and in life is largely determined by our underlying reality, or our mindset. In other words, positive genius isn't just the amplifier of all other forms of intelligences; it's also the *precursor.*

This book does not negate all the research on IQ and emotional and social intelligence. Your IQ teaches you *what* you need to do, emotional intelligence shows *how*, and social intelligence illuminates *with whom*. Those three intelligences are the legs of your "triangle of success." But if you want to amplify your potential, you need to turn that two-dimensional triangle of success into a three-dimensional prism by constructing a positive reality *first*.

After all, you can have all the IQ and emotional and social intelligence in the world, but if you believe that your behavior doesn't matter, then you'll never bother to apply all those cognitive, social, emotional, and intellectual resources to accomplish your goals. Everyone knows someone like this, someone who has all the core intelligences but never uses them because he doesn't believe it would make a difference anyway. Unused intelligence, whether in a smart but unmotivated employee, a brilliant but disengaged student, or a visionary but disaffected leader, does nothing to evoke your potential.

Other people are experts at creating positive realities. These are the people who seem to have the Midas touch at work, the people who turn every opportunity, every relationship, every setback to gold. They are the people who continually find new possibilities to pounce on. They are the ones who discover ways around the obstacles that seem most insurmountable, the ones who solve the problems that seem most intractable.

It's not that they don't see the negative realities in the world, it's that *they also see they have the ability to do something about them.* They can see the tragedy in the earthquake in Japan or understand the difficulty in treating breast cancer or recognize the racial injustices in our educational system—but they are also the ones who search for ways to help the survivors or raise money for medical research or continue to work to invent a more fair system. These people are what I call *positive geniuses*, and in this book I'll show you how you can become one as well.

Only once we can see and construct a reality in which we have the power to create positive change—one in which our behavior matters—can we truly summon and utilize the entirety of our brain's abilities and intelligences to achieve ever-greater success and happiness. *Success, then, is not just about how much intelligence you have; it's about how much of your intelligence you believe you can use.*

This change to the way we approach intelligence changes everything. Every single business outcome—from sales volume to customer retention to revenue growth to career advancement—and even every personal outcome—from relationship quality to life satisfaction to better health—are governed by this basic equation. By mastering the five skills in this book, you will learn to turn your own triangle of intelligences into a prism of success.

Along the way I will share research showing how these skills have been used to quadruple sales at call centers, increase engagement at companies by 31 percent, raise accuracy rates among doctors by 19 percent, lower fatigue by 23 percent, increase customers' likelihood to refer by nearly 30 percent, significantly improve customer satisfaction, increase the likelihood of living to age ninety-four, raise the likelihood of a promotion by 40 percent, and even more.[8]

But that isn't the end of the story. Not only can positive genius help us see a greater range of opportunities, solutions, and routes to success, it can help others—our colleagues, our teams, our families—do so as well. Exciting new research proves that by sharing our own positive reality we can help others architect theirs, exponentially increasing the amount of collective intelligence we have available. You'll learn how to reap the benefits of this later in the book, using a technique called *positive inception.*

And here's some great news: It doesn't matter how many advanced degrees you have or how socially adept you are or how high your IQ is. *Anyone* can become a positive genius by mastering the five empirically validated skills you'll learn in this book.

BEYOND OPTIMISM: SEEING THE FULL PITCHER

In November of 2011, I got an exciting e-mail. The *Harvard Business Review* wrote to tell me that my research on the happiness advantage was going to be on the cover of their magazine for January/February 2012![9] The whole issue would be dedicated to how happiness leads to successful business outcomes. As I worked on crafting the article, I thought to myself, *Finally, this research is making it into the mainstream of business understanding and leadership. We need people to take it seriously. I just hope they don't put a big smiley face on the cover. No way they'd do that.*

When I received my copy just in time for Christmas, I had to laugh. Sure enough, I was staring at a large smiley face, with dollar sign dimples. But then I saw it: look at this cover, what's wrong with this picture? The smiley face has no eyes! It is blind happiness. This is exactly what's wrong with most people's understanding of happiness in the workplace. Happiness is not about being blind to the negatives in our environment; it's about believing we have the power to do something about them.

Once, after I gave a lecture at a large tech company, the cheerful CEO generously offered to take me to the airport so we could keep talking about how to apply my research at his company. I got into his beautiful black Escalade and put on my seat belt. He jumped in, but he didn't put on his, even when the seat belt alarm started chiming over and over. I had just met this CEO, but I decided to ask, "You don't wear seat belts?" And he energetically said, "No, I'm an optimist!"

That's not optimism, that's insanity. Optimism is good for many things, but it will definitely not keep other cars from hitting you or keep you from flying through the windshield. That is irrational optimism. An irrational optimist has a vision of reality based on *desire and delusion*, not how things actually are. Irrational optimism is why financial bubbles form, why we buy homes we can't afford, and why we prematurely put up banners that say "Mission accomplished." Irrational optimists see the world through rose-colored glasses without realizing that those tinted lens don't enhance their vision, they distort it. And as a result, their decisions and actions are Pollyannaish and flawed. You can't sugarcoat the present and still make good decisions for the future.

True success emerges from positive realities, not positive delusions. So how do we architect a reality that is both positive *and* real?

This is the question I've sought to answer in my work all over the world. In 2011, while conducting a study (later published in 2013 in the top social psychology journal) at UBS with Yale researchers Ali Crum and Peter Salovey, I had a breakthrough.

We discovered that if we could change someone's *perception* of the stress they were under, we could actually change how stress affected them physically.[10] By simply showing employees videos about the more positive (and again, real) effects of stress on the body, we observed a 23 percent drop in fatigue and other stress-related symptoms (backaches, headaches, et cetera). I'll explain this study more fully later in the book, but the point is that simply by helping people see *a new but equally true reality* in which stress could be motivating and energizing, rather than debilitating, we could make that more positive outcome actually become real.

Positive genius is not about optimism or pessimism, or seeing the glass as half empty or half full. Because in truth, half empty and half full are not the only possible options. Both optimists and pessimists are so focused on how to interpret the single glass in front of them, they can miss the fact that there is a third, equally true reality—a pitcher of water on the table to refill the glass. Positive geniuses, on the other hand, can see the full pitcher, and with it a greater range of opportunities, possibilities, and paths to success.

HOW POSITIVE REALITIES HELP US SCALE MOUNTAINS

If you are still having doubts that the skills of positive genius can help us surmount seemingly insurmountable obstacles or solve seemingly unsolvable problems or meet seemingly unmeetable challenges, consider the following example.

Two U.S. Army Rangers stand with heavy backpacks looking up at a hill in southern Afghanistan. The hill is precisely 600 feet tall. But after the mental and physical fatigue of fierce combat, the first soldier's brain judges that hill to be around 900 feet. And the soldier does more than just misjudge the hill: he actually sees a 900-foot hill, not a 600-foot hill. What he perceives becomes his reality. The steeper his brain perceives the hill to be, the more fatigued his body becomes. He collapses on one knee, ready to give up despite heavy enemy pursuit. Why soldier on when his brain tells him success is impossible?

Yet all is not lost. His fellow Ranger was recruited because she is a positive genius.

When this second Ranger looks at the hill, despite her injuries and fatigue, her well-trained brain perceives the hill as 600 feet and thus surmountable in time. This gives her the energy and motivation to quickly climb another 50 feet, upon which she notices a less steep and more rubble-free path up the hillside leading to a helicopter extraction point. Her brain is now convinced that a successful mission is possible, allowing her to summon her cognitive resources to map the best path up the hill. Now feeling even more positive and convinced that she will get herself and her partner up to the top of the hill, where they can be rescued by helicopter, her brain releases extra energy reserves, called success accelerants, allowing her to rally her physical and emotional resources to help her teammate to climb. Eliminating all distracting noises both internal and external (doubts and gunfire), she drags her partner toward the extraction point. As they climb, she tells him repeatedly that they will make it until he too finds the energy and drive to keep climbing. It's not long before they reach the top, where they are rescued. Success became their *reality*.

This is not an entirely theoretical story. In fact, it is based upon an actual experiment performed by researchers at the University of Virginia led by Dennis Proffitt, who were looking at how our perception of physical space is constructed in the brain.[11] What they found was that when we are in a negative or fatigued state of mind, our brains actually perceive hills as being significantly higher and backpacks as significantly heavier. And this principle doesn't apply just to hiking; further research has revealed that when we're in a negative mindset, *all* loads feel heavier, all obstacles loom bigger, all mountains seem less surmountable. This is especially true in the workplace, and it's why, when we look at stress, workload, and competition from a negative mindset, our performance suffers.

In the above example, IQ alone would not have saved those soldiers. Neither would emotional intelligence or social intelligence, or any combination of the above—if that Ranger hadn't *created a positive reality first*. After all, the ability to conjugate verbs and calculate standard deviations would not have gotten those soldiers to the top of the hill. Nor would the ability to regulate emotions or navigate complex social dynamics. But a positive reality could and did.

In this scenario, the second Ranger used the five skills of positive genius that you will learn in this book. First, she perceived a reality in which success was possible (skill 1). Then she mapped a route to success (skill 2). Once she made progress on that route, her brain was able to release success accelerants to get her there faster (skill 3), all the while canceling out distracting and destructive negative noise (skill 4). Then, once she had reaped the benefits of her positive reality, she created positive inception (skill 5) by transferring that reality to her teammate.

These are the exact skills you will learn in the following chapters of this book.

1. REALITY ARCHITECTURE
Choosing the Most Valuable Reality

- Recognize the existence of multiple realities by simply changing the details your brain chooses to focus on.

- See a greater range of realities by training your brain to add vantage points and see the world from a broader perspective.

- Select the most valuable reality that is both positive and true, using a simple formula called the positivity ratio.

2. MENTAL CARTOGRAPHY
Mapping Paths to Success

- Identify and set better goals by highlighting markers of meaning in your life and learning to distinguish true areas of meaning from decoys and mental hijackers.

- Chart more direct routes to your goals by reorienting your mental maps around those markers of meaning.

- Keep yourself squarely on the path to success by mapping success routes before escape routes.

3. THE X-SPOT
Using Success Accelerants

- Zoom in on the target (proximity). Make your goal seem closer by building in a head start, setting incremental subgoals, and highlighting progress to date instead of what is left to accomplish.

- Magnify the target size (likelihood of success). Increase the perceived likelihood of hitting your target by creating "champion moments" that remind you of when you have been successful in similar situations, decreasing the perceived number of your competitors, and choosing goals that you have a perceived 70 percent chance of reaching.

- Recalculate thrust (energy required). Preserve and channel your cognitive resources better, think about tasks in terms of objective units rather than in terms of the effort involved, and decrease your focus on things you worry about or fear.

4. NOISE CANCELING
Boosting the Signal by Eliminating the Noise

- Learn to cancel out any negative or useless information (noise) that distracts you from the true and reliable information that helps you reach your fullest potential (signal).

- Hone your ability to distinguish the noise from the signal by learning the four simple criteria of noise.

- Improve your ability to hear the signal through simple strategies for reducing the overall volume of noise by just 5 percent.

- Learn to actively cancel out internal noise of worry, fear, anxiety, and pessimism by emitting three simple waves of positive energy.

5. POSITIVE INCEPTION
Transferring Your Reality to Others

- Once you've created a positive reality for yourself, learn how to transfer it to others and reap the exponential benefits of your collective intelligences.

- Franchise success by creating simple, easy-to-replicate positive patterns and habits and then helping them spread.

- Wield more positive influence and increase the likelihood of your reality being adopted by taking the "power lead" in a conversation and rewriting the social script.

- Plant meaning in others' realities by appealing to emotion and crafting shared, meaningful narratives.

- Create a renewable, sustainable source of positive energy that motivates, energizes, and summons the collective multiple intelligences of those around you.

Once you master these five skills, you will see the difference in virtually every personal and professional realm. You'll be more energized, more motivated, more driven, and more productive. Your ideas will be more creative and innovative and will yield better results. You'll suddenly start seeing new routes around obstacles and faster paths to achievement. Instead of being crippled by stress and adversity, you'll be able to turn them into opportunities for growth. And once you master the final skill, positive inception, you'll be able to refract the light of your positive genius on your coworkers, clients, family members, and others around you.

BRINGING THE RESEARCH TO LIFE

If you're a reader of books on happiness, business, or leadership, you've probably noticed what I've noticed: if they quote research at all, they all tend to quote a lot of the same studies. Thus I've striven in every chapter to bring you brand-new original research done over the past few years, as well as pull from lesser-known but equally groundbreaking studies from my colleagues that haven't seen the light of day in a business book.[12]

But while all these studies paint a revealing and fascinating picture, research is useless unless it is lived. The goal of this book is not merely to entertain and enlighten; it's to show you how to *use* the skills of positive genius to improve your work performance, accomplish your professional goal and ambitions, and raise your success rates. That's why I've also included real-world stories and examples from my experiences teaching these skills in the working world—from raising positive genius at Bank of America after a 40 percent drop in stock price, to training leaders at Johnson & Johnson in the midst of one of the largest recalls in company history, to teaming up with Adobe and Google, to helping Hugo Boss transform its company by creating meaningful social interactions. Between all the science, the stories, and the research-based strategies, by the time you finish this book, you will have a deep understanding of *exactly how* to create a better reality and magnify the volume of happiness and success in your life and, equally important, how to transfer that positive reality to others.

By the time you've finished this book, you will have learned to use this five-step process to *evoke the potential* you have lying hidden and to use it to transform literally every aspect of your world. Visit the companion website at BeforeHappiness.com to see a video of me describing this research, to test yourself, or to get updates on new research since publication.

reality architecture

CHOOSING THE MOST VALUABLE REALITY

I f we want to be able to select the reality that will lead to greater productivity, engagement, and revenue growth, we first need to recognize that we have control over how we *choose* to interpret the objective facts in our external world. I learned this the hard way several hundred feet below the Pacific Ocean.

During year two of my navy scholarship, I and a dozen other future naval officers departed the coast of California on a nuclear submarine. The first night of the tour, my fellow midshipmen officers and I had the opportunity to dine with the commander. We had not met him yet, but already, on the basis of the reports I'd heard from the enlisted soldiers . . . let's just say that this guy was not leading with the happiness advantage. The soldiers were terrified of him and warned us not to make any mistakes around him. *No problem*, I thought naively.

The nicest area on the sub was the small room in which the commander dined at a table for twelve. The cooks had laid out an amazing spread with piping hot bowls of delicious food, but I barely noticed them. That's because I had gotten lost in the labyrinth of corridors on the sub and had arrived a few minutes late to the dinner. As I sprinted in, out of breath and fearful of the captain's wrath, I slid immediately into my seat, without so much as a glance at my surroundings. A split second later, the stoic commander walked into the room, followed by the nervous second in command, the XO (executive officer). The XO's body language confirmed the theory, "The closer to Caesar, the greater the fear."

The XO immediately scanned the room and noticed a horrific breach of protocol just as I did: *someone* had had the nerve to sit down while the captain was still standing. That's when I finally noticed that the rest of the midshipmen and crew were standing respectfully behind their chairs waiting for the commander to be seated before they took their own seats. Panicking, I immediately pushed my chair back to stand at attention with the rest of the midshipmen. But since it was my first night on the submarine, I had not yet been fully briefed on all the aspects of its design: for example, the fact that the chairs on a nuclear submarine are bolted to the floor.

I frantically tried to push my chair back so I could stand up, but it would not budge. Instead I looked as if I was having a minor epileptic fit in my chair while everyone else gave the commander his due respect. By the time I got myself up, everyone had sat down, and I was the only one standing there awkwardly.

While I certainly learned my lesson about arriving late to dinner, I still didn't understand one thing: Why was my chair bolted to the floor? I found out the next morning at 4:00 a.m.

I thought that the captain had already written me off as a bumbling fool, so imagine my surprise when he sent an officer to wake me up in the middle of the night and bring me to the control center. And imagine my further shock when he said he had called me there to give me the opportunity to try my hand at steering the entire nuclear submarine. (As I later discovered, this was all part of a lesson the commander often imparted to young officers—particularly the green ones like myself.)

I obediently took the wheel, and after I had steered the vessel several hundred feet, the commander took a sip of coffee from his "World's Greatest Boss" mug (really) and quietly issued an order: "Dive." Then about four officers—not very quietly, I might add—started urgently screaming, "Dive! Dive! Dive!" Instinctively, I pushed down on the controls, and the entire sub shot down at a sixty-degree angle toward the ocean floor. The hull of the submarine popped, and suddenly I felt the floor quite literally slipping out from underneath my feet. At first my brain was emotionally hijacked, but then, as I looked around, I could suddenly see why chairs had to be bolted to the floor. The room had been turned virtually on its side, and what had once been "the floor" was now at a sixty-degree angle toward what had once been the ceiling. Had the chairs not been bolted down, they would have gone flying. That was when one of the officers explained that I had just unwittingly taken part in a drill called "Angles and Dangles."

The commander then instructed me to pull up on the controls

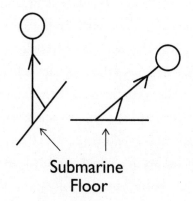

Submarine
Floor

sharply and continue until the submarine breached the surface. After the submarine crested, in what must have been a magnificent scene to someone on the outside, it plopped back underwater like a huge, exhausted catfish, and the control room lurched back to its original position.[1]

This story is not about why chairs on a submarine are nailed down, or why you should always arrive on time for dinner with the commander of a navy submarine. Looking back, I could see that Angles and Dangles had taught me a much bigger and more important lesson about the brain's ability to perceive multiple realities.

Before that day, my brain assumed that "floor = down." Period. That was my reality. But not so on a submarine. On a submarine, as I learned that day, the floor could be up, down, sideways, or at sixty degrees. The captain, through his years of experience, had no problem seeing that reality. That was why he was able to sit there smugly, sipping his coffee, while I flew backward into a bolted-down chair. And he didn't even spill a drop.

Angles and Dangles is a real treat for a brain researcher because it so perfectly demonstrates how our brains take shortcuts (which psychologists call *heuristics*) to create our perceptions of the world. Equating the floor with "down" is the simplest heuristic there could be. After all, it instinctively makes sense: gravity should always pull perpendicular to the floor, and under most conditions this is the case. So brains take the shortcut of assuming that the floor is always "down." But as Angles and Dangles demonstrated, in some instances these shortcuts fail us: if the floor is sliding out from under you, the world can look very different.

That's when I realized that in just about every situation you can think of, there exist *multiple* realities that are just as true as the realities our brains are wired to expect. And as my subsequent research has borne out, developing the ability to override shortcuts and perceive these multiple realities is the first step to expanding our triangle of intelligence to a three-dimensional prism of success.

But don't worry, this isn't nearly as hard as it might sound. Like everyone else, you have a reality that affects every decision you make and every action you undertake at home and at work. The real question is: Does your reality really work?

Research coming out of positive psychology labs across the globe shows that two individuals in the exact same situation and external world can have two completely different perceptions of the world that are both *equally* true. Because your brain can process only forty bits of information per second every minute of every day, you are merely picking and choosing from the eleven million pieces of information your senses are receiving.[2] In truth, there is not one reality: there are millions of possibilities that could be constructed into a reality in every given second. It all depends on which information your brain chooses to process! So if your reality is a choice, the important next question is: Have you chosen the one that will help you harness your multiple intelligences to their fullest potential and lead to greater success and growth? And if not, how can you select a more valuable one?

In this chapter you will learn three proven skills that you can use to improve your reality and become more engaged, productive, and innovative at work.

Strategy 1: Recognize Alternative Realities. One of the first and most important tools of positive genius is the ability to realize that multiple versions of reality exist. Otherwise, your brain will keep re-creating the same negative realities even when the external world changes. Maybe you know people like that in your office, people who always choose to see a negative reality even when the external world has changed to positive. The research I did in collaboration with Yale at UBS demonstrated that by simply changing which facts you choose to focus on, you can significantly improve your response to stress at work and decrease your fatigue symptoms by a stunning 23 percent in one week. For example, by simply adopting a "stress is enhancing" mindset, you can dramatically reduce the negative effects of stress, such as headaches, backaches, and tiredness. Stress is inevitable, but its effects are not. In this section I'll reveal how, by raising your awareness of multiple realities, you can change how the external world affects not only your work performance and success levels but even your health.

Strategy 2: Add Vantage Points. In neuroscience and positive psychology, your *vantage point* is defined as the point from which you observe the facts you will use to create your reality. For example, if you are looking at a door from one vantage point in your office, you will see a door you can easily pull open. From another angle or vantage point—say, the hallway—you might see a door that you need to push hard. But you need not have only one vantage point. In truth, both motions will open the door; it just depends which side of the door you're on. What if a manager could see that pushing people with punishments *and* pulling them with rewards could both work but that sometimes one would work better in the situation at hand? The result would be a more motivated and productive team.

Research shows that a reality at work based on only one vantage point is limited and full of blind spots and that it prevents forward movement. Let's say, for example, that you left your keys on the floor of your car. If you looked in only one window, you might not see them. But if you changed your vantage point, going to another window and peering in from another angle, you could. The same is true of situations at work. My research has shown that the simple act of *adding* vantage points—changing your viewpoint as you evaluate your options—can significantly increase your ability to see new valuable details, which, in turn, broadens your perspective and helps you find a broader range of ideas and solutions. In addition, researchers have found that the ability to add vantage points is crucial to creativity and innovation. By merely adding vantage points, you can begin to combine your emotional intelligence, social intelligence, and IQ to solve bigger problems and achieve more ambitious goals. In other words, if you want to find the keys to success, you might need to look through a different window.

Strategy 3: Pursue the Most Valuable Reality. Once you are aware that your reality is not locked, and you have added vantage points, you can pursue the reality that will help make you more successful. After all, it's not enough just to know that multiple perspectives on the world exist; you have to be able to evaluate and choose among them successfully. Research shows that by simply changing your perspective in the workplace you can achieve greater long-term growth, 37 percent higher sales, and 31 percent more productivity, and perhaps even increase your likelihood of living to age ninety-four. The ultimate goal of this chapter is to help you find and then pursue your most valuable reality in all domains of your life.

STRATEGY 1: RECOGNIZE ALTERNATIVE REALITIES

The economic crisis and recession of 2008–11 created a work equivalent of the navy's Angles and Dangles, as tens of thousands of Americans felt the ground slip out from underneath their feet. I witnessed it firsthand when I was called in to consult with nonprofit groups and temp agencies who were attempting to help the unemployed find jobs. It was sobering to see how many of the newly unemployed suddenly found themselves in a world in which their employers of twenty years had dropped them like a hot potato, they had no backup options, and their retirement account investments had been suddenly cut in half. I saw it also down on Wall Street in New York City when I was working with the survivors of layoffs at companies like UBS that had had three massive restructurings. Those who managed to escape the layoffs may have still had jobs, but they were now doing the work of more people, for lower pay, under conditions of much greater stress. The reality they had believed in—that they would continue growing their money forever—had crumbled. No wonder they were having a hard time staying engaged, motivated, and confident. No wonder their performance was suffering.

That's when I noticed something. The employees and leaders who managed to stay productive and even excel amid this chaos were the ones who were quickest to let go of those predetermined beliefs about what the world should look like. These were the people who clearly saw that there could be other realities than the one to which they had become accustomed—perhaps one in which they would live in a small but perfectly comfortable apartment instead of a mansion, perhaps one in which they would have to stick to a budget instead of spend freely, et cetera—and consciously decided to embrace, rather than run away from, those realities. It was as clear as day: those who embraced their new reality bounced back, while those who clung stubbornly to their old reality became mired in helplessness and defeat (in the same way that if that smug sub commander had clung to the floor as his anchor point for his reality, he would have had a whole lot of trouble steering that billion-dollar submarine).

It was this revelation that inspired me to further investigate how the first skill of positive genius could help businesses stay profitable and employees stay engaged and productive in the midst of the greatest economic Angles and Dangles most of us have ever seen.

RETHINKING STRESS

We've all been through it. Lying awake at night, feeling tense, thoughts buzzing through our heads. Our bodies desperately want to sleep, but our minds just can't shut off. I was having one of those nights when I got the idea for a study that would later be featured in the *Harvard Business Review*.[3]

I had gone to bed at midnight. It was now 2:00 a.m. I was still awake, completely stressed about the book I was trying to write (my last book, which, ironically, was about happiness). In an effort to unwind, I opened my laptop and started watching clips from *The Daily Show*. An ad for a popular sleep aid came on, promising me that if I took the pill, I could go right to sleep. Great, I'm in! Then for the next forty seconds a soothing voice told me that if I took the pill, I might also experience seizures, a sudden heart attack, hallucinations, extreme levels of anger, swallowing my tongue, or suicide. After an ad like that, I knew if I took that pill, I'd be much too stressed about the possible side effects to ever fall asleep. At first I thought this was part of one of Stewart's gags, but it was no joke—it was a real ad. That's when it dawned on me how similar that ad was to all the corporate trainings and talks about stress given at work.

For the past forty years, companies have been bringing in trainers and coaches to try to reduce stress levels among their employees (the idea being that a less-stressed employee is more productive and effective, not to mention a lower health liability). To get companies and employees to take stress seriously, most of these trainers and coaches have emphasized a very grim reality about stress. They highlight the following side effects:

- Stress is linked to the six leading causes of death.[4]

- Seventy to 90 percent of doctor visits are due to stress-related issues.[5]

- Stress negatively affects most of the organs in the human body.[6]

Then they say, "Have a good day and try not to stress!" Are you serious? That's like a pilot announcing to his passengers that the engine is sounding weird, then telling them to have a relaxing flight.

If you are like me, after hearing that list of side effects, you'd go back to your cubicle gripping the hell out of your stress ball and thinking, "Please don't stress, please don't stress!" You'd spend all day long stressing about not stressing, which, ironically, would probably prompt your concerned manager to send you to more stress programs to learn about how bad stress really is!

There is no question, stress can be detrimental to our work and our health. Countless books and entire research journals are dedicated to this topic. But that is not the entirety of the research on stress: in fact, there is a huge body of research showing that, if managed correctly, stress can be *enhancing* to both our performance and our overall well-being. There exists an alternate but equally true reality in which stress is actually good for us.

I was convinced that focusing on the negative impact of stress only makes it worse—just as thinking about the side effects of a sleeping pill would only keep me up at night. So I wondered, as I lay there tossing and turning, what would happen if we reframed the way we thought about stress, focusing on positive rather than negative truths about its side effects. Just as on the submarine the floor isn't always down, stress isn't always debilitating. So if we can use the tools of positive genius to change the way we *perceive* stress, I thought, couldn't we reduce the negative effects of stress on the brain and body? To test that theory, Yale researchers Ali Crum and Peter Salovey and I teamed up with senior leaders at UBS and enlisted 380 managers to help test whether we could turn stress from debilitating to enhancing merely by developing people's ability to see that alternate and equally true reality.

Crum and I showed different three-minute videos to two groups of UBS managers. The first group watched a video that contained the above-mentioned statistics typically cited in corporate trainings on stress and other findings such as the following:

- An estimated one million workers are absent on an average workday because of stress-related complaints.[7]

- "Stress's effects upon reproduction, growth, and immunity identifies it as a threat to the survival of humanity."[8]

The second group watched a video that painted a different picture, focusing on scientific findings that stress can help the brain use more of its capabilities, improve memory and intelligence, and even help the body recover from injury:

- Hormones released in the stress response actually boost performance on cognitive tasks and memory.[9]

- The narrowing of perspective recruits attentional resources and can actually increase the speed at which the brain processes information.[10]

- Stress can fuel psychological thriving by positively influencing the underlying biological processes implicated in physical recovery and immunity.[11]

- Stress and adversity have in some cases been shown to facilitate the acquisition of mental toughness, deeper social bonds, strengthened priorities, and a sense of meaning, a phenomenon called post-traumatic growth.[12]

The important thing to realize is that these researched facts, though less well known, *are equally true*. Research indicates that stress, even at high levels, creates greater mental toughness, deeper relationships, heightened awareness, new perspectives, a sense of mastery, a greater appreciation of life, a heightened sense of meaning, and strengthened priorities. And doctors at Stanford University have found that because stress causes the release of growth hormones, which help rebuild cells, synthesize protein, and enhance immunity, if someone experiences a stress response before knee surgery, he or she recovers significantly faster. These are the facts we focused on in the second video ("stress is enhancing").[13]

Just one week later, we regrouped. To see how the two videos affected stress levels, we assessed the employees using several measures, including the Stress Mindset Measure (SMM), the Work Performance Scale, the Quality of Life Inventory, and the seventy-seven-question Mood and Anxiety Symptom Questionnaire (MASQ), which evaluates individual physical and mood-related symptoms. These are some of the best metrics psychologists have to assess health and stress. The results of our study were highly significant. Those who had watched the video highlighting the enhancing rather than debilitating effects of stress reported a 23 percent drop in physical symptoms associated with distress (such as headaches, backaches, fatigue). What's more, on a scale of 1 to 4, productivity assessment moved from 1.9 to 2.6—nearly a 30 percent increase.

Encouraged by these results, Crum and I then trained two hundred managers in a program called "Rethinking Stress," which showed employees how, instead of stressing about stress, they could actually use it to their advantage at work. The process involved three steps: becoming aware of the stress, looking for the *meaning* behind the stress (for example, "I'm stressed about this project because I know I'll get a promotion if I succeed"), and then, most important, channeling the stress response to improve motivation and productivity. The effects of this experiment were even more dramatic. Not only did distress decrease, but the stress became more beneficial, as evidenced by gains in the managers' work effectiveness and improvements in their health. And it's all because they were able to see that alternate reality in which stress could have positive effects on the brain and the body.

The lesson? Stop fighting stress. *Stress is a fight-or-flight response, and when you fight or flee from it, you only make it worse.* Instead, when stress happens, recognize that stress can materially improve your productivity and performance. Then think about the *meaning* behind the stress you are experiencing. This is easy; after all, you wouldn't be stressed about something if it didn't mean something to you. For example, you are stressed about work because you care about providing for your family or seeing more of the world or having an impact. When we divorce the meaning from the activity, our brains will rebel. So if you are stressed about a job interview, refocus on the chances to advance your career, and if you are stressed about a presentation you have to give to an organization, think about how your involvement with that group is making a difference. Ali Crum uses a neat trick to remind herself not to fight stress but to embrace it: she uses doorknobs as mental anchor points. For example, whenever she opens a door into a meeting, a lecture, or a job interview, the sight of the doorknob cues her brain to think about the possibility that any stress she might feel in that situation could be performance enhancing. Try creating your own anchor points to remind yourself not to fight the stress you might feel in certain situations at work.

I'm not claiming that stress is *always* positive, or trying to debunk the literature that stress does indeed have negative effects. I'm simply trying to show that there are multiple ways of looking at the effects of stress, and that one's mindset regarding stress may determine which response will be produced. Stress at work is a reality. As Patriots head coach Bill Belichick says, "It is what it is." *But while stress is inevitable, its negative effects are not.*

THE COFFEE CUP EXPERIMENT

Being raised by a neuroscientist has its ups and downs. On the one hand, you learn valuable habits like always wearing a helmet when you ride a bicycle. And no one can scare you away from drugs more than someone who can show you a real, drug-rotted cadaver brain.

The downsides are you never get to play professional football (I was so close!), and you get experimented on. A lot.

Here's a benign experiment, similar to one my dad made me do when I would visit his office as a kid (I'll spare you the traumatic details), that can help you train your brain to see multiple realities. It is called the coffee cup experiment. Note that no caffeine intake is required for this experiment, which is probably why my mom gave it the green light (there were definitely some experiments she wasn't told about until after they were over).

> Experiment: On a napkin or a sheet of paper right now, just draw
> a rough picture of a coffee cup and saucer.

Sounds easy, right? You'd be surprised. A few years ago I ran this experiment with managers at Morgan Stanley Smith Barney, and the drawings were . . . How do I say this nicely? Blind, quadriplegic cats, with no artistic training, would have done slightly better. Clearly, hiring at MSSB is not based on artistic skills.

However, when I did the experiment again, this time explicitly asking the MSSB leaders to "be creative," they fared a bit better (though they still couldn't really draw). Now, rather than that same plain mug, I got pictures of mugs that looked like the fake Holy Grails in *Indiana Jones* or had fanciful dragon handles. I got small mugs, big mugs, and many with slogans, like my navy commander's "World's Greatest Boss" mug. From two hundred employees I got two hundred wildly different mugs, all of unique shapes and sizes and with different patterns on them.

Yet for all their individuality, these drawings had one thing in common. All of them were drawn from the side view, rather than from above. Every single one.

Studies have found that when most people draw a coffee cup, they do it from the side, not the top.[14] But why? We've all definitely seen a coffee cup when we were standing above it. So why did none of these people think of drawing the mug from above?

It comes back to the prism of success. When we try to solve a problem using only one type of intelligence, we may see different solutions (or in this case different styles of mugs), but we still see from only one *perspective*. It's only when we combine our multiple intelligences that we can see from a full range of perspectives.

Practicing your own version of the coffee cup experiment can help you do just that. It doesn't have to be a coffee mug, obviously. Take any everyday object, and try to draw as many versions of it as you can envision. Think not just about different shapes, sizes, and patterns but about different angles and vantage points. It may feel silly at first, but developing this skill will pay off because it will help you to draw on your full range of intelligences to see the details, connections, and solutions that no one else sees.

To do this, however, you need to master strategy 2, adding vantage points.

STRATEGY 2: ADD VANTAGE POINTS

If you walk through the main door of the Art Institute of Chicago and enter the medieval art section, you will notice that something is dreadfully wrong. Your vision will seem distorted, as though warped by a two-martini lunch. If you stay in the room long enough, you'll begin to realize that your artificially induced vertigo is caused by the paintings. The more artistic among you will immediately know why. The paintings lack perspective. I don't mean that medieval artists were lacking in emotional intelligence and insight. *I mean that despite how deep their insights and emotions were, their artwork literally lacked perspectival depth.* These artists struggled to portray the world in three dimensions on a two-dimensional canvas. The artists among you will know why: you need multiple vantage points to paint in three dimensions. And without that third dimension, the entire painting is out of proportion; objects in the distance look the same size as objects in the foreground, and vice versa. Without perspectival depth it is impossible to see what is actually large and what is small, what is near and what is far.

Many of us in the working world today suffer from a similar lack of perspective, severely impairing our ability to see our world in the right proportions. Just as the people look virtually (and somewhat ridiculously) the same size as the buildings in those medieval paintings, many among us erroneously see the positives and negatives in our lives as more or less equivalent in size and importance. For example, all too often a minor setback—like losing a single client or screwing up on a tiny detail of a project—can loom disproportionately large over larger accomplishments and successes, like the bigger account we just landed or the last five projects we successfully completed. In 2011, I traveled to London to work with a company that had been rated "one star" in a three-star system (with three stars indicating the highest levels of employee engagement). They had hired some of the smartest people in the industry, and they had done one 360-degree feedback session after another to raise their emotional intelligence. So why was their employees' performance so lackluster? Their picture of reality lacked perspective.

Many of the employees saw only the current economic climate—one in which they were doing a lot of work but achieving only minimal gains in terms of sales. They saw that many of their leaders had jumped ship to another company. They perceived that nothing had changed over the past year, that they were still maintaining their profit levels from two years ago. Just as a medieval painter failed to create a three-dimensional picture of the world, many of the individuals at this company were stuck in a two-dimensional reality. What they were failing to recognize was that even though their numbers were flat, they were outselling all of their competitors, even ones that were far bigger. What's more, they were completely overlooking the fact that the leaders who had left were the dead-weight, uncommitted leaders and that in truth their leaving meant more room for upward mobility of true talent. And many of the employees missed out on the amazing fact that their sales had not dropped during the greatest economic downturn of recent history. If they had looked at the world from these vantage points, they might have recognized a very positive and strong reality in which growth was just over the horizon.

THE PERSPECTIVE IS IN THE DETAILS

As a Harvard guy, I try not to talk about Yale. If you can't say anything nice . . . well, you know. But they do one thing right. My brother-in-law went to Yale School of Medicine, and in the middle of their incredibly intensive medical training, his professor took his class to an art museum. The purpose of this was not to expose the Yale students to culture (if culture was their interest, they wouldn't have chosen Yale in the first place). The real reason for taking them out of the classroom was to teach them the importance of perspective and to help them train their brains to add vantage points so they could see the world in multiple dimensions.

This was a gutsy gamble: taking extraordinarily busy future doctors, who were learning the secrets of biology and anatomy so as to save human lives and cure diseases like cancer, and forcing them to go stare at centuries-old paintings and to diagnose the individuals portrayed in them. But according to Dr. Irwin Braverman, a professor at Yale School of Medicine, and Linda Friedlaender, the curator at the Yale Center for British Art, this exercise helped the doctors improve a skill that actually could save lives. As one medical student in the class said, "It made me notice things that my eyes had just not seen. In going through it in my own mind and with my peers I was able to develop a fuller story, and *that enabled me to put the pieces together in a way that was closer to the reality.*"[15]

This success was not just anecdotal. The *Journal of the American Medical Association* reported that the students who took this class exhibited an astonishing *10 percent improvement in their ability to detect important medical details.*[16] And once they were able to see this wider range of details, they were better able to leverage their IQs and EQs and all their other cognitive abilities to knit these details together and see previously missed connections. Those details, in other words, were the vantage points that broadened their perspective and made them more successful in their work.

For example, take the case of one patient who had had a stroke that had blinded her in one eye. When she came to the Yale–New Haven hospital for an examination, the doctors were understandably focused on the bad eye. They assumed the blindness was the result of blockage caused by the stroke until one of the physicians suddenly exclaimed to the team, "Oh my God, look at her lip."[17] (As a brief aside, I might suggest that doctors also be taught not to exclaim things like "Oh my God" or "What the hell is that?" while examining a patient.) In looking at her lip, that doctor noticed something that others had missed: a clear indicator of a hereditary condition called HHT that eventually robs the lungs of oxygen and is fatal unless caught early. By looking at the situation from other vantage points, that doctor literally saved her life.

In medicine, as in all professions, it is easy to get stuck seeing things from only one vantage point. But by training their brains to see more vantage points, these students learned to approach problems with a broader and deeper perspective. Today, over a decade later, all first-year Yale medical students are required to take that art class, and more than twenty other medical schools now have the course as well.

The ability to better spot and knit together details is incredibly valuable, no matter what field or profession you're in. So don't wait! Go on a tour at a local art museum and take your entire team. Or go with your family this weekend. Ask the guide to point out new details in the paintings or sculptures, then practice looking at the works of art from other angles and vantage points. Obviously this is more than just a trip to a museum: it is about consciously building a skill set that will dramatically increase your team's performance and your brain's ability to create multi-dimensional realities. What would the ability to see 10 percent more details in your work do for your performance? My guess is that it's worth an afternoon at the museum.

Here's another simple exercise to help you add vantage points in your professional life. Let me ask you a seemingly simple question. What is work like for you right now? Write your answer down on a scrap of paper. Now take a moment and think about what you just wrote down. Did your version of reality leave out some important details? If you mentioned a volatile work environment, did you also mention opportunities for promotions? If you mentioned your heavy workload, did you also mention the amount of authority and responsibility you have? If you mentioned high levels of stress, did you mention your social support network and strong relationships with colleagues? Now, using only true statements, offer an alternative description of the exact same work situation. Finally, write down a *third* version of your working life that mentions none of the details you mentioned in the first two realities. This will be hard, and you will feel as if your brain has to stretch, but stay with it. Maybe this list includes a chance to help others with your work. Or the mission you have to serve your clients. Or the excitement of building a new business or inventing a new product. The goal here is to see three realities, all constructed out of facts.

Adding vantage points will help you see new possibilities to pounce on, new entrepreneurial avenues to follow, new client needs to fulfill, new business leads to explore, and new solutions to problems—before other people are even consciously aware of them. And what's more, looking at reality from different angles will not only allow you to open your eyes to a broader range of opportunities, ideas, and solutions but also help you connect more deeply with your team, organization, and family.

In 2009, I worked with thousands of bankers on Wall Street who were furious about not receiving bonuses and depressed about the collapse of their industry. One managing director at one of the largest banks in New York told me that he had found a way to gain some much-needed perspective. That night, instead of taking his family out to a fancy restaurant as he usually did, all the while complaining about the change from better times and resenting the people around him who perhaps had gotten bonuses, he took his wife and children to a soup kitchen to serve the underprivileged. You could hear the pride in his voice return as he recounted to me how powerful it had been to see his children, who had all the toys in the world, meet an eight-year-old kid who was celebrating his birthday at the soup kitchen.

When this executive returned to work, the objective facts were the same—he did not receive a bonus, the economy was continuing to tank—but his reality had been altered by this new vantage point. He now was able to see more positives in his situation—like the fact that he enjoyed the company of his coworkers and the fact that his children looked up to the work he did. If you can open your eyes to more positive details, you will have not only high positive genius but also the greatest possible buffer against down times.

If you are having trouble seeing details in your world that you have previously missed, it also helps to change your patterns. Drive a different way to work, or intentionally talk to one person each day you wouldn't normally talk to. Maybe even try going somewhere new for lunch, or, instead of meeting with a client, meet with someone who chose *not* to buy your product. Researcher Richard Wiseman, in his article "The Luck Factor," says that if you are an apple picker and you keep coming back to the same trees every day, eventually you're going to run out of fruit.[18] The more you break out of your patterns, the easier it will be to find new vantage points.

GAINING PERSPECTIVE IN YOUR SLEEP

In 2011, after spending a month traveling to share my research in seven Latin American countries, I returned to snowy Boston and found it to be a lot colder. But I don't just mean the temperature. Research has found that one of the reasons for higher rates of resilience and optimism among workers in Latin America is their extraordinary social support networks with coworkers, family, and friends.[19] My plane had landed in Boston, but my family and roots were back in Texas. It turned out that this research was on the money: without my network of support, I was not only less happy but less productive, less motivated, and less effective in my work. So as soon as the grueling semester ended, I moved the hub of my research to San Antonio, Texas.

When I got off the plane at the airport in San Antonio, the drive to my sister's house was hellish. I remember being shocked at how desolate it looked. The trees were sparse and scraggly.

Since the soil is only one inch deep, there is bare rock almost everywhere, and after five months in tree-lined Cambridge I found the landscape barren and hideous. The buildings seemed squatty and far apart. I wondered why I had decided to move from the lush cathedral setting of New England to a wasteland.

What I saw was desolate, scraggly, and quite frankly, depressing—hardly a positive and growth-enhancing perspective. This wasn't the Texas I remembered from my childhood. Was my brain simply playing tricks on me, or was something else happening here?

After getting some much-needed rest, however, I started seeing different details in my surroundings. The trees seemed to be a little taller. I noticed that there were greenbelts everywhere, more than even in Boston. Instead of focusing on the patches of barren rock, I became impressed with all the life that could bloom in such a rocky soil. I started noticing the bluebonnet and Indian paintbrush wildflowers and the hummingbirds. The sky looked even bigger and bluer than in Boston. Suddenly I was in a paradise of light and color. Of course, San Antonio hadn't changed. My perspective had.

That's when I realized that on the morning I'd landed I had been awake for thirty-six hours working on a project and was jet-lagged from a quick work trip to Europe on top of it. Digging into the research, I confirmed that our ability to see positive details can indeed be heavily impaired by fatigue. One of my favorite studies found that if you memorize sets of positive, neutral, and negative words, then sleep for seven to eight hours, you will remember around 80 percent of all three lists a day later. If you miss a night of sleep and stay up for thirty-six hours as I did, you still remember most of the negative and neutral words, but you remember 59 percent fewer positive words![20] This is because your brain interprets a lack of sleep as a threat to the central nervous system, then goes on high alert, scanning the world for additional threats—that is, negatives.

So if you want to be able to see the details that will help your brain summon its full range of intellectual and emotional resources, first make sure you get seven to eight hours of sleep a night. Second, *when* you make the decision or presentation or pitch matters. A fascinating new study shows that right before lunch is the worst time to see positive details.[21] In a study of parole board hearings, researchers from Columbia Business School found that right after lunch judges granted parole to 60 percent of offenders, but that right before lunch, when their stomachs were rumbling, they granted parole to only 20 percent. The facts of the cases were, of course, the same; the time of day was the single factor determining whether the judges chose to focus on the cases' positive or negative details. This is because when we are low on fuel, our brains are tired and thus more likely to go on high alert to threats and to remember and focus primarily on the negative. At certain low points in the daily cycle, we literally see a more negative reality, and one that we feel we have less ability to change.

This finding could transform how our companies set goals, make decisions, and even run conferences and meetings. Think about a typical conference or annual meeting. Having observed dozens of them every year, here's how I believe most go. In the morning, after breakfast, are the boring introductions and a talk by the most senior leader (who generally isn't known for his or her speaking ability), followed by a report on what has happened in the past and an update on finances. Then, in the last hour before lunch, we cram as much information and goal setting into those final breakout sessions as possible. Finally, we have lunch and replenish our glucose levels in our brains. Then we hear about a couple of new ideas from vendors or speakers, but nothing we have to act on until about 3:00 p.m., when—just as our blood sugar is beginning to drop again—we break into groups and brainstorm ideas. Finally around 4:00 or 5:00 p.m., before dinner and cocktails, we realize (as with all meetings) that we are behind schedule, and we sprint to map out our plans and targets for the entire next year. In other words, the most critical plans and decisions are made when our brain glucose is most depleted. We are doing conferences backward! Instead, if you are running a meeting or giving a presentation or even bringing a small team together for brainstorming, be sure not to do it right before lunch or dinner. And if you're not the meeting planner and are forced to sit through a long or ill-timed meeting, bring snacks! You'll be not only more positive but also more alert and productive if you regularly replenish your brain's glucose levels with healthy food. If you want to see a single, fixed, negative reality at work, don't sleep enough the night before and make your decisions without food. If you want to find the most valuable reality, you have to take steps to ensure that your brain can perceive possibility.

MASTERING THE SWITCH BETWEEN REALITIES

There is no better demonstration of our brains' powerful ability to see reality from multiple perspectives than the Kanizsa triangle, a famous experiment created by the Italian psychologist Gaetano Kanizsa. (What are the chances that he'd discover an optical illusion with the exact same name as him, right?)

What do you see in the image on the next page? On the basis of the research, you probably saw the black-outlined triangle first. But do you see the solid white triangle? Once you see the white triangle, your brain will be able to switch back and forth

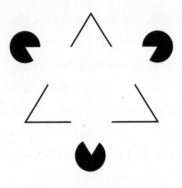

between the two perspectives. In fact, you will be unable to ignore the white triangle now that your perception has expanded.

In the UBS Rethinking Stress study, we found that two true
realities could coexist. And we found that if we could get people
to see *both* realities—not just the reality that stress is debilitating
but also the reality that stress is enhancing—stress could have a
beneficial effect, rather than a debilitating one. But merely being
able to *see* multiple perspectives and realities is only half the story.
If we want to increase our chances of success, we need to develop
the ability to *select the most valuable reality.*

In positive psychology, "the most valuable reality" is defined as
the reality that is most valid (true), helpful (conducive to the best
outcomes), and positive (growth producing). In the next section,
I'll show how you can evaluate the realities you've constructed
and choose the most valuable one to pursue.

STRATEGY 3: PURSUE THE MOST VALUABLE REALITY

In the 1950s, if you had heard of Kimball Electronics, you would
know them for pianos. They were wildly successful: that is, until

electric organs started to gain in popularity. So Kimball invested a ton of its money in organs, only for the demand to suddenly fall flat. From one vantage point, they were stuck. But the leaders of Kimball took a different angle and saw opportunity. Instead of concluding that they were the leaders in a dying field, they perceived themselves at the vanguard of an electronic revolution. They sat down and decided to look not at their deficits but at their resources, and in doing so they realized they had a wealth of electronic experts who now had time on their hands to innovate. So they decided to steer their resources and efforts in a different way, and today they make the electronic steering systems for Fiats, do testing for threat detection and avoidance systems for the military, and manufacture electronics to help hospitals determine levels of hygiene. One reality would have led to a bankrupt division, another reality led to fifty years of innovation and profits. What would have happened if they had seen only the negative reality?

In 2010, HSBC had a fantastic advertising campaign in airports that demonstrated the power of our brains to construct multiple realities based on the same external world. On the walls of the jet bridges in a number of airport terminals, HSBC displayed three identical images of a bald head; superimposed on each picture was a different word. Here's an example.

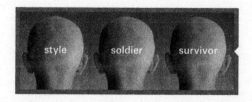

Does the word over the image change how you look at this person? Does one word inspire more pity, while another inspires more awe, or admiration? In this case the words tell you, to some extent at least, what to think about the person in the picture, but in the real world your own brain actively writes words on every single person or image you see. And the words and phrases that our brains write on people, projects, and goals at work change not only your perspective but your motivation, engagement, and creativity.

Let's say your boss walks into the room. Someone with a low positive intelligence is likely to see words and phrases like "stress" or "threat" or "I am powerless." Someone who has learned to add vantage points may still see some of these descriptors, but he or she would also see additional ones, like "human being," "mentor," "opportunity to impress," and "key to promotion." Training your brain to attach more positives to each situation at work will improve your brain's flexibility and significantly increase your ability to find and pursue your most valuable reality in all kinds of personal and professional situations.

If you are feeling that no positive attributes can be associated with your team, company, or workplace, that means one of two things: either (1) your brain is missing something or (2) you need to make some serious changes in your current situation. *Those are really the only two options.* But in all the work I've done over the years, even in the most struggling of companies, with the most beleaguered of leaders and the most pessimistic of individuals, I've never encountered an environment where positive details could not be found.

Try this experiment at home. Focus on an object and see how many attributes, phrases, and labels you can come up with for it in thirty seconds. Ignore grammar and other rules; go for speed.

You get +3 points for every positive descriptor and +1 point for every negative one. Remember, to get the 3 points, the attribute must be both positive and true. Here are a couple of examples:

Object: Your overflowing e-mail inbox.
Phrases: "Overloaded" (+1). "Source of stress" (+1). "Connection" (+3). "Business opportunities" (+3). "Addiction" (+1). "Opportunity for praise" (+3). "Key to job success" (+3). "Invitations for lunches" (+3). "Amazingly fast" (+3). "Tool" (+3). "Never-ending" (+1). "Dopamine rush" (+3). "Record of victories" (+3). "New ideas" (+3).

Object: Dishes in the sink.
(It's amazing how often people pick this object when I do this exercise in talks and speeches.)
    Phrases: "Ugh, a lot of work" (+1). "Messy" (+1). "Pain in the butt" (+1). "Never-ending" (+1). "Not fun" (+1). "Chance to feel productive" (+3). "Opportunity to win points with spouse" (+3). "Way of showing love" (+3). "Chance to do something mindless for a moment" (+3). "Opportunity to meditate for a few minutes" (+3). "Warm water feels good" (+3). "Way to make the kitchen look great" (+3). "Good way to feel control" (+3).

If you just did this experiment, you might be wondering why you got any points at all for the negative descriptors. After all, if we are looking to raise our level of positive genius, isn't it counterproductive to include them? This is the very question an HR leader at Humana, a large health insurance company in Louisville, Kentucky, asked me when I conducted this experiment. And it is a fair one. Wouldn't it make sense that including the negative words would make it easier for your brain to construct a reality around the negatives? But research shows that while listing *too many* negatives is detrimental, including *some* can actually be helpful. The secret, as it turns out, is all in the ratio.

THE POSITIVITY RATIO

This might sound strange coming from a positive psychology researcher, but acknowledging the negatives in our external world can actually be highly adaptive—to a point. Awareness of negatives can motivate us to take positive action, and the act of looking for them can help make our brains even more flexible and nimble. The harder your brain has to stretch and work to scan the world for multiple realities, the greater your creativity, your problem-solving ability, and even your empathy for those who do not see the world as you do. In 2012, I gave a talk to a group of one thousand safety inspectors on the link between positivity and success rates. Afterward, a man came up to me and dejectedly said, "I liked your talk, but it was depressing. I mean, you're talking to a room full of guys whose job it is to go into companies and tell them about all the problems you found that could injure or kill someone and that will cost millions to fix." That's exactly the point. We can't fix problems until we train our brains to see them. So while this exercise rewards you more for coming up with positive descriptors or facts than for coming up with negative ones, the negative ones should still be on the list.

Unfortunately, our brains are wired to naturally seek and find negatives. We, as human beings, are already good at that. This is because in order to survive on the savanna our primitive brains had to respond to threats faster than to emotions like happiness or gratitude. That's why retraining our brains to find the positive descriptors is usually where the real work begins.

The key to managing this delicate balance is what scientists call the *positivity ratio*. Powerful research by the mathematician Marcial Losada and the University of North Carolina psychologist Barbara Fredrickson found that in the working world the most valuable reality is one in which there is *at least* a 3:1 ratio of positive to negative interactions (this is called the Losada Line). In one study, real business teams were observed in laboratories in Cambridge and Ann Arbor. When the amounts of positive and negative feedback that team members received were tallied and the ratio of positive to negative interactions was calculated, it was found that when the P/N ratio was above 2.901 to 1 the teams had significantly higher profit levels as well as improved "360-degree feedback" reports. Below this ratio, engagement plummeted and turnover rates shot up. In fact, Losada found that the highest-performing teams had a 6:1 ratio.[22] So if you or your team are going through a rough period, ramp up the ratio of positive interactions, even by doing something as simple as complimenting someone or bringing in doughnuts.

Interestingly, Fredrickson found that 3:1 was the ratio at which people began to flourish outside work as well. Her research revealed that when people have three positive thoughts to every negative thought, they are more optimistic, are happier, and feel more fulfilled (2:1 was considered "languishing" and 1:1 was "depressed").[23] There's an old saying that "bad news comes in threes." Instead of just accepting this depressing adage, try to balance every piece of bad news with three good pieces of *good* news.

Why a skewed ratio? Shouldn't one positive neutralize a negative? No. Research has emphatically proven that because we naturally give more weight to negatives, it takes more positives to balance them out.[24] We've all felt this. When you get feedback on a project, people could say several nice things about your work, but your brain will still focus on the "one thing you might want to work on." Many leaders I have worked with have sheepishly admitted to me that if they unfairly blow up at a team member or add more work to an already overencumbered employee, they believe they can equally make up for it with one nice comment to or joke with that person. Not so. Positive leadership requires a positivity ratio of at least 3:1.

Once, when I did this exercise at a financial firm, a particularly negative financial advisor tried to outdo his positive peers by writing as many descriptors of his current work situation as possible in the thirty seconds allotted. But with his 3:1 negative-to-positive point ratio, he would need to come up with nine negatives in thirty seconds to "win," whereas the positive geniuses would need only three positives. It's like those Total cereal commercials: "It'd take sixteen bowls of your cereal to get the iron in one bowl of Total." When you're constructing alternate realities, a few positives far outweigh a long list of negatives.

A similar principle applies even in romantic relationships, and it may not surprise you to learn that in this domain the need for positivity is even greater. On the basis of decades of research, psychologist and relationship guru John Gottman has found that there needs to be at least a *5:1* ratio of positive to negative experiences to maintain a sound relationship and that spouses who have lower than a 5:1 ratio have a significantly higher rate of divorce.[25] So for every time a husband says something hurtful to his wife, getting her flowers isn't going to cut it; if he wants to truly atone for his actions, he should buy her flowers not once but *five times* (sorry guys)! What's more, Gottman's research with seven hundred newlywed couples revealed that this ratio can be used to predict, with a whopping accuracy rate of 94 percent, whether a couple will be together or divorced after ten years.

Both at work and at home, if everyone has access to only one version of reality, everyone suffers. Only when you keep your eyes open to many realities—both positive and negative, in the right proportions—can you choose and pursue the most beneficial one. In other words, the more interpretations of the world you can see, the better you can construct the prism of success to achieve the most successful outcomes.

OVERCOMING YOUR BLIND SPOTS

The blind spot is the spot in the back of the eyeball that lacks receptors and thus can't absorb the light coming into the eye. We all have them. We aren't ever consciously aware of a gap in our field of vision because our brains *invent* information that fills it in. But the blind spot in our view of the world is there.

Similarly, in the business world we all have blind spots that distort our perspective and impair our ability to see and choose the most valuable reality at work.

In one fascinating article for Bloomberg's *Businessweek*, Dr. Loretta Malandro names some of the most common blind spots that hold us back in our careers.[26] The primary one among executives, she says, is an inability to rely on other people: when most executives face a massive challenge or stressor, they try to figure out how to solve the problem alone. In my previous book, *The Happiness Advantage*, I wrote that one of the seven principles for creating greater happiness and success is "social investment." While people with the blind spot that Malandro has described lose connection to their social support networks in the midst of challenge, positive geniuses invest *more* heavily in their social support system during these periods. As a result, they reap massive dividends compared to their peers.

The second most common blind spot among business leaders

is impact awareness, or the ability to see the effect their decisions will have upon their teams. Leaders with this blind spot assume that everyone will view their decisions and choices in the same way they do, or they downplay the importance of feedback; as a result, their perspective on problems or challenges is limited.

The final common blind spot is the one Malandro identifies as "bottling it up," or concealing emotions from one's teams, employees, and coworkers. Leaders who are afraid of letting their emotions show are blind to how this can affect levels of trust, engagement, and effective decision making. For years I have worked with thirty chapters worldwide of the Young Presidents' Organization (YPO), a global group dedicated to creating a safe space for CEOs to open up. Its cornerstone is a forum in which CEOs meet monthly to share highs and lows, be accountability partners, and reveal blind spots in each other's thinking. I wish that we all had such highly developed forums that we could join. Through these groups, it's clear that the more the boss learns to open up, the better it is for everyone at the company, in terms of both morale and profits.

One of my favorite exercises for training the brain to see past blind spots is the famous experiment known as the Nine Dots Test.

Without picking up your pen (or, if you're on an e-reader, without picking up your finger), draw four straight lines that go through all nine dots only once.

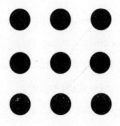

Did you get it? If not, it's because as soon as you saw these dots, your brain immediately registered the word and the concept "square." Your brain defined boundaries that in reality *do not exist*. It created a blind spot in the area *outside* the square.

Can your line go outside of those nine dots? Of course: there's no impenetrable force field preventing you from drawing outside the lines. Trina Kershaw and Stellan Ohlsson at the University of Illinois explain that the reason many people can't solve this problem is that our brains create rules for reality that we do not think we can break.[27] Positive genius is what allows your brain to recognize that there are actually multiple ways of looking at that square.

Here's the answer:

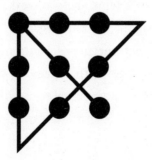

Your brain's ability to use the whole prism of success is what allows you to see the triangle. IQ alone won't help you solve this problem because our knowledge of geometry and shapes can be hampered by the emotional and social rules that we subconsciously set for ourselves, such as "Don't cross lines" and "Don't go out of the box." Only once you harness your social and emotional intelligences to regulate your emotions and social scripts effectively is your IQ able to find the answer. Positive geniuses are better able to think outside this box because they are more likely to have richer associations within existing knowledge structures and to be flexible and creative.[28] They also end up having fewer blind spots while driving down the road of life.

Sometimes simply asking the right questions can help us overcome our blind spots. During the eight years that I worked as a proctor and tutor at Harvard, a lot of stressed and depressed students walked through the door of my office. Instead of asking them, "Do you feel depressed or not right now?" or "Are you happy or unhappy right now?" I asked them a question like "How are you enjoying the social connections you've made here at Harvard?" or "How are you helping others?" By getting them to focus on positive details of their reality, like the friends they'd made or the service organization they'd joined, I got them to see outside the box of their negative thoughts.

So where are your blind spots at work? And more important, what are you filling them with? Pessimists fill them in with what they expect to be there: negatives. Irrational optimists fill them in with sunshine and roses. Both are equally counterproductive. But a positive genius fills in the blind spots with information that is true and valid and that leads to positive growth.

EMBRACING MULTIPLE CULTURES

When I talk about culture, I mean much more than simply race, religion, or nationality. Within even a single group there are literally thousands of combinations of beliefs, customs, dialects, personality types, and so on. This is, of course, true not only of countries, towns, and cities but of companies as well. Yet for all the lip service leaders give to their efforts to build multicultural companies, I find it interesting that when companies talk to me about issues they are struggling with, they often cite "cultural differences" as a stumbling block, rather than a strength. This is something we need to change, because the research is clear: the more diverse outlooks and ideas you are exposed to, the broader your perspective on the world.

Admittedly, cultural differences can be a major challenge for leaders trying to implement uniform policies, procedures, or protocols throughout the company. After all, how can we streamline procedures when the tech department has a different culture from the legal department, which, in turn, has a different culture from the finance department? The answer is that we can't and shouldn't. Instead, we should embrace the cultural differences across the company and draw on them to broaden our own perspective and that of our teams and departments. I'm often called in to work at recently merged companies to help them navigate the clash of corporate cultures. The first thing I tell them is that just as rubbing two sticks together can start a fire, the initial friction between cultures can produce the spark to ignite the flames of positive genius. In work and in life, you can't create harmony if everyone is playing the same note.

Once, after addressing a group of leaders from emerging companies in Shanghai and Beijing, I was presented with a gift of a tiny spoon and a flat bronze bowl etched with Chinese lettering. At first, I didn't understand what it was for, but of course I took it and said, "Thank you," anyway. At first I wondered if the small spoon was a reminder of mindful eating, or if it was a comment on American obesity. But as soon as I rested the miniature spoon on the flat bowl, it started spinning. Ah . . . it was a compass; the spoon was the needle, and the lettering referred to north, south, east, and west! But as the spoon stopped, I realized my gift was broken. Instead of pointing north over Beijing, it was pointing in the "wrong" direction. The CEO of a large Chinese manufacturing company, who had spent several years in the United States,

recognized my cultural confusion. He leaned over and whispered, "Here compasses point south."

On this Chinese compass, the spoon corresponds to our Big Dipper, part of the constellation called the Great Bear, or Ursa Major. A line drawn between the outer two stars of the bowl of the Big Dipper points north to the pole star, and so does the outer lip of the bowl of the spoon in a Chinese compass. So of course the spoon's handle, at the other end of the compass's north-south axis, points south. I suddenly flashed back to my experience on the navy submarine; just as my brain had used the heuristic that "the floor is down," I had once again taken the mental shortcut and assumed "compasses always point north." This was a brilliant reminder that looking at the world from the vantage points of other cultures can open us up to all kinds of ideas, possibilities, and paths to success that we might otherwise have missed.

For example, international diversity on a team can help us find new approaches to solving problems. In *The Geography of Thought*, Richard Nisbett, the preeminent researcher on the effects of culture on cognition and perception, describes an experiment in which he showed groups of Americans, Europeans, and Asians a series of pictures and then used a machine to track their eye movements.[29] This sounds like an odd experiment. Why would eye movements differ? What we see in pictures should be the same, regardless of culture. However, Nisbett proved this wasn't the case. On average, Asians seemed to focus their attention and gaze on the context, setting, and background of the picture, whereas the Westerners focused their attention and gaze on whatever object or person was in the foreground.

This may seem trivial, but it, in fact, highlights a very fundamental cultural difference. The Asians were interested in the *context and setting* of the picture, while the Americans and Europeans were more concerned with whatever was most front and center—a distinction that carries over into how different cultures (generally speaking) view real-world situations. What's more, these differences are not genetic nor biologically bred. Upon further investigation, Nisbett discovered that those born in Asia who grow up in the West will see the world like a Westerner: they focus on the center instead of the context of a picture. What this means is that cultural perspective is not fixed; it can be learned. We can actively expand our cultural vantage points through experiences with different personalities and cultures.

Of course, diversity is broader than culture. It refers to age, background, personal history, and so on. One of the CEOs in the Shanghai chapter of the Young Presidents' Organization told me that when he was back in corporate America and he really wanted to gain perspective, he sought out three types of people: (1) those who had a different personality; (2) those who had a lower position in the company; and (3) those who were outside the company. Looking at the world through the lens of another culture—whether an international culture or a corporate culture—can help us gain a broader perspective and see more details in our external world. This is why, in our work lives, surrounding ourselves with people from other countries, ethnicities, interests, and professional backgrounds makes us more flexible, innovative, adaptive, and primed for success.

As a bonus, diversity can improve employee engagement, since more people feel that their perspectives are valued. In my work in the financial industry, I have seen how important such perspective taking is for leaders, especially in the current business environment that is so rife with uncertainty, regulation, and restructuring. As it turns out, there is a biological reason for this: demonstrating an awareness of another person's perspective can actually short-circuit disengagement in the other person's brain. As Sharon Parker and Carolyn Axtell from the Universities of New South Wales and Sheffield have found, if a manager needs to add an urgent task to the workload of an already burned-out employee, even adding a mere acknowledgment can help the individual feel as if their perspective is being shared.[30] Saying something like "I can imagine that you're swamped right now—I would be feeling overwhelmed" allows part of the employee's emotional brain (amygdala and limbic centers) to quiet down and turns on the prefrontal cortex, which helps him or her approach the task with a more positive mindset and greater energy and investment.

The more vantage points we have for viewing the world, the better our ability to select the most successful path forward. Sometimes the most valuable realities can come from incorporating others' realities into our own.

The first step in becoming a positive genius is learning to see the objective facts in your external world through a lens that is true and positive and that leads to positive growth. In our working lives, adding vantage points broadens our perspective and helps us see a greater range of realities, which, in turn, allows us to select the one that is most valuable: the one that allows us to construct our prism of success and use all our cognitive, emotional, and social resources to their maximum potential. By amplifying the power of our multiple intelligences, our most valuable reality helps us raise our levels of motivation and engagement, see more opportunities and possibilities that others miss, come up with more innovative solutions to problems, reduce our stress levels, and map paths to achievement. In the next chapter, we'll address the latter and show you how to create mental maps for achieving your most meaningful and ambitious goals.

MAKING IT PRACTICAL

1. *Make stress work for you.* Rather than fighting or fleeing from stress, think about what is *meaningful* behind whatever is stressful. You wouldn't be stressed if there weren't something important embedded within the stress. For example, if I told you that a randomly chosen student was failing English, you wouldn't become stressed. But if I told you that your child was failing English, you would feel stress. Stress comes only from meaning. However, stress becomes debilitating only when we forget about that meaning. Reconnect with whatever meaning is there, and set cues in your environment to remind your brain why stress is enhancing rather than debilitating.

2. *Cross-train your brain.* Go on a tour at a local art museum and take your team or family. In this technological age, all the paintings are on the Internet anyway,

so you can even just check out the website of your favorite museum. Look at the paintings from different vantage points and perspectives and try to spot new details, even in paintings you may have viewed dozens of times before. What would the ability to see 10 percent more details in your work do for your performance? Even if you're not an artistic person, my guess is that it's worth an afternoon at the museum. The research proves it too.

3. *Do something prosocial.* Find an altruistic activity, like going to a soup kitchen, offering to pick someone up at the airport or help someone move, or sending a nice handwritten thank-you note. All of these break us out of negative patterns and help us see alternative, positive realities where our behavior matters. The key is to stop vacillating over whether you are happy or not and instead turn your attention to the question of whether you are helping someone else. The greatest buffer against depression is altruism.

4. *Fuel your reality.* To free up your brain's resources to see positive details in your external world, eat and sleep regularly. In particular, make sure to eat *right before* making a big decision. The best time to make decisions or set goals as a team at a conference or during a meeting is right after breakfast and right after lunch. Right before lunch and right before dinner are the worst possible times. And don't make big decisions when you are low on sleep. When Bill Clinton was asked to give advice to then-incoming president Barack Obama, he pointed out the importance of rest.

"Most of the major mistakes I made in my life, I made when I was too tired to know what I was doing—both personally and professionally."[31] If you are well rested and just fed, it will be easier to see the broader range of valuable details, information, and possibilities.

5. *Add vantage points.* Do the Add Vantage Points exercise from earlier in this chapter to see how many attributes—both positive and negative—you can assign to people or situations at work. The more you see, the better, but aim for a 3:1 positive-to-negative ratio. Seeing the multitude of details not only helps you choose the most valuable reality but also keeps your brain flexible so you don't feel boxed in by the external world.

6. *Seek diverse voices.* When you are really searching for the most valuable reality for a big project at work, or a big decision at home, make sure to run it by at least three people who have diverse vantage points in terms of characteristics such as personality, gender, position, or culture.

7. *Remind yourself of the power of change.* Write down the three greatest moments of change in your life that have brought you to being the person you like being today. Then put them up at your desk or in a place visible to you (like a bathroom mirror) to remind yourself that you live in a reality where your behavior matters and that you are capable of long-term positive growth.

Please visit BeforeHappiness.com to watch a video about how to put this research into practice.

mental cartography

MAPPING YOUR SUCCESS ROUTE

As part of my navy ROTC scholarship, one of the very first classes I was required to take was called "Weapons Systems and Navigation." At the time I found it odd. Why would they require incoming freshmen to learn complex navigation systems? Now I understand the reasoning behind this immediate emphasis upon mapping abilities. If you don't have a good map of reality, there is no chance of a successful mission.

Whether you realize it or not, right now your brain is using a map. Powerful, yet usually hidden, mental maps are what guide your actions anytime you make a decision, face a challenge, or set a goal, be it large or small. Your mental map is what helps you spot the most useful opportunities, seize the most valuable resources, and chart the best route toward your goals at work. But not all mental maps are created equal. If the mental map you are using lacks "meaning markers," it is incomplete and inaccurate and can lead you astray. Meaning markers are quite simply those things in your life that matter to you: career advancement, a new business, your kids' admission to a desired school, better health, your faith, and so on. No matter what goal or challenge you set for yourself, if you want to be able to channel your full range of intelligences toward achieving it, your personal meaning markers should be points on your mental path. So if you're currently finding your work less meaningful, your obstacles less surmountable, or your goals less attainable, chances are you need to redraw your mental map.

Truth be told, we could *all* really use help finding more meaning in our lives. In *The Happiness Advantage*, I defined happiness as "the joy we feel moving toward our potential." A lack of meaning in our reality robs us not only of that joy but also of our ability to use our multiple intelligences to increase our success. But as we have seen, a high IQ or EQ alone won't help us find meaning along our paths. During the eight years I spent counseling students as a proctor and then as a house tutor at Harvard, 47.4 percent of students reported experiencing depression over the previous year. And in the 2003 University Health Services survey of 2,250 Harvard students (a sample including a full third of all the undergraduates), 10 percent had contemplated suicide.[1] This is absolutely heartbreaking and horrifying. These kids have such high potential, but because they aren't able to see or remember the meaning behind that potential in the midst of competition and stress, they feel hopeless and unable to reach it. A life without meaning markers does not seem worth navigating.

Harvard students are not alone in this. Only 29 percent of American employees report that they are thriving at work, and internationally this number is even smaller.[2] After all, can we expect to succeed at anything or create lasting happiness, whether at school or at work, when we are distracted all the time by negative information, when we take no joy in the positive results we do achieve, when any moments we might take to reflect on meaning are consumed with e-mails and text messages and other noise, and when we have demands on our time that keep us from the people we care about? And research has conclusively shown that those who fail to find high meaning and engagement at work are three times less likely to have life satisfaction and happiness outside the office. This is a vicious cycle, but luckily it is one you can break by using the skills you'll learn in this chapter.

The second skill of positive genius is learning to use positive markers of meaning in your life to draw mental routes to success. Research shows that when your mapped success routes are based upon meaning markers, not only do your stress levels drop dramatically, but productivity can increase 31 percent, accuracy and completion rates on goals rise significantly, energy and engagement at work skyrocket, sales rates improve, and you are able to utilize the entire prism of success at work. In fact, research I did at the Institute for Applied Positive Research in collaboration with our partner Mindshare Technologies demonstrates that if you reorient your map successfully, you can increase your likelihood of a promotion by nearly 40 percent and *triple* your rates of job and life satisfaction. When we have meaning, our brains release a storehouse of resources to help make us more successful. Mental maps without meaning, on the other hand, lead to apathy, depression, burnout, and ultimately failure. That's because success without meaning is hollow and not worth the effort.

In my research, I've found that there are several common mistakes we make, albeit subconsciously, when drawing the mental maps that guide our daily decisions and actions. Sometimes we haven't highlighted enough meaning markers and thus can see only a limited number of routes to success. Sometimes we've highlighted the *wrong* meaning markers and chosen a path studded with negatives, rather than the things that we truly care about. Other times we have mapped *too few* paths to success, or mapped the most congested ones, on which opportunities and resources are scarcer. And all too often, we map *escape routes* before we even begin to look for paths to success. When we are so busy mapping escape routes because of stress and fear, the very negative outcomes we most fear end up becoming self-fulfilling prophecies. The research on this topic is stunningly definitive: when we expect the worst, we ignore important opportunities, squander valuable resources, and miss the viable solutions—and thus end up with the negative outcome we most fear. In this chapter, you'll learn how to avoid or reverse these common pitfalls and draw better and more effective mental maps.

On the basis of research I did first at Harvard and then out in the corporate world, I have isolated three strategies that lead to better mental map making.

Strategy 1: Highlight Your True Meaning Markers. The best mental map is one whose paths steer us toward accomplishing meaningful goals. But we can't chart those paths until we've identified and mapped the things in life that matter most to us. In this section I'll show you how to create a diversified portfolio of meaning and how to distinguish your true meaning markers from the decoys and hijackers that derail your paths to success.

Strategy 2: Reorient Your Mental Map. Every mental map has a focal point that dictates where the majority of your brain's resources will be allocated. In this section I'll show you how to reorient your map around the meaning markers you identified in strategy 1 so that you can harness all your intellectual, cognitive, and social resources to their fullest potential.

Strategy 3: Map Success Routes Before Escape Routes. What you focus on becomes your reality: if you are focused on avoiding routes to failure, you will completely miss the roads to success. In this section, I'll explain how mapping for success first can dramatically increase the likelihood of your road leading there.

As you'll read in this chapter, orienting your mental map around meaning is key to becoming a positive genius because it allows you to channel your full range of intelligences toward solving the problems that most frustrate you, upholding the values most dear to you, and achieving the goals you most care about. I don't claim that mastering these rules of mental cartography will answer the question of the meaning of life, but I do promise they will help you create a life of more meaning, happiness, and success.

STRATEGY 1: HIGHLIGHT YOUR TRUE MEANING MARKERS

One of my proudest moments growing up was also one that got my parents in trouble with the police. Let me preface this by saying my mom and dad were the most loving, calm, and patient parents one could ever imagine. I say that only because this story might make you think otherwise.

My parents rarely argued, but one midsummer night in Waco, Texas, they had a minor disagreement about their weekend plans. My seven-year-old self decided this could not stand. So I calmly sat down and wrote the following ransom note: "To The Parents, you are fighting all the time. I'm running away from home. Love, Shawn. P.S. I'm taking Amy" (my sister, who was five at the time).

But a few minutes later, before I had a chance to make my great escape, I realized my parents had stopped fighting (or maybe hadn't been fighting in the first place), so I tore up the note, threw it in my trash can, and wrote a new and slightly more chipper note: "Dear The Parents, I am going on an educational exkurSHAWN [this deliberate misspelling was a phrase my parents would use to refer to a trip to my dad's neuroscience lab at Baylor, or the zoo]. Don't call the police, or I will not come home. I'm watching you. Love, Shawn. P.S. I'm taking Amy." Then I strategically placed the note where they were sure to find it first thing in the morning, and went to bed.

At 4:30 a.m., my alarm clock went off. I diligently woke my sister, who was happy enough to comply with my plan, and snuck out to the garage to gather supplies: a SeaWorld fan (it was summer), a Fisher-Price compass with a nonmagnetic needle (rendering it completely useless), fishing poles (you'll see why in a minute), and a French-to-English dictionary (just in case).

Now, no one expects a seven-year-old to have a spatial map of adequate range to get him into too much trouble. And generally, they are correct. That's why many moms let their seven-year-olds walk alone to the bus stop and why, when most seven-year-olds run away, they run away to their next-door neighbor's house. But children's brains are capable of much more. That morning, Amy and I walked 7.2 miles away to a secluded portion of Lake Waco where my dad would always take us fishing. (It was also where an unsolved triple homicide had recently occurred. When I recall stories like this, I really cannot wait to have kids!)

As Amy and I hiked cheerfully to our beloved fishing spot–turned–crime scene, my parents woke up peacefully, had coffee, found the note, and called the usual suspects (above-mentioned next-door neighbors, grandma, and so forth). Then, getting more and more nervous, they phoned the police—who said they couldn't help until we were missing for twenty-four hours (turns out they say this in real life, not just on Lifetime Television). I'm not sure what transpired on the call, but whatever it was, moments later the police decided to make an exception to this policy.

The police came immediately, searched our home, and found my first note, torn up in a Transformer trash can. After meticulously piecing the note back together at the kitchen table, the officer read the note revealing that my parents were "fighting all the time" and that I had been forced to take Amy with me. They then began to interrogate my already distraught mother, who was now under suspicion of abuse and abduction.

Meanwhile, 7.2 miles away, Amy and I were contentedly dragging empty hooks through the water at a fishing hole where my dad had helped me catch my first and only fish (in case you are wondering, it was a magnificent three-inch perch). The walk there had been arduous. I now give runaway tours to my friends from out of town, and it takes forever even by car. It was 105 degrees by the time my father found us five hours later hiding in the bushes under a drainage bridge. My parents have requested that I mention here that our only punishment was having to face a silent, crying mother. It worked. To this day, Amy and I have yet to run away again.

Although we did not know it at the time, our ability to make that 7.2-mile journey—seemingly impossible for a seven- and a five-year-old—lies in one of the most incredible capabilities of the human brain. I was able to find and get us to that fishing hole because I had mapped my route on the basis of a "meaning marker." In other words, my seven-year-old brain had been able to channel all its resources toward reaching our destination because I had chosen a destination that meant so much to me emotionally, thanks to my early memories of fishing with my father.

According to a landmark article in *Nature*, our brains start this process of mapping meaning in the world as early as eighteen months of age, right about when we learn to crawl.[3] But as this story demonstrates, the young brain is capable of using its mapping ability for much more than just figuring out where to find one's toys.

Using one of its most primitive functions, my brain had created a mental route to that fishing hole, much as a prehistoric gatherer's brain would create a mental route to a patch of berry bushes. Unconsciously, every time we drove home from fishing, my brain recorded all the landmarks and points of reference along that 7.2-mile path. So when it came time to run away on my educational "exkurshawn," I had a complete mental map at my disposal to steer me to my destination.

Similarly, in our professional lives, our brains are constantly storing and recording information that guides us toward our goals. Called *meaning markers*, these mental signposts can be anything that you consider important or valuable, any aspect of life that you feel a deep emotional connection with. These markers could be something as simple as feeling that you've accomplished something at the end of the workday. Or it could be the satisfaction of helping people solve complex problems quickly to save them time and money. Or the emotional connection of having a beer with a colleague after a long workday. Perhaps the meaning we get from work comes from the ability to help our community, or the opportunity to use an obscure skill. Or perhaps your most meaningful marker has nothing to do with work at all—like taking time out to read with your children every night. It doesn't matter what the marker is, as long as it holds true meaning for you.

Although we rarely think about it, every goal we set for ourselves in both our personal and our professional lives is based on meaning. Luckily, because we're wired to channel more of our energy, drive, focus, and emotional and intellectual resources toward the things that matter most to us, the more we care about that goal, the greater the chance of a successful outcome.

It's impossible to overstate the importance of meaning in our professional lives. Researchers from Wharton Business School demonstrated that we experience up to three times higher levels of motivation, engagement, and productivity when our work is centered on our positive meaning markers.[4] What's more, they found that employees who *didn't* find their jobs meaningful had higher stress levels and blood pressure during the workweek than those who were able to map meaning at work. And another study found that when people started finding work meaningful, their chances of getting depressed or feeling high anxiety two years later dropped dramatically and that lack of meaning markers was one of the main predictors of depression.[5]

The good news is you don't have to be rescuing puppies or saving orphans to find meaning in your professional life. In fact, meaning is less about the specific job you have than the personal significance you attach to it. In one study, Yale University researcher Amy Wrzesniewski found that the difference between individuals who see their occupation as a "job," a "career," or a "calling" is based upon the meaning they find in their work, rather than job title or position. For example, they found that janitors at retirement homes are just as likely as Wall Street bankers to find their work to be a calling—as long as both can see how their work is helpful to others, perceive how their strengths are needed to do well at the job, and de-emphasize the monetary reward for working.[6] This is because meaning is created by the *individual*, not the job, which is good news because it means that we all have the ability and power to imbue our professional lives with more meaning.

In 1958, the Gallup organization collected data revealing that the average age of retirement was eighty among men who lived to ninety-five years old.[7] This prompted George Gallup to wonder, What kept these men working for fifteen full years after the average age of retirement, which at the time was sixty-five? When he polled them to find out, a staggering 93 percent of them responded that they kept working because they found their work meaningful, and 86 percent said it was because they found their work fun. Yet what was most interesting was that their jobs weren't exciting or glamorous or even what most people would generally consider enjoyable. These men weren't directing blockbuster movies or flying airplanes or hanging out with Playboy bunnies. They were working in offices, in supermarkets, in manufacturing. But because they cared about what they did, to them, their jobs were meaningful and engaging and, yes, even fun.

Think for a moment about what *you* find most engaging or fun about your average workday. Are there aspects of your daily routine that you secretly enjoy, even if others around you find them mundane? What's the first thing that excites you when you wake up in the morning? Now think about what attracted you to your current job in the first place. How did you hope it would make you feel? What are some of the things you hoped to accomplish or achieve? While you're at it, think about what you hoped to accomplish or achieve by reading this book. What are the skills you most wish to improve? The areas in which you most wish to excel? If you could wave a magic wand, what's the one thing you'd change about either your personal or your professional life? The answers to all these questions will help you draw mental maps oriented around your deepest and truest sources of meaning.

A SECRET MAP OF HARVARD YARD

The best psychology professor I had at Harvard was Brian Little, a nontenured, twitchy-browed, self-professed introvert from Canada who somehow inspired every person in his class to dream of being a great psychologist someday, regardless of how bad his or her grade was in the class. As his teaching fellow in "Personality Psychology," I often performed an experiment that revealed a key insight about mental mapping. The experiment was simple: I simply gave students three minutes to draw a map of Harvard Yard and Harvard Square on a sheet of paper. (It is sadistically fun to ask perfectionist students—who hate to make a single mistake—to draw. Just for fun I may have also mentioned, in passing, that the students would be graded on their accuracy.)

Though the maps themselves always differed, the result of the experiment was always the same. Consciously or not, the student always drew the most important part of his or her world at the physical center of the map. If the student loved hanging out in his dorm, he drew his dorm at the center of the map. If the student was on the football team, his map prominently featured the field and fieldhouse at the center. If the student frequented the same pub every night, well, you can guess what building was smack-dab in the middle of her map.

But what was even more fascinating about the students' maps was how they drew the areas of campus that clearly were *not* at the center of their emotional universe. For some overachievers, Widener Library was the biggest marker on the map; but for those who were less studious, the second-largest library in the world was minuscule or tellingly absent. Shops or restaurants that the student never went to were either tiny or left off the map altogether. For students who rarely left campus, Boston, just down the road from Cambridge, didn't even make it on the page. And tellingly, not a single student drew any of the "civilian" houses or apartment buildings around Harvard Square. For them, life was the university, and literally nothing else.

This is exactly how we all map our mental worlds: those things that matter most to us loom largest and in the center, whereas the things we care less about are smaller and pushed out to the periphery, if included at all. But while it's true that we are often better off setting our goals and charting our paths according to things that do hold meaning for us, sometimes, like those Harvard students who never set foot in the library, we fail to assign meaning to things that perhaps we should. So what you *don't* map can be as important as what you do. Could your map be missing important markers that would help you navigate your path to success?

Try out this experiment: take one minute and draw a picture of your workplace (or, if you are a student, of your school). Did you draw only a handful of key locations, like your office or the cafeteria? Try now to think about all the places you left off, and it will become immediately obvious what you value and what you don't. For example, maybe you drew your boss's desk but not the tech department. This map might serve you well in most situations, but what if you were working on a crucial project that required technical support? To be successful, you'd need to redraw your mental map to include that department.

Now let's take this one step further. Take a few more minutes, and draw a map of your world—your entire reality. Where do you go on a daily or weekly basis (work, home, the gym, church, et cetera)? What do you do, both personally and professionally (meetings, networking events, kids' soccer games, and so on)? Whom do you see (your spouse, your boss, your yoga instructor, your friend down the street)? The places and people that loom largest on your map are likely those that hold the most meaning. This exercise will be harder than simply mapping your workplace, and it's inevitable that your map will be missing some things and probably overemphasizing others. But we can't draw new routes to success until we uncover which things in our lives hold the most meaning and which meaningful things have been left unmapped.

If you're still having trouble spotting those hidden meaning markers in your life, try another experiment I designed in 2011 for Pfizer, in which I asked employees and managers to think about the past year and then sketch a "happiness graph," which is simply a line graph with two axes: happiness and time. So, for example, if you got a promotion in January and that made you happy, that should be a high point on the graph. Or if you were miserable in January, but then in early February your football team won the Super Bowl, you'd draw a spike on the graph. Then if in April you had a series of bad things happen at work, including not getting your expected raise, you'd likely draw a big dip. Then you label those events that dictated how you drew the graph. For example:

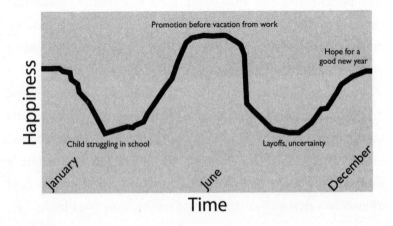

The events or markers you included can uncover important yet hidden nodes of meaning in your life. In the Pfizer study, some of the managers' graphs fluctuated around events in their family life, both good (like their child winning a soccer tournament) and bad (like finding out their teenager had an eating disorder). Others were more oriented around world events, like the results of an election or the resolution of a conflict in Asia. For others, the events on the graph were entirely work related. Whatever our individual graphs look like, they help us understand what parts of our lives our happiness (or conversely, our unhappiness) depends upon. And in doing so, they help us see the areas that are clearly meaningful but that for some reason—whether our busy schedules or misaligned priorities—may not have made it onto our mental maps. For instance, a graph dominated by family events might reveal that we consider our relationships with our children highly meaningful, but if we are not currently putting a lot of time and attention into those relationships, that's a sign those markers are missing from our mental maps. Take a minute to reflect on your happiness graph. What do you find meaningful that is missing from the reality map I just had you draw?

By finding these hidden sources of meaning, we can raise our levels of engagement, productivity, and efficiency at work. Just think about how much faster you could accomplish boring tasks or projects at work if you found something in them you cared about. When I was in divinity school, I had to read some really dense and dry texts by dead people arguing about things that I frankly couldn't have cared less about. The assignments would take me forever. But I knew I had to read them, so eventually I learned a trick. I would take the book, and right inside the front cover I would write three interesting things I hoped to learn from it, or why reading this text was important beyond just my grade.

Sometimes I would have to do a bit of research online to find out why this text was important or to ask the professor why we were reading it. When I did, I always discovered that these texts held a lot more meaning to me than I'd initially realized—it was simply a question of finding the markers and adding them to my mental map. Suddenly, not only did the reading go much faster, but I understood and retained more of the information and, in turn, performed better on papers and exams.

DIVERSIFY YOUR MEANING PORTFOLIO

The more markers we add to our mental maps, the more paths to success we open up to ourselves. But if all these new markers are clustered in one corner of the map, we'll still lack success routes in other areas of our personal or professional lives. If you are finding that your happiness seems to be entirely dependent upon one corner of your life, that means that you have left too much of your world *unmapped*. Once, when consulting at Morgan Stanley Smith Barney, I talked with a financial advisor who told me that his entire happiness graph revolved around events in the stock market. Ironically, he was doing the opposite of what he would recommend to his clients: his happiness portfolio was not the least bit diversified. Just as a more diversified portfolio of stocks is more likely to succeed in the stock market, the more diversified your portfolio of meaning, the better your chances of creating long-term success in your career and your life.

Diversifying your meaning marker portfolio begins with identifying the area or areas of life that are currently dominating your reality map. For example, that financial advisor's meaning markers were completely clustered in the area of work. So he began creating meaning markers in his social life. He planned outings with his college buddies. He asked a few women out on dates. And he found that when he had an event with his friends to look forward to, and his happiness was not solely dependent upon stock tickers, he was better able to harness the full suite of his intelligences to be more positive and effective at work.

Now go back to the map of your reality that you drew a few moments ago, and try segmenting it into sections representing different areas in your life, like work, family, health, money, and so on. Which sections are most crowded? Which look like ghost towns? Are any areas of your life completely empty, or absent from the map? If so, how can you add them? Remember, the more diverse your markers, the more routes you will have to steer you to your goals.

WATCH OUT! MAP HIJACKERS

Sometimes, however, our mental maps can become corrupted by hijackers, which are negative attitudes in our lives that *lower* our overall levels of happiness and derail our paths to success. Often cleverly disguised as meaning markers, map hijackers can skew our reality, rather than improve it. If you are currently feeling frustrated with people at your job, having trouble making progress in your career, or failing to achieve your goals or benchmarks at work, it's probably because your map is being hijacked.

Let's say you've determined that advancing in your career is the most important meaning marker for you. Now ask yourself: *Why* is that meaningful? What are the positive effects it has on your life? Maybe it allows you to achieve more of your potential as a leader. Maybe it offers more opportunities to make a difference in the world. Maybe the accompanying bump in salary will lower the levels of stress at home. All of these answers would indicate that career advancement is a valid marker. But if you find you can't answer that question or, worse, can think only of its *negative* effects—for instance, that you are working so hard to get promoted that you are stressed and grumpy when you come home—you are probably going head-to-head with a map hijacker. And it should go without saying that if the desire for career advancement is leading to unethical acts at work, like backstabbing, cheating, or tearing down others, it is most certainly a map hijacker.

Map hijackers are very commonly found in the health area of your map. Let's say you want to lose weight. Now ask yourself *why* you want to lose weight and what effects you expect weight loss would have. When I do this exercise in my talks, people often reply that it's so they can start liking themselves again. That meaning marker is not effective (as I proved in *The Happiness Advantage*) in getting you to change your habits. In fact, it hijacks those efforts because it's grounded in a negative reality: you do not currently like yourself. An answer indicating a true meaning marker would be that you want to live longer, set a healthier example for your children, or have the energy to do other activities that are meaningful, like go on that bike ride through the south of France. Map hijackers don't only derail your progress, they sap your life of meaning and happiness. So how do we go about spotting these sneaky hijackers and banishing them from our mental maps?

A few years ago, a friend, who happened to work for the attorney general of New York, gave me a birthday present that I didn't initially want: DVDs of the HBO series *The Wire*. He told me that it was all about the drug trade in Baltimore and that I would personally find a lot of meaning in it. I got nervous. Why did someone working for the attorney general think I would care so much about drugs?

In any case, I waited to watch it until I was sick and stuck on the couch with nothing else to do. And to my surprise, *The Wire* was amazing. It combines the power of incredible storytelling and meticulous research to bring the pulse of an entire city—from drug dealers to politicians to educators to the media—to life.

Not only did I quickly realize what a great show I'd been missing, I also realized why my friend thought I would find it particularly meaningful. One of the plotlines was connected to some new research about how we map our mental worlds. In real-life Baltimore, Kenzie Preston and David Epstein from the National Institute on Drug Abuse at Johns Hopkins University, along with biostatistician Ian Craig, were attempting to create a scientific version of what the police were doing on *The Wire*: tracking heroin addicts in Baltimore. Their goal wasn't to break up a powerful organized crime ring but rather to make the first-ever computer model of the mental map of an addict. If they could map the mind of the typical addict, they reasoned, they could help these addicts find meaning markers that could help them avoid the hijackers that were keeping them stuck in negative, self-destructive patterns of crime and addiction.

So they did something rather unprecedented: they gave drug addicts PDAs with GPS systems so they could track and record exactly where the addicts roamed every day over the course of a year.[8] In and of itself that was fairly useless information (unless you were trying to decide where you did not want to buy a house) until Ian Craig stepped in. Craig, a native to Baltimore, had previously used census data to map the city according to metrics like income and race. Then he augmented this map using information compiled by Debra Furr-Holden at Johns Hopkins, who had previously sent teams to walk the city and to score city blocks on the basis of the numbers of broken windows, shell casings, incidents of public drunkenness, unsupervised children, street memorials for recent killings, et cetera.

The result of these three overlaid maps provided a window into how certain markers in an environment mired addicts in negative patterns or paths. It revealed what physical routes those addicts who broke free from the drugs took—what streets, neighborhoods, shops, and so on—and what environmental triggers led them (tragically) right back. Does seeing spent handgun shell casings and "dead soldiers" (used drug vials left on the street) remind an addict that the world is negative so he might as well shoot up? Does walking past a clinic or a clean block remind recovering users that there is hope? These data answered such questions and more, allowing the researchers to literally see which roads led to triumph over addiction and which paths led to violence, failure, and despair.

This methodology is called ecological momentary assessment, or EMA. And I believe EMA could one day have huge implications not only for drug addicts but for workaholics, pessimists, procrastinators, and anyone else stuck in a negative or destructive reality in his or her personal or professional life.

Just as certain environmental triggers hijacked those addicts' attempts to avoid crime or get sober, so can certain triggers hijack our best efforts at work. For example, I spoke with an analyst from TD Ameritrade at a conference in Vegas who had been trying to write a book about financial investing. The problem was, every time he noticed that the stock market was down, he found himself unable to concentrate on writing. His pattern went something like this: he would go online, see the Dow Jones was down, then go on CNN to get more information, which led to his surfing the Web to get his mind off it, which led him to e-mail, where he got absorbed until he realized he wasn't working . . . which frustrated him, causing him to eat junk food. I have followed a similar pattern: when I got frustrated writing, I would start unconsciously surfing the Web; then, to relieve my frustration over not working, I would end up playing chess on my iPhone until I won—which took forever, frustrating me more. In truth, this behavior is not unlike that of the Baltimore heroin addicts that the Johns Hopkins study observed. One single trigger threw their entire day off course.

The only way to banish these kinds of hijackers is to replace them with meaning markers. In the example of the analyst, it would mean perhaps replacing his morning habit of checking the state of the markets with another, more meaningful habit, like e-mailing a friend or family member or reading his favorite blog. By starting the day with the positive, he would become more motivated and energized about his writing and less prone to procrastination.

Another common hijacker at work is a negative boss who tries to drive productivity through intimidation and fear. In *The Happiness Advantage* I described two parts of the brain I called the Jerk and the Thinker. The Jerk is the amygdala, the most primitive part of the human brain, which responds to threats. The Thinker is the prefrontal cortex, which helps you make good decisions. Fear is a map hijacker because when you activate the Jerk, you shut off the Thinker and thus waste your valuable and finite brain resources on avoiding and fleeing from that fear instead of pursuing your goals. So instead of letting yourself be infected with the boss's negativity, you should actively look for an element of meaning in the work the boss has assigned. This will shut off the Jerk and allow the Thinker to channel your brain's full suite of intelligences toward accomplishing that goal or task.

One of my personal hijackers when I'm writing is worrying about negative reviews. To combat this, I started putting positive reviews or comments I got about by my first book into a folder in Gmail. Now, before starting to write each morning, I pop into that folder to read one of those meaningful e-mails. This reminds my brain why I'm writing, giving me the drive and confidence to move ahead. It has worked so well that I now have notes all around my office from people who have used my research to improve their lives. So when I look around my office, I literally see meaning everywhere. If you have a difficult project to accomplish, I highly recommend stacking the odds in your favor by surrounding yourself with similar reminders.

Environmental triggers can hijack our mental maps outside the office as well. One example might be eating out at a favorite restaurant. For most of us, eating out is a meaning marker because we associate it with good food, good company, and being social. The problem is, eating out may also mean unhealthy eating and drinking. One strategy to avoid this kind of hijacker might be to have people over for a dinner party or to meet with friends to play basketball instead of having pizza and beer. That way you banish the unhealthy hijackers while still preserving the meaning.

What are your mental hijackers at home and at work? If you're not sure, take just two minutes to write down five triggers that consistently lead to counterproductive or destructive behavior. Are there certain people in the office who sap your drive and productivity? Certain friends who exert a negative influence? Certain places where you're likely to let good habits slip? Are there activities that tend to bring down your happiness or distract you from your goal? Only once you know what your hijackers are can you replace them and chart faster and more direct routes to that promotion, or that sales goal, or that ideal weight.

This chapter is all about learning to construct a meaning-filled reality map that harnesses your full suite of intelligences and motivates you toward continual positive growth. But identifying meaning markers and banishing hijackers is only the first step. Now let's find out how to amplify the effect of meaning markers by better orienting your map around them.

STRATEGY 2: REORIENT YOUR MAP FOR SUCCESS

Meaning markers are what point us in the direction of opportunity and possibility, steer us toward a state of positivity and full engagement, and highlight crucial intellectual, emotional, and social resources. If you have created a map full of meaning but are still having trouble harnessing your intelligences toward achieving your goals at work, it's probably because your mental map is not properly *oriented* around those points of meaning. To demonstrate the importance of orientation, I sometimes show in my lectures a simple physical map:

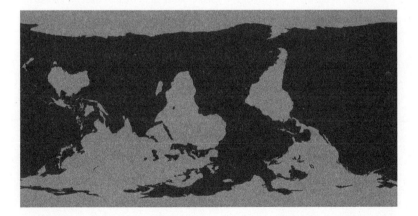

When I show this to executives, they usually say, "Got it, an upside-down world map." Which means that they didn't "get it."

In truth, there is nothing "upside-down" about this map. Think about it: the world is round! That means there *is* no "up" on the map of the world any more than there is an up and a down on a soccer ball or baseball. Yet hundreds of years ago cartographers from Europe decided that Madrid was above Rio de Janeiro and that Australia should be way "down under." From then on, we have always looked at the world from the same fixed viewpoint. I have even had technicians during AV checks tell me that they fixed my slides because one of them was upside down!

Just as the floor is not always down on a submarine (as I learned the hard way), there is no reason at all why Europe should have to be north and Africa south. While, of course, our standard map is accurate, it masks the fact that there are other equally accurate ways to map the world.

So the problem isn't that my map is an "upside-down" map; the problem is our brains' difficulty in seeing it from any other orientation. As cognitive psychologists Amy Sheldon from Stanford and Timothy McNamara from Vanderbilt aptly point out, the brain is unable to perceive location if it is not oriented to some sort of familiar reference point.[9] As a result, our brains assign fixed orientations to objects in the universe when those orientations should remain flexible. This is a problem because the more flexible and adaptive our mental maps, the more paths to success we can find in our external world. Have you ever watched someone using Google Maps on an iPhone turn the phone on its side to better see whether he needs to turn left or right? In essence that person is orienting around the different reference points. Similarly, when it comes to mental mapping, keeping our orientation flexible allows us to see different approaches, solutions, and resources we might otherwise have missed. The orientation of our maps can dramatically change depending on whether we see a positive or a negative reality, and thus it can have a huge impact on our ability to harness our positive genius at work.

If your map at work is oriented around discouragement and lack of control, then all you'll see is one big ocean of failures, rather than all the resources and routes to success. But if you orient your map around the positives, then you can see how all the opportunities and resources are connected, and you can begin to chart a path around them.

What if you could reorient your mental map to depict a world full of opportunities, meaning, and, most of all, happiness? Exciting new research coming out of positive psychology labs all over the country tells us that the question is no longer "what if" but "how."

FROM DISORIENTED TO ENGAGED

You've already taken the first step in changing your map's orientation: identifying your meaning markers. If getting a promotion at work is the goal you want to map toward, and you've identified *why* this goal is meaningful to you, next you'll need to orient your map to find the best and fastest way to get to that end result.

First, I suggest doing a few exercises to train your brain to more naturally shift toward a positive orientation. Try using some of the positive habits I outlined in the *Happiness Advantage* lecture for PBS: practice writing down three new things for which you are grateful for twenty-one days in a row, or journaling for two minutes once a day about the most meaningful experience of your day, or writing a two-minute positive e-mail to someone in your social support network. The things you write down might not be directly related to the goal at hand, and that's okay, because, as I described in the PBS program, the simple act of writing down these meaning markers literally rewires the brain to more quickly perceive a positive orientation of the world, while also keeping your brain flexible, nimble, and adaptive. For more positive habits, check out Martin Seligman's *Learned Optimism* or go to HappinessAdvantage.com.

Now think about something you want to accomplish in your professional life, whether it's starting your own business, getting the corner office, or leading your team in sales. Take out a sheet of paper and write down all the resources you currently have that can be used to get you toward that goal. By resources I don't just mean money. I mean intellectual, emotional, and social resources—like your leadership skills or your ability to stay calm under pressure or your good relationship with someone in the corporate office. This will help you shift to a more positive orientation by forcing your brain to focus on all the reasons why you *are* likely to get the promotion, rather than to waste its finite resources worrying about reasons you might not.

Here's another technique for reorienting your map around the positives: literally folding up your mental map. Why is this useful? Because it can help you see a (true) reality in which your goals are much closer than they originally appeared so that you can chart shorter and more direct routes to get you there. A good way to visualize this is the famous Dymaxion map:

Look what we can do to the world by literally carving up the map. Notice how many new realities emerge when we free ourselves from the rigid and *arbitrary* rectangular framework. See how oceans are suddenly less wide, and continents suddenly closer together, on this (equally accurate) version of the world map. Similarly, folding your mental map at work can help you see your destinations as closer and your challenges as less vast. But remember, we want to create the most adaptive map. Let's revise the Dymaxion map again, this time searching for connected water sources.

I love these maps because they are opposite but both accurate; they just use a different lens or focal point to portray the same information. The Dymaxion map may look weird to the inflexible brain, but it is an accurate portrayal, one that lets you see how continents and oceans are connected in different ways. Just flex and invert a Dymaxion map, and you end up with an equally valid view of the world. All that differs is the orientation. The new perspective caused by a change in focal point can yield a much more helpful mapping of reality.

Keeping your map flexible in this way not only helps you see new routes to your endgame but also allows you to change your *focal point*, or orientation. Just as the above map could be reoriented so that Europe or Greenland or the Pacific Ocean lie in the center, so can you reorient your mental map to center on the area of your life or work where you want to focus. Do you want more social connection at work? Are you aiming to raise your revenues? Improve your writing skills? You can make any of these your focal point simply by reorienting your conventional map.

Remember, the most valuable realities are those that are both positive and true.

ORIENTING YOUR MAP AROUND OTHERS

Research has found that altruism is one of the greatest buffers against depression.[10] Doing something for someone else raises our levels of hope, joy, and happiness—and, in turn, our success rates. To reap these benefits, we must shift the focus off ourselves and onto others. Think about it. When you are most negative— when you are feeling depressed, when you are frustrated about how bad your day has been, when you are feeling inferior compared to your peers—that's when your world is most contracted. Your entire world is *you*. You're so zoomed in on yourself, you're not even at street level, you are at the "only you" level. It is hard to see possibilities and opportunities, much less ways to help others, when all you can see is yourself. Putting others at the center of your map isn't just about altruism, it's about expanding your world so you can see more routes to your destinations.

Given that you're the one drawing your mental maps, it makes sense that you are usually in the center. But when we become too laser focused on the self, our brains waste a good deal of valuable energy, attention, and intellectual and emotional resources that would be better spent elsewhere. A common example of this is what happens when we make a faux pas at work. Once, when I was out speaking at an Adobe CEO retreat in California, toward the end of my talk, amped up on three hours of coffee, I was pacing back and forth on the stage and accidentally kicked the table leg, spilling a cascade of water and coffee off the stage and onto the CEOs' table. Mortified, I immediately lost my concentration and focus and completely fumbled through the rest of my presentation. I was sure that my little accident was all that people were going to remember from that talk. But when I returned six months later and mentioned how I had knocked an entire table of water pitchers onto the CEOs' table, hardly anyone remembered what I was talking about. I then realized that no one in the room had been paying attention to that incident. My embarrassment barely registered on their mental maps at all, as they were fully, and rightfully, focused on how to use the research with their teams or families.

In his book *Finding Flow*, the famous psychologist Mihaly Csikszentmihalyi wrote, "The Eskimo, the hunter of the Amazon basin, the Chinese, the Navajo, the Australian Aborigine, the New Yorker—all have taken for granted that they live at the center of the universe."[11] This is true for mental maps, too; our brains construct our world around the "blue dot" of us. But if we can actively expand or shift the focal point of our maps to include our colleagues and our families and our communities, we suddenly unlock more of our brains' resources and open up a much broader range of possibilities. There are two easy ways to do this.

First, we need to change how we judge people. One of the first things students learn in "Introduction to Social Psychology" courses is the concept of fundamental attribution error (FAE), which is the human tendency to judge our own behavior based on *context* but to attribute others' behavior to their *character.* For instance, if you cut someone off while driving, you might think: "Well, that's because I was running late to work because there was traffic." But if someone cuts *you* off, you think, "What an inconsiderate jerk! He's willing to risk someone else's life to save two seconds." This phenomenon happens all the time at work. Someone doesn't execute a project perfectly, and you decide he's lazy or incompetent. However, if you make a similar error, you chalk it up to how tired you were that day (probably because of your jerk boss), or how you were given incomplete instructions. In both cases, you have decided that others' behavior explains what they must have been thinking, whereas you use your thinking to explain away your own behavior. We need to give others the same benefit of the doubt that we give ourselves. Not doing so is a counterproductive error that results from putting ourselves at the center of our maps. But by consciously choosing to reorient our maps so that we try to explain others' behavior on the basis of context rather than character, we can slowly begin to expand the borders of our mental universe.

This change of focus can yield huge returns in the workplace, making us better marketers, salespeople, and managers. Jordan Brock, one of the top salesmen at Dell, once told me that because novice salespeople are constantly worrying about what clients and customers are thinking about them, they tend to talk incessantly to overcompensate. This can be very off-putting to potential clients and customers. But expert salespeople, he said, seem far more confident and self-assured because they've realized clients aren't scrutinizing their every word—they are way too busy thinking about their own reality to be analyzing the foibles of the salesperson.

Another way to reorient your map around others is to work to offer social support, rather than merely to receive it. When scientists try to assess levels of "social support" (the depth and breadth of your social relationships), they tend to look at how much support you are receiving, not how much you are giving. This is a mistake.

It's true that the perceived social support we receive is one of the best predictors we have for job satisfaction and engagement (which correlate directly with productivity).[12] So you would think the best way to be more connected and therefore more productive would be to receive more social support from others at work, right? Turns out, not exactly.

Some of the greatest discoveries in psychology arise when we decide to ask questions in a different way. Social connection is my favorite research topic, but I recently realized that until earlier last year I had been looking at it all wrong. On the basis of a study I performed on 1,600 Harvard students in 2007, I had discovered an 0.7 correlation between perceived social support and happiness. (That number may not *sound* high, but it is. In fact, it is significantly higher than the connection between smoking and cancer.) And the more my colleagues and I studied social support, the more we found it to be crucial to every single business and educational outcome.[13] Studies even show that social support affects your health and high levels have been found to be as predictive of longevity as regular exercise, while low levels are as damaging as high blood pressure. We put warning labels on smoking packs; maybe we should put warnings on companies that have low social support.

Since social support was clearly crucial to happiness and productivity, my team and I, including Dr. Max Weisbuch, from the University of Denver, set out to find a way to measure the amount of support people had in their lives. We started with the kind of questions scientists had been asking for the past twenty years: "Are you *receiving* meaningful connection and support in times of trial from your friends? Are you *receiving* support and a belief that you have a high potential from your parents? Are you *receiving* a congenial and supportive environment at work? Are you *receiving* the benefits of social engagement from your managers at work?" See a common pattern here?

The past two decades of research on social support have mistakenly focused on how much you *receive*, not how much you *provide*. It turns out that giving feels better, does more for you, and provides greater returns in the long run than getting support does. We had been asking the wrong question.

We began to look not at how much your colleagues were helping you but at how much you were helping your colleagues. So we asked people about how much effort they *put into* their work relationships, whether by, say, inviting coworkers out for drinks or commenting on their Facebook posts or taking the initiative to get to know them better. We didn't ask how much support their parents were providing them, but how much love and encouragement they were giving their parents. We looked not at whether their friends were there for them, but whether they were there for their friends.

The findings were extraordinary. After surveying over three hundred research participants from various occupations, we identified several distinct types of social support providers, including "work altruists" (who provided the most social support at work) and "work isolators" (who provided the least). Here's where it gets interesting. When we looked at the correlation with work engagement, we found that only 5 percent of work isolators were extremely engaged in their jobs and that work altruists were *ten times* more likely to be highly engaged than work isolators.

What's more, over half of the work altruists got along "extremely well" with coworkers, as compared to only about 20 percent of isolators. Work altruists were twice as likely as work isolators to be satisfied with their jobs, and almost two-thirds of work altruists reported excellent relations with supervisors.

Most important, though, was the impact that the giving of social support had on their success rates: *only 7 percent of isolators had received a promotion in the previous year, compared to about 40 percent of each of the other groups.* The conclusion was clear. If you're not giving at work, you're not getting ahead either.

I believe this finding is critical to our understanding of positive genius. In an era of doing more with less, we need to stop wasting mental energy lamenting how little social support we *receive* from managers, coworkers, and friends, and instead channel our brains' resources toward *giving* more social support.[14] In *The Happiness Advantage*, I wrote about how one of the greatest predictors of success and happiness at work is social support. We now know that one of the greatest predictors of positive genius is providing social support to others.

All it takes is consciously remembering that we need to include others in our reality.

Remember, the reality you experience at work and at home is a constellation of meaningful facts that your brain has wrapped together. Finding meaning in the social support we give to others is one of the best ways to harness our cognitive resources and intelligences to become more engaged, motivated, productive, and successful in our professional and personal lives.

As St. Francis of Assisi in the thirteenth century said it best, "Grant that I may not so much seek to be consoled as to console; to be understood as to understand; to be loved as to love. For it is in giving that we receive."[15]

STRATEGY 3: MAP SUCCESS ROUTES BEFORE ESCAPE ROUTES

In the summer of 2011, I walked into a nondescript building in San Antonio, Texas, to conduct what I thought would be a routine webinar on happiness for the IRS. I was ushered into the building and into a room where I would be doing the webinar from a government-issued laptop. Then the two very kind women in charge sat me down to explain what apparently was the only important thing to know before I began my webinar: where the fire escape routes in the building were located. I'm serious. Not just one fire escape route either. They felt that it was their professional responsibility to inform me about *multiple* escape routes. Really, how badly did the IRS expect my talk to go?

Of course, literal escape routes are important in case of an actual fire. But often in our professional lives we get so focused on mapping mental escape routes that our brains are left with little energy for mapping paths that lead to growth. For example, every bit of mental energy we spend thinking about what we'll do if our big presentation tanks is energy that could be spent reviewing our slides, perfecting our speech, or rehearsing our notes. Similarly, every minute we spend trying to figure out how we'll fund our new business if the venture capital dries out is time we could spend meeting with investors, drumming up resources, or reinvesting our existing capital. And this principle holds true for virtually any challenge in any job and industry.

It is amazing how much of our brain resources is spent on finding escape routes away from situations or environments where success is still possible. That's why, if we spend too much time and energy mapping escape from the negatives in our lives, rather than movement toward the positives, we dramatically lower our chances of finding opportunities. Given that our brain has a limited amount of resources, what we decide to map *first* has the greatest chance of becoming our reality.

In a *Harvard Business Review* article entitled "The Happiness Dividend," I described research about how 75 percent of job success is predicted by three things (aside from intelligence): belief that your behavior matters, social support, and the ability to *view stress as a challenge instead of a threat.*[16] If you view stress as a threat, your brain will be continually looking for escape routes, and you will miss seeing those signs and seizing those resources that could help you succeed. I have seen countless people at countless companies fall into this trap. After the 2008 banking collapse, for example, managing directors at the world's top banks told me that their teams' performance had taken a nosedive because employees were spending inordinate amounts of time thinking about whether they should flee the firm, or what job prospects and compensation packages would be like elsewhere, instead of focusing on what they could do to improve their situations where they were. Just think about all the ways this tendency undermines us in our everyday lives. How often have you spent more time thinking about how to get out of a phone call or lunch date than it would have taken to just do the call or have the lunch?

I once spoke with a CFO from Holland, Michigan (the clog capital of America), who told me, "I can't be happy unless I've thought through all the things that can go wrong, because then and only then do I know that I am prepared for any eventuality." But in mapping only for escape, he *wasn't* ready for every eventuality, only for failure. When I asked him how much time he spent preparing for success, the CFO looked thoughtfully down at his shoes (sadly not clogs) and said, "Huh, that's funny, because our problem in 2007 was that demand for [their product] way outstripped our ability to produce them." His company had been prepared for every eventuality—except that their product would be successful.

Pessimists assume that imagining worst-case scenarios will help protect them in case of problems. But in truth, the more time we spend imagining what might go wrong, the less time and resources our brains have to spend planning for things to go *right*. When I worked with the National Association of Safety Professionals, one of the members came up to me after an event and told me, "I have trouble having fun at dinner with friends because I'm constantly scanning for how the beams above us look shoddy or whether the fire exits are too far from my table if there was an explosion in the kitchen." But how could he expect to accomplish anything at work if his mind was so constantly consumed by worst-case scenarios that he couldn't even enjoy dinner with friends?

Like using a world map where Europe is always on top, using a mental map that always points to escape limits the opportunities, possibilities, and resources you can perceive. Worse, if all we map are routes to failure, we'll inevitably end up stuck on those routes. Then that failure will become our reality, confirming our very worst fears and leading to more hopelessness and pessimism. For example, a negative employee may construct a reality in which people are constantly criticizing her or never giving her her due. When facts emerge that fit into this orientation (since she hasn't mapped for any other), she may feel validated, thinking her prediction came true. In actuality, though, there exist alternate realities that are equally true; she just hasn't mapped them. Individuals with a negative mindset keep flipping their orientation of the world until it justifies their pessimism. A positive genius avoids falling into this vicious cycle by looking for paths to success *before* escape routes.

Once when I was out speaking at Google in Palo Alto, one of the managers described someone at his previous company who kept telling everyone about how he expected to get passed up again for a promotion. The dejected employee would say, "Oh, I'll probably just get passed up again. That's what always happens." Then, when the manager didn't give him the promotion (and who could blame him!), the employee went around spreading even more negativity to the team by griping, "See, I told you I would never get that promotion." The manager told me point-blank that while the employee had had the technical skills and the intelligence, he didn't get the job because he didn't have a vision for success. The manager said, "That guy was affecting the team's performance a ton, just in the wrong direction. How could I trust him to lead a team to success when he didn't even trust his own chances of success?"

Defensive pessimism, or assuming the worst until you are proven wrong, seems like a very safe position at work. That way, you are never surprised by negative events and even have a plan ready in case they happen. Sounds safe, right? The problem is, your brain constructs a world based upon how you expect it to look. So if you can't anticipate accomplishment, meaning, praise, and gratitude, you are doomed to a reality devoid of those things. Remember, you have to live in your reality, so why construct it with negative expectations?

One of the biggest discoveries coming out of positive psychology is the revelation that negative people literally see a narrower range of opportunities and possibilities. In her book *Positivity*, Barbara Fredrickson writes about her research showing that when a brain is negative, it operates in fight-or-flight mode. But when your brain is positive, it can use its full range of intellectual, social, and emotional resources to "broaden and build" and find new ways of seeing and doing things. This finding was later confirmed by researchers at Brandeis University. They used an eye-tracking machine to literally track and record everything our eyes, and thus our brains, are focusing upon. They found that when people were in a negative mindset, their attention was focused mostly on what was in the center of the computer screen. When people with a more positive orientation looked at that screen, however, their range of vision expanded to include the entire picture, rather than just one or two pieces of information in the center.[17] Thus a positive employee is more likely to perceive avenues for job advancement in his company, a positive entrepreneur is able to see more open niches in the marketplace, a positive student is able to see more fellowships or scholarships to apply for, a positive athlete will see more players to pass to on the field, and so on.

Which kind of map have you created for yourself? Does it look more like an emergency exit map or a treasure map? Do the paths merely steer you away from failure, or do they navigate you toward success? No matter what goal you are mapping toward in your personal or professional life, you should always look for the path to your desired outcome *before* you devote any cognitive resources to planning how you'll survive failure. *It's not that anticipating problems is inherently bad. But because what you map first is more likely to become the reality, you should spend your brain's valuable resources looking for an escape route only once you have mapped multiple paths to success.*

So if you are thinking about running a marathon, don't start out by thinking about the injuries you could sustain or about how embarrassing it would be if you didn't finish. Instead, start by planning a training schedule, thinking about how good you'll feel as your miles start increasing, and anticipating that nice dinner you and your family will eat after the race to celebrate your accomplishment.

Or if you want to start a new business, don't start by playing out scenarios in your head about what will happen if no one likes your product, or your capital dries up, or what your friends will think if you fail. Instead, start by looking at the market and gathering data, phoning investors and growing your resources, and enlisting your friends to cheer on your efforts.

If you want to write a novel, don't start by thinking about how many people don't get book deals, how slow your writing is going, or how few books become bestsellers. Instead, start by reminding yourself how passionate you are about your idea and how many contacts you have to help guide you on your path, and by making a timeline for when you think you can finish each chapter.

Mapping for success first will allow you to better harness your full suite of intelligences and construct a prism of success.

A CARTOGRAPHER'S JOB IS NEVER DONE

Keeping on track toward your professional goals requires checking and rechecking your map periodically. This is critical: flawed reality maps, with paths that are no longer viable, are responsible for some of the greatest disasters, not just in business but on the world stage.

In 1999, the CIA bombed the Chinese Embassy in Kosovo. When the dust literally settled and an international outcry began, it was discovered that the pilots had been using a hard copy of a map from 1996 when they designated their target. Unfortunately, the Chinese Embassy had moved in 1997.[18] The pilots' maps were tragically one year outdated.

A year before, on a cold February day on the beautiful ski slopes in the Dolomites of Italy, when a U.S. military EA-6B Prowler plane's right wing struck and cut through a gondola cable, twenty people plummeted two hundred feet. All of them died instantly. In the subsequent investigation, the new maps that marked the cables were found unopened in the cockpit of the plane. The maps the military had been using were old and did not mark the "killer wires." This is not uncommon; between 1980 and 1999, fifty-nine collisions occurred between military aircraft and unmapped obstacles.[19]

One last true story from the *New York Times*: a Nicaraguan military commander named Edén Pastora almost incited war with Costa Rica when he mistakenly dumped several tons of river sediment on the wrong side of the Costa Rica/Nicaragua border.[20] Costa Rican president Laura Chinchilla thought that her country, which doesn't even have a military, was being invaded; it turned out that Pastora had simply been using Google maps, which had drawn the border slightly off.

In business, too, outdated maps of reality can lead to unintended and negative results. To save costs after the economic collapse of 2008, a large European bank at which I consulted decided to combine the HR and learning departments of the three business units—private equity, banking, and wealth management. However, while the official borders between these departments were removed, the mental and cultural borders remained. So while the leaders in the company were navigating according to these new borderless maps, the company employees continued to use the maps that were now outdated regarding whom they should talk to and how to treat different people in the company. The result was a quagmire of culture clashes, miscommunications, and interpersonal conflicts that ended up costing the company in both productivity and profits.

One of the best-regarded book editors in New York once told me a story illustrating how important it is to continually update our reality maps. She told me that she had gotten into her line of work because she loved editing and wanted to rise higher in her profession and become a big-time editor. So using these meaning markers to guide her path, after she graduated college, she was willing to do all the thankless grunt work as an intern, knowing this was a necessary step toward her goals. But eventually she realized that if she kept traveling along the same mental route she had drawn as a recent college graduate, at some point in her career there would be a problem. If she got the next level of promotion, she would have a higher position, but she would no longer be editing books. She would only be deciding which books to buy and when to bring them to market. So she went back to her map and updated it.

Drawing a career map but then failing to look back at it or update it is a fairly common phenomenon in the working world, as *most people strive for promotion after promotion without stopping to think about whether they would actually like their new job or role more.* If you don't periodically step back to evaluate whether your old meaning markers are still leading you toward the specific place you want to go in your career, you may end up veering way off course.

So take time each month to make sure that your short-term plans are still leading you toward your career and life goals. There are a few ways of doing this. One is to look at your map from another viewpoint. By this I mean, ask a friend, a colleague, or even a career expert to give you an objective opinion on where he or she thinks your career is headed. Another strategy is simply to ask yourself a simple question: Does my behavior today lead toward one of my meaning markers? If not, you've identified a road that need not be traveled. Third, make a regular time, maybe even just an hour on the first Saturday of each month, to reflect upon the map I had you draw earlier in the chapter. Does it still reflect your goals and your plans? Are there new meaning markers to be drawn, new paths to be added? I suggest even keeping a journal or a Word doc to track your goals for the next year and periodically check them against your map. You can have the greatest map in the world, but if you aren't keeping it updated, you may be miles off course.

Above all, remember that if you map toward your goals and ambition, your brain will have a path to follow. Now that you've learned how, you're ready to learn the next strategy: how to harness success accelerants to get you there faster.

MAKING IT PRACTICAL

1. *Diversify your meaning portfolio.* Write down a list right now of as many meaning markers in your life as you can. Aim for at least ten, and be specific. Instead of just "money" or "family," yours might include "Be a positive role model for my son" or "Find time to read more" or "Do more adventuresome travel with my family." And be sure to look for meaning markers in

all areas of your life, not just a few corners: the more diverse your portfolio of meaning, the more roads will lead to growth and the less chance you will have of getting lost as you navigate through all your work.

2. *Do a daily "meaning orientation."* Ask yourself each morning as you start your day, "What is one action I will take today that will get me closer to my meaningful goals?" Even if you were going to do that task anyway, highlighting the fact that you are doing a meaningful action daily will train your brain to constantly and automatically readjust and reorient your map around meaning.

3. *Map your life.* Draw an actual map of your current workplace, neighborhood, or city. What areas or people did you draw largest? Which are closest to the center? Now think about what's missing. Are there important people or places or resources—like the quiet but fiercely smart engineer on your team, or the library brimming with professional tools— that you overlooked? If so, chances are you are over-looking them in your actual work life as well. Think about ways you might better utilize these people and resources.

4. *Spot and stop the hijackers.* Identify three map hijack-ers that you know pull you off your path (for exam-ple, getting e-mail alerts, hanging out with negative people, envying others' possessions, gossiping, hav-ing more than two drinks a day, shopping online). What can you do today to avoid those hijackers?

What positive, meaningful habits can you replace them with? If you're worried about the hijackers rearing their ugly heads, give a copy of the list to a close friend, a colleague, or your spouse to help you stay accountable.

5. *Use a treasure map.* For the next big meeting, project, or presentation you have, make a mental treasure map instead of an escape route map. Commit to focusing your brain on what it would take to nail it, rather than what to do if you fail. If others start focusing on the problems or worrying, steer the conversation back to the positive: "Let's figure out how success is possible before talking about what might go wrong."

6. *Update your map.* Take a monthly, one-hour sabbatical to reflect on your mental map. Pick a Saturday or a Sunday, at some point in the day when you are not occupied with family or work responsibilities, and spend some time just thinking about what your current ambitions are and whether you are still on track. This brief respite is crucial to ensure that your map is up-to-date and accurate. You don't know how many people I work with who create maps, then just keep following the path they drew a decade ago without thinking about whether that's still the destination they want to get to.

the x-spot

FINDING SUCCESS ACCELERANTS

There are few better ways to witness the sheer power of human potential than to watch a runner cross the finish line of a marathon. It's incredible to see the months and years of physical training, determination, and self-discipline culminating in that one moment of pure achievement. What's always fascinated me about those final moments of a marathon is that I have never once seen a runner slow down as he or she approaches the finish line. Despite how exhausted they must feel by that point, marathon runners actually *speed up* and sprint with the full force of their remaining energy across the finish line. How?

When runners are 26.1 miles into the 26.2-mile race, a special brain event occurs right at the spot, called the X-spot, where runners turn the corner and can finally see the finish line. Their brains release a flood of endorphins and other chemicals that give them the energy to accelerate through that final leg of the race. If you are a runner, or any kind of athlete, you have probably experienced some form of this. When your brain sees that *success is not only possible but now probable*, the reaction is physically powerful—so powerful, in fact, that a very small handful of marathoners can't handle it.

Incredibly, in the entire grueling 26.2-mile race, the X-spot is the most likely place for a cardiac arrest to occur. This is why, at the Philadelphia Marathon, Dr. Lewis Maharam, board chairman of the International Marathon Medical Directors Association, brilliantly places medics right at the X-spot. He knows that in some rare cases ultrafatigued bodies can't handle the incredible surge of neurochemical accelerants dumped into their bodies, and he's right. Maharam has had ten successful resuscitations right at the X-spot in 2011 alone![1] But of course, the discovery of the X-spot is not about stopping the rare heart attack. The X-spot reveals one of the most important attributes of our brains. At the precise moment your brain realizes that attaining your goal is not only possible but probable, it releases a potent stream of chemicals that help you speed up.

The X-spot illustrates how powerful the finish line can be in terms of increased energy and focus. As soon as that goal comes into view, our efforts ramp up. That's because once our brains are convinced that we will finish, they release these powerful accelerants. Similarly, in football running backs are known to run faster and harder the closer they get to scoring (this is why they are said to have a "nose for the end zone"). With the reward right there, their brains sanction the release of greater energy, rather than reserving it for later rewards. And the body is thus rewarded with increased vigor, speed, mental clarity, and toughness. So if you want to accelerate your success rates, you need to find your X-spots early and often.

Of course, this phenomenon doesn't occur only in sports. No matter what your goal is—whether it's finishing the marathon, completing a big project at work, or losing twenty pounds—your brain behaves in the exact same way. As soon as your brain registers that you are going to achieve your goal, it releases these same chemicals that give you the extra boost you need to accelerate. *The closer you perceive success to be, in other words, the faster you move toward it.*

What if we could access that increased energy, focus, and drive as we approached not just the finish line but any point in the race? And what if we could apply those same techniques to speed toward any goal we wished to accomplish in our professional lives?

Positive psychology research reveals that we can. The brain releases its accelerants, not just when a runner *sees* the finish line, but as soon as the runner *realizes the probability* that he or she is going to succeed. What that means for all of us in the working world is that we don't need to be at the end of the race to reap the cognitive rewards of the X-spot. By changing our *perceptions* of the distance to the finish line, we can prime our brains to release those chemicals earlier to accelerate our success. The goal of this chapter is to make your possible, positive reality seem more probable.

PAINTING THE TARGET

As part of my training for my navy ROTC scholarship, I spent a summer during college training in different warfare specialties. One week during the training, my fellow cadets and I were invited to go out on one of the navy's crown jewels: an Aegis class destroyer. These extraordinary ships were the first of their kind to be built entirely around the cutting-edge Aegis combat system and SPY-1 phased array radar, meaning that they were basically a super-high-tech floating guided missile system. These 9,200-ton behemoths had over ninety missiles and would use a series of interconnected weapon systems to scan for potential threats to the ship and neighboring countries and then shoot them down.

The technology employed by these ships is beyond the scope of this book (and my understanding), but at the basic level, when a missile fired from a ship neared its target, it was able to detect the scattered energy coming from that target and adjust both its trajectory and its momentum on the basis of these data. This was called "painting the target," and these ships could do it with incredible precision.

Why am I telling you this? Because "painting the target" is exactly what your brain must do anytime it desires to accomplish a goal. Once your brain has mapped a path toward a goal you want to attain or a target you want to hit at work or in your personal life, it is constantly reading signals about what it will take to get you there.

By now you have learned how to set goals rooted in meaning and how to map your way toward them. But if you are truly interested in becoming a positive genius at work, the next question should be, How can you construct realities that help you achieve those goals *faster*? In other words, how can you not only achieve successful outcomes in your life and career but accelerate them? What you need are success accelerants.

Your brain is a goal-oriented machine. At work, when you set sales targets, assign project deadlines, or set any other kind of objective for personal or career growth, your mind subconsciously makes a number of assessments about how far away that goal is (proximity), how likely you are to achieve it (the size of the target), and the effort (thrust) it will take to do so. As you work toward the goal, your brain is constantly calculating and recalculating these three variables, just as the Aegis missile system is constantly reevaluating the position of its mark. But here is the thing: research coming out of neuroscience labs all over the world is finding that these variables are not based only on objective measures; in fact, they are based largely on our *perception* of the facts. Think about it this way. Unless you can see into the future, you can't possibly know or control how far away your goal is, how likely you are to attain it, and how much effort it will take. But you *can* control how you *perceive* the proximity of the goal and the effort required to succeed. That means you have the power to accelerate the speed at which you hit your targets—whether they are sales goals, productivity gains, career benchmarks, or personal resolutions—simply by changing your perceptions.

In Part One, I described how the question of whether a glass is half full or half empty doesn't matter as much as the question of whether there is a pitcher of water on the table. That's because how you choose to interpret that 50 percent mark is in many ways a subjective judgment. If you are at the 50 percent mark of a marathon and not feeling too tired, you will probably be encouraged by your progress and motivated to run even harder. If you are 50 percent of the way through a marathon and are worried about your knee pain flaring up, that remaining 50 percent will probably seem daunting, and you may get discouraged and give up. The same is true with your professional goals. Your success is largely determined by how you *perceive* your current progress.

For example, did you know that your performance on a test like the SATs can be influenced by the number of people you see in the room taking the test with you? Did you know you're more likely to hole a putt in golf if you surround the hole with a circle of smaller circles to create an optical illusion that makes the hole look bigger? Or that if you highlight reaching the 70 percent mark as you progress toward your goal, you can speed up? Creating more positive perceptions of our goals can dramatically increase our engagement, focus, productivity, and motivation and thus increase the speed at which we attain them.

In this chapter, you will learn three skills to help you do exactly that.

Strategy 1: Zoom in on the Target (Proximity). Research shows that the closer people get to a target, the harder and faster they work. Changing your brain's perception of the distance to a target—whether a sales goal, the completion of a project, a promotion, or any other professional goal—provides drive, focus, and motivation and gets your brain working at maximum capacity.

Strategy 2: Magnify the Target Size (Likelihood of Success). In archery, the bigger a target is, the more likely you are to hit it. By the same token, the bigger a target *looks*, the more your brain *believes* you will hit it. Various studies have demonstrated that when people perceive their chance of hitting the target as higher, success increases significantly: golfers putt more successfully, baseball players hit more home runs, employees are more likely to stay with a big work project, and team productivity rises as much as 31 percent.

Strategy 3: Recalculate Thrust (Energy Required). To achieve any goal, professional or otherwise, a certain level of energy is required. But different types of goals have different mental costs. The lower the mental costs, the faster you speed toward success. Research has shown that by changing your perceptions of these costs, you can increase your speed toward your target by as much as 35 percent.

Everyone, pessimists and optimists alike, sets goals. The difference is that positive geniuses construct the facts in their reality so that those goals seem well within their reach. As a result, they are able to harness all their other mental resources and intelligences to accomplish those goals faster and more effectively than their pessimistic counterparts. You too can learn to do this by using the three strategies you'll read about in this chapter.

STRATEGY 1: ZOOM IN ON THE TARGET (PROXIMITY)

It is said that those who do not learn from history are doomed to repeat it. This is even more true in science. When I took psychology courses in college, professors would often scoff at research that was only ten years old. With a knowing and derisive laugh, they would dismiss those studies as passé, outdated, old-fashioned. Their opinion was clear: we had advanced way beyond the scientific discoveries of the previous decade.

We as scientists get so excited about learning new information that we often forget the importance of previous discoveries. That is perhaps why, when I talk to educators, only a handful have heard of Robert Rosenthal and Lenore Jacobson's famous Pygmalion effect from 1968, which found that students perform at the level expected by the teacher, even if the teacher never verbalizes that expectation.[2] That is why, when I spoke to doctors at retirement centers, few had heard of Harvard professor Ellen Langer's 1979 study in which she was able to reverse the effects of aging merely by having seventy-five-year-old men pretend for a week that it was twenty years earlier.[3] And that is why you have probably not heard of Clark Hull's goal gradient theory, though it affects virtually every business, educational, and personal outcome.[4]

THE INCREDIBLE HULL

Clark Hull was born in 1884, which meant he grew up right as modern science was coming of age.[5] Hull did not have an easy life. As a boy, he contracted typhoid and almost died. Miraculously, Hull lived, but typhoid left him with a parting blow, impairing his vision and memory capacity for life. Yet Hull persevered, and when he graduated from college, despite his terrible recall and eyesight, it seemed that he had finally overcome adversity. That was when the unlucky twenty-four-year-old was diagnosed with polio.

Polio ravaged Hull's body; one of his legs would never work properly again. But Hull would not abandon the goals he had set for himself. While some people use life's burdens as a crutch, or as a rationale for giving up on their high ambitions, Hull made a literal brace for himself so that he could continue to chase his. It took him ten years to get his PhD in psychology, for he had to quit several times to get extra jobs to pay for his education. This tremendous feat accomplished, Hull could easily have relaxed and slowed his pace. But he was just getting started. The more goals he accomplished, the less time it took him to achieve the next one.

We have a joke in the field of psychology that you end up studying whatever your reality is. We call it "mesearch." If you study depression, you're probably prone to depression. If you study the psychology of obesity, you're probably overweight. If you're studying anger management, well . . . we're usually too afraid to tell you why.

So what did Hull study? If daily life is a constant struggle because of a diseased or sick body, yet you persevere to accomplish great things anyway, you might be interested in studying why some people accomplish their goals when others do not. You might want to study the impact of high-order processes like drive, engagement, motivation, and energy on a person's success rate. In 1926, Hull wrote, "It has struck me many times that the human organism is one of the most extraordinary machines—and yet a machine." He believed humans were machines that could be tweaked or adjusted for improved speed and accuracy.

At the time, it was unheard of for a psychologist to conduct behavioral research on real human machines. So Hull had to settle for the next best thing: rats. And what better way to study goal attainment than to watch rats trying to find their way to a reward at the end of a maze?

After over ten thousand hours of observation, Hull started noticing a phenomenon that must have seemed very familiar: the closer the rats got to the end of the constructed maze, the faster they seemed to get. To confirm these findings, Hull designed electric sensors all along the maze to get precise readings of the rat's speed over time. And what he found was that the rats did indeed speed up as they approached their goal—just as marathon runners do when they reach the X-spot.

Have you ever noticed that you start reading faster when you get close to the end of a book? Or that you start talking faster when you know a phone call is about to wrap up? Or that you work more diligently and efficiently when the completion of a big project is in sight? This is Hull's goal gradient theory in action: the closer to your goal, the faster you go.

Hull was a behaviorist, meaning that he believed that our brains rely on objective rules of behavior. But I'm a positive psychologist, which means I believe our brains are powered not only by objective measurements but also by perception. On the basis of my research—not with rats in cages but with real live employees in businesses and offices, and using not mazes but real-world goals and teams—I contribute one important addendum to Hull's hypothesis: we work harder and faster not only when we get objectively closer to our goal but also when we *perceive* that we are closer to our goal. In other words, *the closer we perceive success to be, the more successful we become.* And by carefully painting our targets closer, we can spur ourselves to unleash the drive, energy, focus, motivation, and cognitive resources that will help get us there faster.

So now let's look at exactly how you can create X-spots to accelerate projects, increase productivity, raise profits, and improve personal and professional results.

RAT MAZES AND FREE COFFEE

In 2006, researchers at the Columbia University Graduate School of Business did a series of fascinating studies that brought Hull's hypothesis into the business world. One, which would later be published in the *Journal of Marketing Research*, looked at whether the goal attainment hypothesis could be used to accelerate consumer spending. But how to replicate Hull's research with real live consumers? No one runs mazes in the real world (unless it's on *Wipeout*). They needed a situation that would simulate goal attainment in a retail context.

Cleverly, they decided to look at rates of participation and purchase in a customer reward program at a local coffee shop. Here is how it worked: all customers were given a stamp card and were told that every purchase would count toward a reward; in this case ten stamps would equal a free beverage. Then they simply recorded the dates people made the coffee purchases to see if people would come in and buy coffee more frequently as they got closer to winning their free coffee. And indeed, that was exactly what happened; just as Hull's hypothesis predicted, the closer the customers got to the goal, the faster they would race toward the finish line.

This is where the research takes a really interesting turn. The researchers repeated the coffee shop experiment, but this time half the customers got a "buy ten coffees and get one free" card, and the other half received a "buy twelve coffees and get one free" card—with the first two already stamped. So in both cases a person needed to buy ten coffees to get a free one—the goal was equally far away—but group 2 was given a *perceived* head start. Think about it this way: before even buying a single coffee, group 2 seemed to be one-sixth of the way toward the reward, whereas group 1 hadn't even started their long road to a free coffee.[6] If you were in group 1, your first coffee would bring you only one-tenth (10 percent) of the way toward your reward, whereas in group 2 it would bring you one-third (33 percent) of the way there. How did this affect purchasing behavior? Fascinatingly, the people in group 2—those who *perceived* the goal as closer even though it was the same distance away—burned through those ten stamps significantly faster than the people in group 1.

This series of studies is precisely why the Hull hypothesis has to be revised. What predicts your behavior is not objective proximity to your goal but your subjective *perception* of that objective reality.

As you can imagine, this has enormous implications for businesses, given that customers who buy more frequently will obviously buy more over time. So, the researchers wondered, would this also apply to consumer behavior online, where the stakes for businesses are even higher? After all, with online shoppers' short attention spans and all the competing noise, it's critical to get consumers to that "buy" button as quickly and as frequently as possible. To find out, researchers designed a reward system, similar to the coffee shop's offer of one free drink for every ten that customers bought: people would receive gift certificates for rating a certain number of songs. Once again, they found that the closer people got to earning their next certificate, three things happened: (1) they rated more songs per visit to the website, (2) they visited the website more often, and (3) they persisted longer in the rating effort. In other words, they worked not only faster but longer and harder as they got closer to the goal.[7]

Even more important, these studies hold some very useful lessons for businesses and for anyone dealing with clients or customers. The first is obvious: if you want to incentivize your customers to visit you more frequently, make sure to design your reward programs so that people (1) have a perceived head start and (2) can perceive great progress.

These findings also have huge implications for how we should set and structure goals for ourselves as individuals and for our teams. For one, give yourself a perceived head start by designing your goals with some progress already worked in. For example, if your New Year's resolution is to raise $1,000 for a charity, don't start with the fundraising thermometer at zero; instead, start with some money you've already accumulated through some other means so that you can feel as if you're already partway toward your goal. Or instead of starting sales targets at 0 percent each quarter, structure them to include the previous month or week of sales. The distance to the goal may still be the same (for example, if your original target was $10,000 and you're starting with $1,000, you can simply raise your target to $11,000), but you and your team will work faster and harder to get there because the target *seems* closer—just as it did for the customers who received a twelve-punch coffee card with the two-stamp head start.

No matter what industry you work in or what your job responsibilities are, the best way to turn a marathon of work into a sprint is to change your perception of the finish line. Create X-spots for your team whenever and wherever you can, and show them how close success could be through repeated positive feedback, shorter goal horizons, and graphic/visual displays of progress. This could be as practical and simple as making weekly goals, rather than yearly ones. Or try making daily habit charts where you check off each positive habit or action, rather than discrete tasks, which often take longer and involve multiple steps. It's a lot easier to see the finish line when that finish line is "Respond to boss's e-mail," rather than "Get through e-mail inbox."

Break up big projects into smaller, incremental goals. But also create X-spots by setting mileposts for yourself at the 70 percent mark. For example, if the incremental goal is $1,000,000 in revenue, set a reminder to highlight to yourself and your team when you hit $700,000. Or if the goal is to return ten client calls, be sure to note when you've completed that seventh call. Simply knowing that you are nearing the finish will cue your brain to release those success accelerants that will increase your drive and productivity and speed up your progress.

One of the best ways to create X-spots at work I learned from an employee at Microsoft in Europe. He said when you make a list of things to do during the day, write down the things you have already done that day and check those off immediately. Just like the reward card given to a coffee drinker with two stamps already done, your daily list of tasks can create that X-spot benefit. And include three things you know you are going to do anyway, like attend your weekly staff meeting, then check those off as well. This increases the likelihood of an X-spot experience because it highlights how much progress you've made over the course of the day. What matters is feeling that you are moving toward the finish instead of focusing on how far you still have to go.

LOOK BACKWARD

The newest research coming out of goal theory labs adds another important dimension to the X-spot theory. It sounds counterintuitive, but Minjung Koo and Ayelet Fishbach at the University of Chicago have found that in situations where you're less committed or motivated, the best way to accelerate growth is to look, not ahead to the finish line, but *behind* you, at what you've already accomplished.[8]

It makes sense that the more you care about a goal or target, the more energy and effort you will invest in achieving it. Turns out that this works in the other direction too; the more you invest in a task or challenge, the more you begin to care about it. This is called "escalation of commitment," and you have probably seen it at work many times. The more money, time, and energy you have sunk into a project, even one that is ill advised, the more you feel that you have to keep putting in the extra effort to make sure you get something out of it. The further along you've gotten in a boring book, the more likely you are to read to the end. The more time you put into learning a new skill, the more determined you become to master it. Even if you weren't fully committed to the task at the outset, highlighting your progress to date and the effort you've already invested tells your brain to release more success accelerants, giving you more energy and focus to keep going.

Looking back at all the energy and resources you've already put toward a goal can be an incredible motivator, particularly when the goal is one you weren't particularly engaged in or committed to in the first place. It's a strategy that can be incredibly useful in the working world, where we're often involuntarily placed on a project or committee or assignment that we aren't necessarily excited about. Think of an important goal at work that you are having low commitment to. Maybe you've been given the task of staffing a new department, but the new hires won't be reporting to you—and you hate conducting interviews. Instead of looking at how many more résumés you have to sift through and how many candidates you have yet to meet, look at how many are already done. Maybe you are having trouble eating more healthily during the workday. Your commitment to the goal of losing weight is way lower than your commitment to buffalo wings and bagels. So try to find points of progress—think about those two pounds you lost last month, or that time you chose fruit for dessert over chocolate. Researchers have found that when people start exercising, they sometimes start eating more healthily, because once they've invested the brain resources to exercise, it seems like a massive loss of investment to then go eat a cupcake.

Whatever the target, and no matter how frustrated you feel about progress, take a few minutes to write down all the work you've done and the strides you've made so far. Look at how far you have come, or how much you have already invested in this project. Make those points of progress your X-spots. Reminding yourself of past success will help your brain perceive that you are closer to the ultimate target, which will energize and motivate you to speed up.

STRATEGY 2: MAGNIFY THE TARGET SIZE (LIKELIHOOD OF SUCCESS)

The proximity of your goal isn't the only thing that matters to your brain when it comes to constructing a reality. Just like those state-of-the-art Aegis missiles, your brain is constantly calculating the *size of the target, or how likely you are to hit it.* Here's something that is important to understand about this skill: *target size* refers to the perceived likelihood of attaining a goal, not how big or important or how ambitious the goal is. Ironically, some of the biggest goals have the smallest target sizes. For example, becoming the CEO of Apple is a huge goal, but the target size is extremely small—realistically speaking, your chance of attaining it is slim to none. Think about darts. The larger the bull's-eye, the more likely you are to hit it. Does that make hitting the bull's-eye a great accomplishment? Not particularly (though I know some undergraduates who'd beg to differ). But it does make it more achievable.

The good news is that new research over the past five years shows that changing how you perceive the size of your target— that is, how you perceive the likelihood of succeeding—can have the same cognitive benefits as increasing your perceived proximity to it.

One of my favorite experiments on this particular success accelerator involves golf. In this study, participants were asked to putt from 1.7 meters away from the hole.[9] Using a video projector, the researchers shone an image of a ring of either five large circles or eleven tiny circles around the hole, creating the famous Ebbinghaus illusion. In this diagram, which middle circle is bigger?

The answer of course is neither: *they are the same size.* In the Ebbinghaus illusion, a circle simply *looks* bigger if it is surrounded

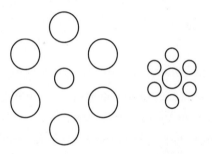

by smaller circles, and vice versa. So to recreate this illusion, the researchers surrounded a golf hole with large circles to see if the golfers would *perceive* it as smaller, even though they, of course, knew consciously that the hole was the same size. Then they looked at whether the golfers' perception of the size of their target would affect their performance.

Indeed it did. Though both holes were exactly the same size, when the hole *looked* bigger (because of the projected images of the smaller circles), the golfers made significantly more putts. When the hole looked smaller, they missed significantly more shots.[10]

This is a very important study because it shows that when we perceive a reality in which success is likely, that success become a self-fulfilling prophecy. What kind of reality do you see when you are faced with a challenge at work or in your personal life? Does it seem that your chances of success are small or large? Fortunately, there are some very simple ways of improving your chances of succeeding, simply by increasing that target size.

Let's say that you are struggling to finish a complex and challenging project for work that was assigned by your boss at the last second. At first, the hole—your chances of completing the project well and on time for success—may seem small. But what if you remind yourself of all the other projects you have accomplished in the past that were even more difficult and rushed than this one? Suddenly, success will feel more likely, and your brain will channel all of your experiences and strengths and intelligences toward hitting that larger target.

A study involving one of the oldest video games, Pong, offers a great way of understanding how this particular success accelerant works. In Pong, you move a horizontal bar, generously called the paddle, left to right to block a ball from getting past. It's like playing air hockey, except that the goal is the entire side of your screen. The longer you survive, the faster the ball goes. The faster the ball, the greater the challenge to intercept it and bounce it back to the other side of the screen.

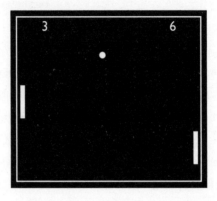

In one clever study, researchers Jessica Witt and Mila Sugovic made some simple changes to the game to manipulate participants' perceptions of target size.[11] Some of the participants got to play with a larger paddle (which makes the game easier), and others got a shorter one (which makes the game harder). Though the size of the paddle affects how likely you are to win the game, it has absolutely no effect upon the speed of the ball. Yet when the participants were asked to gauge how fast the ball was moving, the ones with the longer paddle thought that the ball was moving much slower than those in the short paddle group did. In other words, their estimate of the ball's speed was colored by whether they already perceived the task as easy or hard.

The point is, when faced with a challenge at work, whether it's about tackling a complex project, dealing with a difficult manager, or trying to grow revenues in a down economy, if you perceive your paddle—that is, your ability to overcome these challenges—as small, the objects in your working reality seem to come at you faster. But if you perceive your ability, or paddle, as large, the objects in your working reality seem to come at a manageable speed, and you can face those challenges with greater energy, confidence, and drive. One of the easiest ways of doing this we've already discussed: make a list of your current resources and a few "champion moments" that remind you of when you have been successful in similar situations. Several athletes I've worked with tell me that their secret to not choking at the end of a championship is to remember times when they have been in similar situations and they were successful. Find your work championship moments, even if they are not as dramatic, and use them to increase the size of your target.

THE N-EFFECT

Remember, the X-spot is about not just how far you are from the goal but how achievable your goal seems. One of the most fascinating corollaries to the X-spot is a psychological phenomenon called the "N-effect." Any science geeks among you will know that N refers to the number of participants in a study. If you are a researcher, you want your N to be as high as possible because the higher the sample size, the more reliable the data. (For example, if you were testing whether someone liked Coke or Pepsi and you had an N of only five people, it's possible that the first five people would just happen to all like Pepsi, and you might erroneously conclude that 100 percent of all people liked Pepsi more than Coke.)

Why is this important to our discussion of target size? Because, as it turns out, N is one of the factors used by your brain to determine the likelihood of success, and as a result, the size of the N—the number of people in a study—actually affects how participants perform.

This holds true for performance in the real world, not just the laboratory. In one study, Stephen Garcia and Avishalom Tor correlated the number of students at each testing location with the College Board's 2005 SAT scores.[12] Of all the things that we think matter to SAT scores, the number of test takers in the room is never one of them. What do you normally think is most predictive of SAT scores? Scores at the school over the past decade? The amount of federal funding received? The percentage of minority students? Socioeconomic class? Nope. The N, or number of test takers. Amazingly, the researchers found a −0.68 correlation between the N of test takers per location and their SAT score, meaning that the more test takers in the room, the lower their SAT scores. And that is a huge effect. A correlation of −1.0 would mean that test takers' *entire* SAT score was determined solely by the number of people in the room and that none of it was based upon their intelligence and education. A −0.68 correlation is massive. Holding all things constant, one of the easiest and most effective ways of improving your SAT score is merely to take the test in a room with fewer people.

Why would the number of people in the room lower one's score? The reason lies in target size. The authors of the study explain that if there are fewer people in the room, your brain *perceives* the competition as low, and your perceived likelihood of coming out on top goes up dramatically. If you are surrounded by a ton of other competitors, on the other hand, you unconsciously perceive a lower chance of being in the top percentile. In other words, *when we perceive there are fewer competitors, we believe there is greater likelihood of success, which results in more engagement and concentration and improved performance.*

For further confirmation of this theory, the researchers had participants answer a series of short quizzes. Before taking the quiz, all the participants were told that if they ended up in the top 20 percent, they would receive $5. Then they were split randomly into two groups. Though each person was placed alone in a room to take the test, the participants in group A were told they were competing against ten other individuals, whereas the participants in group B were told they were competing against one hundred individuals.[13]

Now, as a savvy reader, you realize that the N should have no effect upon a person's actual likelihood of success, since in both cases one has a 20 percent chance to get the reward. Nevertheless, the participants in group A finished significantly faster than group B overall. That's because the people in group A perceived that they had to beat out just eight people to get their reward, whereas the people in group B perceived they had to beat out eighty. That monumental challenge loomed higher, and thus chances of success seemed smaller. Just like those golfers putting to the perceived bigger hole, the people in group A perceived success to be more likely, so they worked harder toward the reward. This could have fascinating implications about whether it is good to work in a large company or a small one, to compete in Division I or II sports, or to let our kids be small fish at a really good school or big fish at a less good school.

So how do we utilize this knowledge when faced with a competitive situation or challenge? You need to find ways to make your brain perceive the N, or the number of competitors, as being as low as possible. If you are applying for a job, schedule your interview for the beginning of the morning, when there aren't likely to be as many other applicants waiting in the lobby. If you're starting a business, consider setting up shop in a part of the city where you won't have to walk past your competitors' offices every morning. If you are studying for a big test, do not study in a huge room with a lot of other students studying for the same test. If you are an author, nothing can be more discouraging than walking into a Barnes and Noble, where you are instantly reminded that there are already more books than any human being can possibly read in a lifetime. I can tell you from personal experience that this reminder will significantly slow down your writing progress.

MOVE THE FENCES

If you have ever stepped on a major league baseball field, you know that the stadium seems cavernous and the home run fences seem a mile away. But a baseball field looks a little different to Prince Fielder (his real name). Prince Fielder spent seven years knocking home runs out of Miller Park in Milwaukee as easily as I would hit a T-ball out of a sandbox (though our pay would be very different). Fielder is a power hitter. His job is to hit home runs. No matter what stadium he is in, he is aiming for the fences. But not all players swing for the fences every time. If you're in the major leagues and you are a normal or consistent hitter, who is sometimes capable of hitting home runs but generally gets on base with singles and doubles, you have to choose how to hit each ball. Do you hit for a single or swing for the fences? That choice is based upon your perception of your target.

One thing I love about baseball is that it is so much about science and numbers (on the other hand, baseball is slow as a drunk tree sloth, so there's not much else to do but think about the numbers). According to sports statisticians, different stadiums are better for hitting home runs than others.[14] And it's not just the size of the park that matters: the "park factors" that affect the likelihood of a ball sailing over the fences also include wind, building features that block the wind, temperature, altitude, humidity, and so on.[15]

Players know exactly which stadiums are good for hitting home runs and which aren't. So what happens if a player is moved to a team whose ballpark has higher park factors than his current one—say, 28.6 percent better? Statistically, one would expect that he should hit 28.6 percent more home runs. But one analysis has found that the player's ratio of home runs to times at bat actually more than doubles; he hits 60 percent more home runs.[16] Why?

The answer lies in the target size. If you are in a ballpark where you think you have a higher likelihood of hitting a home run, you are more likely to swing for the fences. But if you perceive a more negative reality, in which your chances of hitting the ball out of the park are smaller, your brain will send you signals to just try for a single to get on base.

In business and life, just as in baseball, our perceptions can affect whether we swing for the fences, or give something our all. But the baseball research shows us that what matters is not the actual distance to the fence but what our brains *perceive* that distance to be. Look around at your work and your current life. Are there domains in your life where you believe you could never hit a home run because the fences seem a mile away? Simply move the fences so that it seems easier. One way is to set reasonable goals. If we believe we have less than a 70 percent chance of succeeding at creating a new habit or achieving a goal, our likelihood of sticking with it plummets. *So structure all your goals so that you can believe you have at least a 70 percent chance of making them.*

For example, let's say you want to increase the number of clients from fifteen to twenty-five in the next month, but you believe you have only a 50 percent chance of adding those ten clients in that time. Why not move in the fences and set the seemingly more doable goal of adding five new clients in two weeks' time? The number of clients you have to add within a certain time frame hasn't changed, of course, but because adding five clients at a time seems less daunting, success suddenly seems more possible. Or you could resize the target another way. Maybe you wanted ten more clients because you thought that might lead to $50,000 more, a goal that seems more attainable than adding the ten clients. Simply make the $50,000 your goal, and your brain will release more energy, engagement, and focus to accomplish it.

STRATEGY 3: RECALCULATE THRUST (ENERGY REQUIRED)

The third accelerant of success is thrust. Thrust is the amount of energy your brain perceives is necessary to hit your target. Research shows that not all demands upon the brain are equivalent: we perceive certain tasks as requiring far more mental energy, effort, and resources than others. Research also shows that the more thrust, or mental effort, we believe is necessary to accomplish a goal, the more likely we are to give up.

For example, in one study, researchers led by Dennis Proffitt at the University of Virginia found that if you place an object up on a hill, people are less likely to expend energy to go retrieve it.[17] How often do we misperceive some task or challenge as an uphill battle, only to find out that making that sale or winning that negotiation or landing that promotion was much easier than we thought? I saw this in my work with the National MS Society. Researchers had previously found that when you put an object down a long hallway, someone with chronic neuromuscular pain will (understandably) perceive the hallway as much longer than a person who has no trouble walking. In their reality, that hallway *is* longer because they have to exert so much more effort to walk down it. But the good news is that we have the power to change our perceptions of the amount of effort, or thrust, needed to overcome our greatest challenges or obstacles.

In 2011, I had the opportunity to give a talk at a major animation studio in California, and one of the attendees observed, "When I'm doing normal work, I usually have tons of energy after work to go work out. But when I'm being creative working on a new project, I have a boost of energy, but then I feel too exhausted to work out. I sat at my desk the same amount of time, but it's like I put in three or four days of work." Corporate coaches have the same issue. They have no problem running training sessions for eight to ten hours a day, but make them give a forty-five-minute keynote, and they often feel wiped out. You have probably seen this effect in your own work many times—maybe you can sit for five hours nonstop writing computer code without breaking a sweat, but staying focused on this chapter is taking up huge amounts of mental energy. Why is this happening?

The reason is that cognitive functions are like muscles. If you are doing tasks that you know well and that use the part of the brain you work out often, you can put in eight hours and not feel exhausted. But any time you have to use skills, intelligences, or parts of your brain that you use less frequently, an hour can seem as depleting as three or four normal days of work.

The reason for this lies in your brain's levels of glucose, its primary source of fuel. Because difficult tasks require more glucose than simple ones, trying to use parts of your brain that are out of shape, and thus have to work harder, comes at a high cognitive cost. Susan Weinschenk, president of the User Experience

Network, has dedicated her time and research to understanding how to reduce cognitive costs, or thrust, associated with business and social interactions. According to Weinschenk, mental costs increase as you go from physical (i.e., moving a mouse), to visual (i.e., scanning and observing), to cognitive (i.e., logic, decision-making) processing.[18] The following goes beyond the focus of her research, but on the basis of my work with Fortune 100 companies, I would add one more process to the most expensive side of her spectrum: "emotional and social processing." Some examples could include agonizing over how to phrase something in an e-mail to your boss or trying to read the expressions of the people sitting across from you in a meeting.

Just as, when you're physically fatigued, walking up a flight of stairs can seem as exhausting as running a marathon, when you're mentally fatigued, even a task as simple as writing an e-mail or looking over a report will automatically seem harder. This is why, if you are facing a difficult or daunting challenge at work, *avoiding mental fatigue is key to reducing your brain's perception of thrust.*

Since every choice you make requires some cognitive effort, and you have only a finite amount, the key to avoiding getting burned out when it matters is to budget your cognitive resources wisely and hoard them for those tasks and challenges that take priority. For example, avoid having lunch with a difficult coworker on a day when you have to work on an important project. Don't read a dense academic article right before going to a networking event where you need to be "on."

Further, as researchers Kathleen Vohs and colleagues have found, if you are required to make multiple decisions before having to regulate your emotions, your brain wears out faster, you are more likely to procrastinate, you have lower energy, and you are more likely to quit the task early.[19] So the more you can routinize unimportant tasks at work, thus eliminating the need to make conscious decisions, the more thrust you'll have to complete the important goals. Try to routinize what time you get to work, what you have for breakfast, when you take coffee breaks, and so on. This way, you don't have to waste valuable mental energy deciding on whether to eat a muffin or oatmeal, or whether to take your break at 10:30 or 11:00.

Second, put the most important work early in the day (it doesn't have to be the first thing you do), and never schedule two really important meetings or mentally taxing tasks back to back. Researcher Roy Baumeister has found that your brain's self-regulation, or willpower, is exactly like a muscle in your arm. You can strengthen your willpower, but only if it is rested. You wouldn't try to help someone move furniture immediately after lifting weights at the gym. So why would you try to do your most important work after making lots of emotional and cognitive decisions?

Remember, it is your *perception* of the amount of effort involved that matters most. If you are getting overwhelmed by a task or a goal at work, you might be misperceiving it as harder than it is. One solution is to think about tasks in terms of objective units, rather than in terms of the effort involved. For example, if your inbox is overflowing, calculate how many e-mails you need to respond to, instead of fixing your mind on how much effort it will take to reply to that one difficult e-mail you've been avoiding. If running an errand seems as if it will take forever because your destination is way across town, Google-map how many minutes it actually takes. If you feel that it is ridiculously hard to get all the information you need to make a decision or solve a problem at work, write down the names of the people you need to talk to. In almost all cases, thinking about a task in terms of discrete units will make it seem much less difficult and daunting.

WATCHING THE CLOCK

Mental effort isn't the only thing that shapes our perceptions of thrust. In the same way that the belief that a task will require extreme effort drains our enthusiasm and motivation, so does the belief that the task or project will take a long time. Interestingly, our experience of time is dictated not as much by the clock as by our brains. Philip Zimbardo, the Stanford psychologist who became known for his famous prison study showing the lengths people will go to obey authority, later wrote a book called *The Time Paradox*, which explores how humans perceive time. His basic premise is that *the more mental energy you have to exert during a given period of time, the longer that period seems.* If you are doing a menial task at work and you have nothing to think about but the task, it may seem that time is going very slowly. But if you are on an elliptical machine and you are watching your team play the final quarter of a close game, time will pass very quickly and you will find that your twenty-minute workout felt like no time at all.

This has huge implications for businesses and employees who deal directly with customers, because the more mental processing you require customers to do—the more fine print they have to read, the more selections they have to make—the longer those tasks will feel. And in today's era of instant gratification, if customers perceive doing business with you as requiring too much time and effort, they simply won't bother, just like the participants in the study who didn't retrieve the object up on the hill.

An executive at Google once told me about the time he wanted to get some pump-up music for running, so he Googled "best NFL pump-up songs" and found a site (in the endnotes if you want it) that boasted one hundred pump-up songs.[20] But he had to click to see each one, then wait for each page to refresh on his phone with the new picture and description. He joked that by the time he made it to song #98, he was so mentally exhausted that he decided not to go running after all (and he has yet to get exercise into his routine). I went to the site and found that he was right: I didn't even make it past the top ten songs. To my brain, the thrust seemed too much.

The longer you think it will take to accomplish a challenge or task, the more difficult you perceive that challenge or task to be. And as we've seen, the harder your brain thinks something is, the harder it will actually be to achieve it. In *The Happiness Advantage*, I wrote about how just a three- to twenty-second delay between you and the activity you are trying to make yourself do can often be a solid deterrent. *I'd like to e-mail that potential client, but I don't know where I put his e-mail address . . . so I'll do it later. I would like to eat a piece of fruit, but it's in the kitchen, and these jelly beans are right on my desk . . . so pure sugar it is.* But I also described the "Twenty-Second Rule" to help your brain craft a path of least resistance toward positive habits and away from negative ones. I mentioned how I stopped watching three hours of TV a day by keeping my remote control batteries twenty seconds away in another room, and how I finally created a life habit of morning exercise by going to sleep in my gym clothes for twenty-one days. Both were essentially techniques for reducing the perception of thrust.

Emotional expectations also play a large role in shaping our perceptions of time. If you have a client on hold and your company's automated system says someone will pick up in under a minute, but it takes four minutes, the client will find that four-minute delay interminable. But if the customer is told the wait time is ten minutes and the customer service rep picks up in four, that same four minutes doesn't seem so long at all. If a train is late by five minutes in Germany (where the trains "always run on time"), people get antsy and angrily keep checking their watches. But if the subway is five minutes late in New York, you thank your lucky stars. Today, if a website takes seven seconds to load, we'll be long gone, whereas twenty years ago we would have marveled at the miraculous speed of our brand-new modem.

The point is that time is a very subjective and relative experience. If you've ever wondered why a week can feel like an eternity to an eleven-year-old but the blink of an eye to a fifty-five-year-old, think about it this way: twenty-four hours for an eleven-year-old is one-four-thousandth of his life.[21] For a fifty-five-year-old, that's only one-twenty-thousandth of her life. Similarly, a one-year economic downturn might seem more survivable to a sixty-year-old entrepreneur for whom that year is one-fortieth of his working life, but it seems utterly catastrophic to a twenty-five-year-old for whom a year constitutes one-third of her time in the business world.

In one fascinating study, researcher Peter Mangan found that when people working on a task were asked to estimate when three minutes was up, eighteen- to twenty-five-year-olds were quite accurate, but sixty- to eighty-year-olds overshot by forty seconds. In other words, time seemed to the older group to pass 20 percent faster.[22]

This may seem like a meaningless finding, but there are a lot of practical benefits to perceiving time like an eighty-year-old. For example, if you have been working on a project for eight hours, but it only *feels* like six, you will have more energy and endurance to keep going. If you've been running on a treadmill for twenty minutes, but you perceive it to be only thirteen minutes, you're more likely to have seven more minutes of stamina. Have you noticed how your energy gives out right when you expect it to? Like you plan on running for twenty minutes, and as soon as the twenty minutes are up, you feel like you can't run another minute. Or you plan on working on a project until 5:00 p.m., and after that you "just can't look at it anymore." If you want to harness the energy to work longer and harder, all you need to do is change your perception of how long you've been working.

Ironically, the key to managing time is to lose time—or, more precisely, to lose track of time intervals. We've all experienced how time seems to fly when we're fully immersed in something. This happens because when your brain is fully engaged, its "time-keeper," located in the cerebral cortex, diverts its resources to the parts of your brain that are working hard. It therefore doesn't have enough resources left to keep up with its job: keeping track of time. As a result, time seems to go faster, allowing you to work harder, faster, and longer.

Mihaly Csikszentmihalyi, in his seminal research on happiness, describes this state, in which an individual is completely absorbed in a task and nearly 100 percent of conscious cognitive functioning is aimed at that task, as "flow."[23] Csikszentmihalyi argues that flow correlates with the greatest levels of happiness, suggesting that there is scientific truth to the saying "time flies when you're having fun."

One very practical way to purposely lose track of time is simply to turn the clock around so you don't look at it, or to take off your watch. When I run on the treadmill, I intentionally put my towel over the clock function because, otherwise, that's all my brain focuses on for the entire run. The more you focus on time, the slower it will feel and the less present and engaged you will be. This same is true for any experience or activity you find dull or boring. If you don't believe me, watch how many times you check the clock during the next boring meeting you are attending.

Moments of fear, worry, anticipation, and boredom keep your timekeeper on high alert, making it impossible to focus on anything *but* time. That's why when you are waiting for 5:00 p.m. before summer holidays, or when you are delayed on a tarmac, it seems to take forever to pass. It's why, when you have to wait a day for test results from your doctor, the day seems like a week. It's also why soldiers report that when they are in combat, it seems as if they have been fighting for hours when it's only minutes. The more you can decrease your focus on the things you worry about or fear, the easier it will be to lose track of time so you can direct the entirety of your brain's resources toward succeeding at the task at hand.

TRAJECTORY MATTERS

As I learned during my stint in the navy, a weapons system can have the fastest missile in the world, but if it's not locked on its target, it will whiz right past it. Similarly, at work you can have all the success accelerants you want, but if you aren't on the right trajectory, you won't accomplish what you want to accomplish.

One rough, cloudy morning in Maui, I joined a surfing school. There were very few amateur surfers out that windy day, as the water was choppy, but I had never surfed before and was determined to try it before my lecture that afternoon. If positive psychology researchers have one commonly held character flaw, it's overconfidence in our ability to master new skills almost instantaneously through the power of our minds. Unfortunately, since I'd grown up in Waco, Texas, my sea legs were about as good as a drunk cow's with vertigo, so I was at a slight natural disadvantage.

After paddling out with me through the increasingly irritable whitecaps, and just before giving me a helpful push toward the breaking wave, the instructor yelled, "It's okay to fall, just don't hit the rocks." That's when I saw that the entire beach seemed to be covered by huge boulders, except for a small sandy spot about fifty yards to the right. "Just look at the sandy beach," he yelled above the ocean spray. "Where you look, the board will take you." Then he pushed.

A huge swell of water came behind me, and I gripped the board, then pushed myself up. It is with overwhelming pride that I report that I stood up my very first time on a surfboard. Of course, my moment of pride was soon interrupted by a wall of rocks. I would have been smarter to hop off the board, but I was so impressed with my surfing abilities that I kept going, even though I was on a direct trajectory toward the rocks. I knew the instructor had said to look at the sand, but at that moment it seemed to me that the sand did not need to be looked at, the rocks did.

But my instructor had also said, "Where you look, the waves will take you," and he was right. The wave pushed me fast and hard right at the boulders. I tumbled, my neck hit the rocks just under the water, and I tried to stand up just as my surfboard, trailing behind me on my wrist cord, hit me right in the chest. I was lucky: I could have broken a limb or been paralyzed, but all that was bruised was my pride. When the instructor saw me sheepishly paddling back out to him, he just shook his head and muttered, "Keep your eyes on the sand." (In my defense, why in the world was a beginners' class surfing in front of dangerous rocks?)

In my work with companies, I have seen this pattern over and over again: we spend our working lives trying to avoid the rocks, and as a result we end up steering right into them. The more we focus on the outcomes we fear—losing the client, the merger falling through, not getting promoted, not getting into the school, and so on—the more our brains dwell on and process this information, and we end up on a trajectory aimed straight for our pessimistic assumption. And the more our reality conforms to our worst assumptions, the more time and energy our brains spend fearing the worst in future outcomes.

I saw this vicious cycle being lived out by a sixty-year-old investment banker from a prestigious firm in New York. We shared a car after a talk at an investment conference in Phoenix. Ten minutes into the ride, he had told me his net worth and had stated that he still worked eighty hours a week. I think he thought I was a workaholic like him (since I told him I traveled all the time for my research and lectures) because he opened up and told me that when he was growing up, his family hadn't had much money and that their lack of money had caused a lot of strife and had eventually resulted in his parents' divorcing. His cash-strapped childhood had been so painful, he told me, that he had vowed to avoid repeating it at all costs when he became a father. That's why he had gone into banking. Yet his fear became all-consuming. He said he constantly felt very anxious about making money to spare his kids the difficult family life he'd experienced. But the more he worried about making money, the more he worked, and the more he worked, the less time he spent with his family. Pretty soon he went from missing piano recitals and baseball games to missing birthdays and other important life events. In the end, his wife couldn't take it and filed for divorce. He'd kept his eyes on the rocks, and as a result he'd headed squarely toward them.

What we focus on becomes our reality, which is why it is so

important for our brains to focus on real, meaningful, and positive goals. This is true in just about every realm of life you can think of. A top college basketball coach from California once told me that if a player is thinking, "Don't miss this shot," he is almost certainly doomed to miss that shot. Rather, the player should be focusing his brain on what making the shot looks like. Similarly, Jamie Taylor and David Shaw did an experiment where they had participants visualize either making or missing golf putts. Sure enough, those who had mentally envisioned and mentally experienced missing were more likely to miss than those who had visualized succeeding (their scores were significantly worse).[24] No matter what your goal or challenge is, visualizing what success would look like will help steer you to the beach instead of the rocks.

Another technique to help you stay focused on your goals is to put visual cues in your environment to remind you of your meaning markers. One of the most misapplied ways of doing this is the "vision board." "Vision boarding" is a strategy in which people dream their wildest fantasies, cut out magazine pictures of those fantasies, then put them on a corkboard in their bedroom or office. The problem with this technique is that these boards almost always reflect an unrealistic, commercially motivated vision of what people think their life "should" look like (remember, the definition of a most valuable reality is one that is positive and also *true*). Not only is this unproductive, but it can have a *negative* effect on our future. As researchers at New York University have found, putting unrealistic, fantastical goals onto a vision board actually makes us feel worse about ourselves because it makes us think we are missing out on life.[25] Unrealistic fantasies are the siren calls that tempt our boats toward the rocks. But that does not mean vision boards are bad; they can be helpful if done correctly using (1) realistic goals that are (2) based upon your real meaning markers and (3) possible in the near future. If done properly, the process of vision boarding can help us to determine what our real goals are (eating more healthily this year than last) versus the ones society wants us to have (like getting a six-pack).

It is quite amazing what a powerful effect the simple act of positive visualization can have on our reality. The Cleveland Clinic Foundation funded a study in which one group of healthy volunteers spent fifteen minutes a day practicing "finger abductions," which are basically like a biceps curl but with one finger. A second group of healthy volunteers was asked to practice *visualizing* doing finger abductions for that same time period, and the rest did nothing. After twelve weeks, the people who worked out their fingers every day showed, on average, a 53 percent increase in finger strength. The control group, unsurprisingly, showed no change. But the fascinating thing was that the people in group 2, who literally did not move a finger (except in their brains), showed a 35 percent increase in strength. Incredibly, mentally practicing an action increased physical strength.[26]

Why did this happen? Because when you mentally practice something, whether it's a thought or an action, and whether it's positive or negative, your brain increases a cortical output signal for that thought or action—that is, it becomes more proficient at creating that result. Of course, visualization doesn't take the place of action; if you just spent all day visualizing working out, you would not be nearly as strong as if you actually worked out. Visualization is not the means to your goals. It is the accelerant that gets you on the right trajectory toward those goals.

So don't waste time staring at the sky or the rocks all day, but instead keep your eyes on your true goal, that sandy beach. Remember, positive genius is all about focusing more of your brain and its resources on success rather than on failure.

. . .

Whatever your personal or professional goals may be, keep your eyes on the target and create X-spots using the three accelerants (proximity, target size, and thrust), and your brain will corral the energy, drive, intelligences, and cognitive resources you need to succeed.

MAKING IT PRACTICAL

1. *Identify your X-spots.* X-spots help your brain believe that success is close, possible, and worthwhile. They need not be near the end of successfully completing a project; they can be found all along the way. When you are at work, design minigoals that you can achieve *daily* so that you can be sure to reap the benefits of mental accelerants each and every day. Set markers to highlight for yourself when you're 70 percent of the way to each minigoal—that will cue your brain to release the productivity-enhancing chemicals that will speed up your progress. And for particularly challenging or mundane tasks, focus on "progress to date" rather than "what's left to do." One of the best ways to do this: when you make a list of things to do during the day, write down the things you have already done that day and check those off. And write down things you know you are going to do anyway, then check those off too. This increases the likelihood of an X-spot experience by highlighting how much progress you've made over the course of the day.

2. *Give yourself a head start.* Design your goals with some progress already worked in. For example, if you have just started exercising and you want to continue it by making a habit chart, design the exercise check-off list with several days already checked off instead of starting at day 1. If your New Year's resolution is to raise $1,000 for a charity, don't start with the fundraising thermometer at zero; instead, start with some money you've already accumulated through some other means so it feels as if you're already part of the way toward your goal.

3. *Be objective.* If you're getting overwhelmed by a task at work, think about it in terms of objective units, rather than the effort involved. For example, if you're going on a client meeting or sales call that seems as if it will take forever because it is across town, Google-map how many minutes it actually takes. If you feel that it is ridiculously hard to get all the information you need to make a decision or solve a problem at work, write down the names of the people you need to talk to. When your brain uses objective units, you can avoid becoming emotionally hijacked by the perceived effort—or thrust—involved.

4. *Use champion moments.* If you or your team is facing a daunting project, create "champion moments." *Before* starting on the task, write a list of three instances when you've succeeded in similar situations in the past. When your brain is reminded that success is likely, given past successes, achieving your goals will seem that much more possible. Your brain will be

better able to channel all your multiple intelligences and resources toward that project or challenge.

5. *Keep your eyes on the beach, not the rocks.* Mentally practice and visualize accomplishing the small steps you need to take to get to your goal. Your brain will naturally steer you toward whatever you focus on, so instead of visualizing failure, visualize what success could *realistically* look like.

6. *Make 70 percent your goal.* Design goals or mini-goals that you genuinely believe you have more than a 70 percent chance of achieving. If you doubt your likelihood of success from the beginning, then you dramatically decrease your chances of hitting your target. If you honestly believe you have less than a 70 percent chance to complete the goal, adjust it to make its likelihood of success more than 70 percent.

7. *Make your goals visible.* Create a realistic and mean-ingful digital slideshow or wall in your office with pictures or words representing goals you would like to accomplish. The most practical way I've found for doing this is to keep a series of photos on my computer desktop or in a revolving screen saver. Remember, these goals must be (1) realistic, (2) meaningful, and (3) possible in the near future. It takes fifteen minutes to find pictures of your goals from your smartphone or laptop (one of mine was a picture of a book I'd been wanting to read) and to put them in a folder on your computer. You can then set your screen saver to run pictures from that folder. If you don't know how to do this, I've put a link in the notes.[27]

noise canceling

BOOSTING YOUR POSITIVE SIGNAL BY ELIMINATING THE NEGATIVE NOISE

When I was a freshmen proctor at Harvard, the United States went to war with Iraq. When a massive protest was promptly organized on campus, some national news stations came to film the unrest. One crew, immediately upon arriving on campus, followed all the noise until they found a huge commotion around the freshman dining hall. Students had surrounded the building, holding posters and chanting loudly. The cameras began rolling, and the news reporter began describing the pandemonium that had erupted in response to President Bush's decision to send troops.

Midway through the live newscast, a student dressed up (coincidentally as it turns out) as a plush elephant walked behind the reporter screaming something unintelligible before sauntering off. The newscaster again referenced the students' rage over the Republican president's decision, pointing to the posters, which bore messages like "We Didn't Want You Anyway" and

"Quaded" (which she must have presumed to be a reference to a single-term presidency). The newswoman finished her report, the cameras were packed up, and the story was uploaded to the news website five minutes later. Ten minutes later it was yanked off the Web.

As it turned out, the news team had made a rather embarrassing mistake. They had, in fact, filmed not the Iraq war protest, but the annual Housing Day ritual, in which freshmen students are randomly assigned to upperclass houses (think the "sorting hat" from Harry Potter, but with more noise). Freshmen are dressed up as mascots, screaming upperclassmen wear war paint, and, by the time breakfast is served, students find out whether they will be living in the luxurious River Houses or relegated to the Quad. That morning, the ritual had devolved into complete chaos. So when the news team showed up and followed the noise, it led them to this ridiculous Housing Day riot rather than the war protest on the other side of the campus.

The point of the story is that noise can be a huge distorter of reality. Vegas casinos know this; that's why they overload your brain with sounds and lights to distract you from the reality that you are losing money. But noise is much more than just a distraction; it blocks out signals that can point you toward positive growth.

While noise can lead to a negative reality in which your potential is limited, a positive signal can help you create a more valuable reality, map paths to success, and accelerate you toward your goals. But because of the sheer amount of information we're exposed to in today's world, it isn't always easy to hear the signal through the noise. Luckily, amazing research in positive psychology and neuroscience has found that by consciously decreasing the flood of information your brain receives by just 5 percent, you can substantially improve your chances of finding that positive signal.

But it's important to understand that it is not just the outside world that makes noise. Your own brain is a huge noisemaker. Harvard psychologist William James once said, "Part of what we perceive comes through our senses from the object before us, another part always comes . . . out of our own head."[1] In other words, much of our reality is created not by outside facts but by our own internal voices. And when those voices are a deafening chorus of worry, anxiety, negativity, and fear, our engagement and success rates plummet. So if we want to create the most valuable reality and be more effective in our personal and professional lives, we also have to find a way to block out not just the external noise but the internal noise as well.

In this chapter you'll learn simple strategies for canceling negative noise and boosting the signal that will point you to better decisions, more innovative solutions, more robust sales, improved health, and greater achievement.

Strategy 1: Recognize the Signal. In this strategy, I'll show you how to recognize noise by four criteria and train your brain to pick out the signal from the noise.

Strategy 2: Stop the Addiction to Noise. In this section, you'll learn practical, daily steps you can take to reduce your overall noise level and increase the strength of your signal by up to 25 percent.

Strategy 3: Cancel the Internal Noise. In the final section, you'll learn how to boost your signal by actively eliminating the internal noise of fear, pessimism, and self-doubt. You will learn how to boost the signal by silencing anxiety and negativity through two simple habits.

STRATEGY I: RECOGNIZE THE SIGNAL

Let's begin by recapping the definitions of signal and noise.

Signal is information that is true and reliable and alerts you to the opportunities, possibilities, and resources that will help you reach your fullest potential.

Noise is everything else: any information that is negative, false, or unnecessary or that prevents you from perceiving a world in which success is possible.

Noise is anything that distorts your positive reality and distracts you from harnessing your multiple intelligences that chart a path toward your goals. It can be anything from the memory of the high school guidance counselor telling you that girls really don't go into engineering, to that boss berating you for being one day late with a report, to the one negative review you received on Amazon. (I heard there are only two types of authors: those that are affected by negative reviews and show it and those who are deeply affected but don't show it.) The signal, on the other hand, is the A+ you got in engineering, or the kudos you received from your boss on the last five reports, or the hundred positive reviews your book garnered on Amazon. There is also signal in pieces of information that might seem negative but contain important knowledge. For instance, authentic, helpful constructive criticism might not initially feel great to the recipient but can spark a change that leads to immense personal growth. The key is figuring out what deserves your attention.

Your brain is receiving all types of information right now, from the temperature of the air to the smell of your coffee. Most of that information, like the fact that your coworker is wearing a fashionably irresponsible short-sleeve business shirt, is meaningless noise. The more your brain focuses on this meaningless or negative noise, the harder it becomes to hear the signal. The problem is that in our overstimulated, information-saturated, loud world, it can often be challenging, if not impossible, to tell the difference between signal and noise. Yet if we can decrease the overall noise in our lives by just 5 percent, we can greatly increase our chances of picking out the signal. And it's worth the trouble because, as it turns out, the ability to differentiate noise from signal not only can make you happier and healthier but could even make you millions.

RICHER THAN OPRAH

In his *New York Times* bestselling book *The Greatest Trade Ever*, Gregory Zuckerman describes how, in 2006, John Paulson, owner of one of the world's largest hedge funds, saw the signs that the housing subprime markets were going to collapse and made a whopping $19 billion—$15 billion for his firm and $4 billion for his own pocket—by betting against, or "shorting," the market. Nineteen billion dollars: that's more than Oprah's, Tiger Woods's, and J. K. Rowling's net worth combined.

So how was Paulson able to sift through all the stock prices and predictions coming across his trading desk, all the twenty-four-hour news prognosticators shouting at him from his television, and all the conventional "wisdom" echoing in his own brain to hear a faint signal that the vast majority of brilliant and experienced economists, traders, lawyers, congressmen, financial experts, and media people missed? Because not only was he attuned to the signs that there was deep trouble in the market, but he was willing to *accept* the signal, which was something that the rest of America did not want to hear.

Paulson was relatively unknown to most of America until his

huge windfall in the markets made headlines. On the other hand, another economist, Irving Fisher, was a living business legend, the Warren Buffett, Bill Gates, and Steve Jobs of his time. His academic pedigree was impeccable, his IQ off the charts. Milton Friedman, the world-famous and Nobel Prize–winning economist, called Irving Fisher "the greatest economist that the United States has ever produced."

Students of economics reading this may know of Fisher. But there's a reason most people today haven't heard of him. He disastrously missed the signal. On October 21, 1929, "the greatest economist that the United States has ever produced" proclaimed, "Stocks have reached what looks like a permanently high plateau."

Three days later, calamity would strike, effectively wiping out 40 percent of the wealth in the nation and catching the United States completely off guard. That day, October 24, 1929, dubbed Black Thursday, was the worst stock market crash in history. So how could such a distinguished economist as Fisher completely miss the signs? Because, unlike Paulson, Fisher bought into irrational optimism, the belief that a high market would forever remain high. He dismissed the warning signs from more rational economists as noise, and in doing so he completely missed the signal.

Twelve years later, as World War II raged in Europe, the U.S. intelligence services started picking up chatter that Japan might preemptively attack the United States. The most elite brains in the U.S. military swiftly decreed that this chatter was nothing to worry about—just noise. That may explain the following quote from the U.S. secretary of the navy, Frank Knox: "Whatever happens, the U.S. Navy is not going to be caught napping." The date was December 4, 1941.

Three days later, Japan attacked Pearl Harbor, catching the

United States completely off guard and destroying 40 percent of the nation's battleships.[2] In a short time, the U.S. Navy, like the economy in 1929, was dealt a devastating blow that would require years and years to repair.

So how could such smart people have gotten it so wrong so many times in history? The problem was not that they weren't intelligent but rather that they were using the wrong type of intelligence. IQ may have helped them design aircraft carriers or develop complex financial models, and social intelligence may have helped them foster teamwork within their battalions or collaborate with fellow economists, but it takes positive intelligence to effectively differentiate signal from noise.

But wait, you might be thinking, isn't the signal supposed to be *positive*? At first glance, these signals—that the market was about to crash, that the United States was about to be attacked—don't sound positive at all. But here's the thing: negative events can be positive signals *if they inspire action that leads to a more successful outcome*. In these cases, if Fisher had alerted the powers-that-be in Washington that financial doom was impending, or if Secretary Knox had put the men at Pearl Harbor on high alert, the outcome of those events could have been far less disastrous. Only when we are able to see the reality in which our behavior matters, even in the face of major calamity, can we harness all our intelligences to pick out the signal through the noise.

Remember, positive genius isn't about seeing the world through rose-colored glasses. Positive geniuses can see problems just as well as pessimists; the difference is that when a pessimist sees a problem, he foresees only more problems, whereas a positive genius foresees *overcoming* that problem and thus works harder and smarter to find solutions and avenues for doing so. Of course, not even a positive genius can always *predict* the signal;

positive genius is not a crystal ball. But what it does do is help your brain absorb the information and ideas and resources you need to succeed (the signal), while tossing out the negative, extraneous, or flawed information that hinders growth (the noise).

BRAIN OVERLOAD

Your brain filters out information all the time. It has to; the human brain simply doesn't have the capacity to absorb all the noise that assaults us daily in today's world. As we learned earlier, researchers have found that our senses can receive up to eleven million pieces of information *every second*.[3] However, your conscious brain can effectively process only about forty bits of information, which means the rest is either processed by your unconscious brain or eliminated as "spam." So our brains have to actively decide what to toss out and what to listen to and absorb. We can choose either to hear negative, flawed, or irrelevant information or to absorb information that will help us accomplish our goals. But because the amount we can hear is limited, there is a trade-off; the more negative information we take in, the less positive signal we can hear, and vice versa.

To see how your brain filters information in real time, try this quick experiment. See if you can focus on ignoring the nonbolded words and reading only the bolded words. See how quickly you can do it.

If **Among** *you are* **the most** *constantly* **spectacular** *listening to* **cognitive** *the noise,* **traits** *your is brain* **your** *cannot* **ability** *find* **to** *the signal,* **quickly select** *which* **one** *means* **message** *you* **from** *will* **another. For** *miss out* **example,** *on* **you** *possibilities* **can** *in your* **detect** *environment* **this** *at work.* **message**

For **that** *example,* **the** *hidden* **weather** *beneath* **tomorrow** *your* **will** *seat* **be** *right* **rainy,** *now is* **that** *a* **the** *box* **stock** *that* **market** *contains* **will** *a* **never** *treasure* **go** *map* **down again,** *that* **and** *leads* **that** *to* **it** *a* **is** *chest* **best** *filled* **to** *with* **always** *one* **plan** *million* **for** *dollars'* **the** *worth* **worst** *of so gold.* **that** *We* **you** *need* **are** *to* **never** *cancel* **surprised** *the* **by bad** *noise* **things!**[4]

How well did you do? Congratulations! If you are like most people, you succeeded at filtering out the nonbolded words. Your brain should have been able to easily eliminate the noise (in this case the nonbold words) and focus on the signal (the bolded words). But don't congratulate yourself fully just yet; while our brains' ability to do this can be advantageous in some situations, it can also be very dangerous. I revised this experiment from one described at the W Blog in a special way. I changed the nonbolded text. Why? Reread the italicized text and you'll see where I'm going with this. Did you miss the treasure? In this example I purposely had you focus on the noise and filter out the signal to show how easy it is for our brains to confuse the two and what can happen when we do: we run the risk that our brains will automatically filter out important or valuable information.

To see how this affects us in our everyday lives, let me ask you a simple question: Is Splenda good or bad for you? Search for the answer on Google and you'll get at least 170,000 hits, most of them wildly contradictory. Or take any other subjective question. Is the death penalty fair or unfair? Is the stock market going to go up or down? The responses you'll receive are limitless. So how do you decide which to listen to?

Lawyers know the power of noise. Want to confuse a jury? Overwhelm them with information so they have to go on emotion rather than logically thinking through the argument. Want to stymie the prosecution? Give them a million files for discovery and watch them try to wade through them. Bob Gomes, former CEO of Renew Data Corp., a forensic company that helps companies, including law firms, manage and sort data, is quoted as saying that "one of our clients has forty-two thousand backup tapes holding *2,500 terabytes of data.*" To put this in perspective, the Library of Congress has only 10 terabytes of data, says Gomes. That's one client with *250 times the amount of data* in the sum total of all the books in America. Finding the signal in even a tiny fraction of these data is simply too much for the human brain to handle unaided.

In the working world, where we're subject to a constant and endless stream of information, noise can be particularly dangerous. If you attend to the noise, your reality at work will be made up of the wrong information: information that will only hijack your motivation and decrease your focus. Worse yet, because our brains' capacity for information is limited, when we focus on this negative information, it comes at the direct expense of the valuable information that will help us spot opportunities and solutions in our environment. In short, there is a direct trade-off between hearing signal and hearing noise, and this is why, to be successful, we need to learn to boost our *signal-to-noise ratio.*

But first things first. Before we can begin to boost our ratio, we need to hone our ability to wade through the astronomical amount of information that assaults us daily and learn to tell the difference between signal and noise.

THE FOUR CRITERIA OF NOISE

Learning to distinguish signal from noise isn't easy. In an article called "The Evolution of Superstitious and Superstition-like Behaviour," published in the *Proceedings of the Royal Society of London*, biologists Kevin R. Foster and Hanna Kokko offered an evolutionary explanation for why humans are innately wired to find it difficult.[5] Because the cost to our prehistoric ancestors of missing a signal—like a signal that a tiger was about to attack— was so high, our primitive brains simply couldn't afford to filter out or ignore *any* information. That's why, thousands and thousands of years later, we have to fight against our primitive natures if we are to filter out false or misleading information (noise) from the information that's truly important (signal).

But while this may not come naturally to us, it can be done. Thanks to recent advances in psychology and neuroscience, my colleagues and I at the Institute for Applied Positive Research have been able to isolate four guidelines to help you identify the meaningless or distracting information that reduces your output, leads to errors, and slows your trajectory toward your goals.

If information coming into your brain fits just one of the following four criteria, it's almost certainly noise.

1. *Unusable: Your behavior will not be altered by the information.* If the information won't spur you to change your behavior, it is extraneous. Once you start applying this mental algorithm, you'll realize that, sadly, most of the information that floods into your brain on a daily or even an hourly basis fits into this category. An excellent example is our tendency to obsess about events we see on the news. An earthquake in Burma,

for example, is tragic but completely out of your control. So unless you plan on doing something to help the victims, filling your day with updates on that story is nothing more than surrounding yourself with noise. If, on the other hand, you will send aid, pray for the victims, or vow to live your life in a more meaningful and purposeful way, then that news is a helpful signal. When you are distracted or depressed by some piece of information, if it doesn't spur you to change your behavior, then that information is unusable and thus noise.

2. *Untimely: You are not going to use that information imminently, and it could change by the time you do use it.* If you bought stocks that you want to hold for the long run, then checking the NASDAQ every day is not only creating noise but wasting valuable mental resources and energy that could be spent doing something productive to create real wealth. If the information will become irrelevant by the time you are ready to use it, do your brain a favor and stop seeking it out.

3. *Hypothetical: It is based on what someone believes "could be" instead of "what is."* Classic examples of this are most weather forecasts and market predictions. What if you could have back all the minutes of your life you've spent listening to the predictions—90 percent of which turned out to be wrong? Research shows that even most "expert" predictions fare no better than random chance. Take, for example, a study of weather prediction by the BBC for Cambridge, England, which showed that forecasts for *the next day*

(never mind three days or a week into the future) were only 53 percent accurate.[6] Weather predictions are almost entirely noise, or, as researcher J. D. Eggleston was quoted in a Freakonomics blog, "It is unfortunate that 13 percent of each news telecast (actually about 20 percent if you discount the commercials) is dedicated to a weather forecast that is mostly time-consuming fluff."[7] Hypothetical predictions, in almost all cases, are noise that drowns out useful information you could be using to make better decisions.

4. *Distracting: It distracts you from your goals.* Think about the goals you have mapped for yourself (based on your meaning markers): getting promoted, getting better grades, saving enough money to retire comfortably, being a good mother, and so on. Now watch the flood of incoming information. Does it relate to one of those domains? If your goal is to get your work done so you can spend more time with your family, reading ESPN .com all afternoon is noise (unless, of course, you work as a sportscaster, or a bookie).

Not only will these four rules of thumb help you spot the noise, but as a bonus they will save you time! I used to spend about two hours every day surfing the Web, reading about politics, checking the news, and watching analysts on TV. But using these criteria, especially the one about whether the information would change my behavior, I realized I could eliminate most of that noise (keeping just enough to stay relatively informed) and focus on research, my business, my family, and a charitable cause I believed in—all the areas where my behavior did matter.

Now that you've learned some criteria to tell the difference between the signal and the noise, in this next section you'll learn how to raise your signal-to-noise ratio by canceling out just 5 percent of the noise.

STRATEGY 2: STOP THE ADDICTION TO NOISE

When I give talks, I often get questions about why the media are so negative or sensational or biased—or, in a word, noisy. As a psychology researcher, the prevalence of noise in the media—or society in general—doesn't surprise me, given that our ancient brains are wired for negativity. This isn't just theory. Our brains are wired to respond faster to threats in the environment.[8] Remember that we learned that high-performing teams need more than 2.9 positive experiences per negative experience to maintain higher levels of performance.[9] We also learned that we need over three positive events in our working and personal lives to outweigh one bad event.[10] To understand why this is so, let me take you back a couple of million years.

LIONS VERSUS RABBITS

I'm assuming that since you've read this far in the book you are not a prehistoric rabbit, but let's pretend for a moment that you are. You are contentedly chewing on some grass and you hear something rustling in the bushes. Is it a predator? If you think it's a predator, you will run and will most likely escape to safety. If you do not run, and it is a predator, game over. If you do run, and you were wrong, you don't get to finish your lunch. Losing your lunch is nothing compared to losing your life. So you may be hungry, but at least you survive, enabling you to pass your genes down to subsequent generations of bunnies.

Most of you reading that will say that the rabbit, though skittish, was right to run at any sign of a predator, however faint. But what if you were a lion instead of a rabbit? If you know you're at the top of the food chain, there's no need to run from predators, because you're going to be able to handle whatever comes.

Most of us are at the top of the proverbial food chain in our professional lives, even if we don't always realize it. By "top of the food chain" I don't necessarily mean the corporate hierarchy; you can be the work equivalent of a lion, whether you are a CEO or a midlevel manager or even an entry-level assistant. What I mean by top of the food chain is that you are a smart, competent, valued professional—and if you have read this far into this book, you're also well on your way to being a positive genius. So why do we so often believe otherwise? Why do we allow our brains to see not making one sale, not getting one promotion we wanted, or having one negative interaction with our boss as evidence that we don't deserve to succeed?

Because as cavemen we were not at the top of the food chain, and thus we had to learn to run from any sign of danger, just like the rabbit. As a result, our primitive brains have been programmed, over thousands and thousands of years of evolution, to be highly attuned to threats in our environment. This is why negative noise registers so much louder than signal and why negative events affect us more than positive ones.

While being attuned to threats in the environment may have

been advantageous to our tiger-fleeing ancestors, in today's modern era we pay for it in more ways than one. When we read the news, we absorb and remember the sensational stories better than we do the more measured ones. When we watch television, we more readily take advice from the loudest and most vocal pundits and personalities than we do from the more credible ones. In other words, to our brains, noise registers five times louder than signal.

Take Jim Cramer, host of *Mad Money*, one of the most entertaining financial experts and prognosticators. He makes his case so forcefully and charismatically that whenever I used to listen, I would feel stupid for not having *already* followed his advice. But in 2008, when analyst Michael Zhaung, in an article from *Seeking Alpha*, evaluated Cramer's expert advice from the previous year, he found his combined accuracy to be 35.6 percent—in other words, 15 percent less accurate than a coin toss.[11]

This is not to bash Cramer, who clearly possesses a great deal of conventional intelligence (having graduated magna cum laude from Harvard). And that statistic evaluates only one year of his predictions. Yet listening to his advice clearly violates rule 3 of our noise detection criteria—it is based on what someone believes will be instead of what is. This would be fairly harmless if we were to take no actions based on his predictions (i.e., if you merely listened to advice you would not use, violating rule 1). But let's say you heeded every investment tip he imparted in a year. If you started in January with $100,000 and invested it all, come December you would have lost two-thirds of that, or $65,000.

I would be sad if a reader came away thinking that this is about Jim Cramer. I like him and think he's smart and entertaining. My goal here is not to knock his track record but to demonstrate that just because information is loud that doesn't make it valuable.

Not only can noise lead you to poor (and expensive) decisions, but research shows that it can decrease company profits. In 2000, Stanford and Columbia social psychologists Sheena Iyengar and Mark Lepper conducted an ingenious, creative study looking at how noise affects a consumer's decision about whether to make a purchase.[12]

The researchers set up shop at an upscale grocery, disguised as employees offering free tastings. For half the day, they displayed six different kinds of fruit jams for people to try; for the other half they displayed no fewer than twenty-four different jars. When the cornucopia of twenty-four was displayed, 60 percent of people stopped to taste the jams, whereas when there were only six jars, only 40 percent of people stopped. So if you are a jam maker and your goal as a company is to get people to taste things for free, more choice—that is, noise—is clearly better. But no one is in that business (or if they are, they won't be in business for long). Clearly, the goal of business is to sell more. This is where the results got interesting: while 31 percent of the people who tasted at the table of six bought a jar of jam, *only 3 percent of the shoppers who stopped at the twenty-four-jar table made a purchase.*

Why? All those extra choices overwhelmed the customers, drowning out the signal that would have otherwise pointed them to a purchase. It's just one of many examples of why success in business rests on the skill we're about to learn next: reducing the overall noise in your external environment.

YOUR BOSE BRAIN

Over the past five years, I have given more than five hundred talks in more than fifty countries. As a result, I'm on planes quite a bit.

When I first started traveling so much for work, I thought I would get a lot of writing done while on planes. But I very quickly found that I could barely even focus on a Sudoku puzzle because I kept getting distracted by all the announcements, crying babies, loud talkers, and even engine noise. (I have met enough flight attendants with bad hearing to be convinced that the engines alone are causing hearing loss.) So I bought a pair of Bose noise-canceling headphones, and suddenly I found it much easier to focus on my writing. I began getting more and more done. What if there existed a similar noise-canceling technology to help us improve our focus and productivity in our work lives? Research coming out of multiple fields suggests that there might just be.

Scientifically speaking, there are two ways to cancel noise: *passively* and *actively*. Putting in earplugs is an example of passive noise canceling (even though you have to actively put them in your ears) because their purpose is to simply *block* the noise. My noise-canceling headphones, on the other hand, are an example of active noise canceling, because they actively emit opposite sound waves (as you may remember from high school physics, sound waves are just energy) that cancel out the ambient noise.

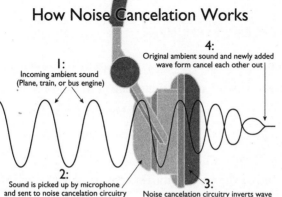

How Noise Cancelation Works

1:
Incoming ambient sound
(Plane, train, or bus engine)

4:
Original ambient sound and newly added wave form cancel each other out

2:
Sound is picked up by microphone and sent to noise cancelation circuitry

3:
Noise cancelation circuitry inverts wave and sends it back to headphone speaker

We passively block out sound all the time. I'm sure you've had the experience of being so engrossed in a TV show, for example, that you didn't even notice that your spouse was yelling at you from the other room. It's not that you couldn't hear him because the TV was too loud (though you might use that as your excuse); it's that when our brains are hyperfocused on something—whether it's the TV or a book or an iPhone—we become oblivious to the outside world. Of course, you can passively cancel all the noise just by closing your eyes and ears, but then you run the risk of missing the signal too. What we should do instead is reduce the overall amount of information we take in. By reducing the amount of noise we take in by even just 5 percent, we can greatly increase our chances of hearing the signal.

There is nothing magical about 5 percent. It is just a small enough increment to not overwhelm your brain (see the Zorro Circle from *The Happiness Advantage*). If you can do more than 5 percent, great, but as readers of *The Happiness Advantage* know, real, lasting change is incremental, and positive growth builds on positive growth. So even small change adds up over time to higher and higher levels of positive intelligence.

THE 5 PERCENT EXPERIMENT

It will come as no surprise that there is a lot of noise in the modern world, but just how much may shock you. Roger Bohn and James Short, two researchers from the University of San Diego, have compiled an extensive census of the amount of information consumed by American households (*not* including work). According to the census, the per capita time spent consuming information rose 60 percent between 1980 and 2008, from 7.4 hours per day in 1980 to 11.8 hours in 2008.[13] That's almost four more hours a day, and remember, that excludes working hours!

This is even more staggering when you think about the fact that, according to the Bureau of Labor Statistics, in 2008 half of the U.S. population worked (kids, stay-at-home parents, the unemployed, and the retired made up the rest), and the average workweek was forty hours.[14] So with an average of four hours a day working for both groups combined, and seven hours a day sleeping, *the average American spent 75 percent of his or her waking time at home overloading his or her brain with information.*

In another study, researcher Ithiel de Sola Pool estimated that in 1990, Americans consumed *4,500 trillion words* if you include TV, print media, books, and handwritten letters.[15] (I had to look on Wikipedia to find out what "handwritten letters" were—they sound precious.) In 2008, Bohn and Short calculated that the number of words consumed had increased to 10,845 trillion words, about *100,000 more words per day*! (Ironically, for researchers concerned about the amount of information consumed, when I did a word count of their write-up, it worked out to 20,000 words.)

In today's world of Google, smartphones, and always-on media, we have become addicted to information. As every addict knows, the first step in recovery is recognizing that we have a problem. The next step is to extricate ourselves from tempting situations. Just as a recovering alcoholic should stay away from the bar, or keep liquor out of the house, so should noise addicts (which is all of us) avoid noisy situations.

Let's pretend you are at a neighborhood party (if you are actually currently at a party, put the book down), and Bob comes up to you and starts talking about a recent car accident in the neighborhood, then a murder he saw on the news, then a new study that talks about how alcohol kills brain cells and makes people stupid. What would you do? Well, first you might put down your glass of wine (thanks a lot, Bob); then you would probably wave to an imaginary person on the other side of the room and excuse yourself, and you would spend every future party actively avoiding Bob, without even thinking twice about it.

So why do we have so much trouble avoiding this same kind of negative information in other contexts? Why do we spend hours watching the news coverage of the latest earthquake in Asia? Or focus on all the negative numbers in the quarterly reports at work? Or indulge our spouses when they come home from work complaining about the traffic or the long line at the supermarket or their annoying boss? Unless we are going to take immediate action to improve these situations, dwelling on them creates noise and should therefore be avoided. So for the next week, start treating those negative noisemakers like Bob at a party. It doesn't mean you have to completely turn a blind eye to the news or to the morning reports or to your spouse; it just means you force yourself to *disengage from conversations or media that meet any of the four criteria of noise: unusable, untimely, hypothetical, or distracting.*

Your brain will surely be throwing up some defenses, just as an alcoholic's brain might in the equivalent situation. *What if I miss something big?* This is the most common question I get when I talk about noise reduction, and it's no surprise, given that we are wired with an evolutionary need to check out every noise.

Intuitively, this fear of missing out makes sense. What if ignoring the advice of a financial expert caused you to miss an investment that could have made you thousands of dollars? Or what if ignoring the thundershower warnings on the Weather Channel caused you to drive three hours to the beach, only to spend the afternoon sitting in your car?

As Jim Collins writes in *Good to Great: Why Some Companies Make the Leap . . . and Others Don't*, every event is always predicted by *someone*. Every day in the markets, someone is always right, and there has never been a stock market crash that some contrarian didn't predict. Like a broken watch that is right twice a day, every noisemaker will be right occasionally, and we tend to remember noisemakers only when they are. But if we want to preserve the mental energy to pick out the valuable, reliable, and positive information from the information that is only as accurate as a broken watch, we need to cut back on our overall information consumption.

Let's try an experiment I've now performed at companies like Facebook, Google, UBS, and Freddie Mac: for two weeks, try to decrease your information intake by just 5 percent. This doesn't mean cut any old 5 percent: cut specifically the information that fits one of the criteria for noise.

The key to this experiment is to decrease your *INFOtotal*, or the total amount of information your brain is trying to process, so you can free up more energy and resources to pick up and process the important stuff. I have, in fact, been striving to do this in my own life. I told you earlier about how, in *The Happiness Advantage*, I described an attempt to watch less TV that involved taking the batteries out of my remote control and leaving them twenty seconds away in my bedroom. More recently I decided to try new strategies. I canceled my cable so I don't mindlessly surf channels, and I hooked up a computer to the television. So now if I want to watch something, I have to specifically seek it out by going to an on-demand site. Sure, I'm still watching the occasional mindless episode of *Glee* on Hulu, but I'm getting my INFOtotal down in small increments.

Here are some other practical tips for reducing your noise consumption by 5 percent that I've learned from leaders both in positive psychology and at companies worldwide. None are hard and fast, but I have tried them, and they work.

1. Leave the radio off for the first five minutes of being in the car.

2. Turn off the car radio while talking to people.

3. Mute TV and Internet commercials. (Don't get freaked out if you are a marketer; when I do this, I intentionally turn back on the sound for commercials that look funny or relevant).

4. Remove news media links from your bookmark tool bar (amazing that typing in three letters like "CNN" seems to take forever compared to clicking on a bookmark).

5. Limit watching of prediction news ("experts" trying to predict what will hypothetically happen in politics or the markets).

6. Do not read articles on tragedies that you cannot or will not affect with your behavior.

7. When working, listen to music without lyrics.

These seven strategies are great ways to boost the frequency of the signal by passively blocking out ambient noise. But as I mentioned earlier in the chapter, it's not just the external world that creates noise; our own brains create noise as well. So if we want to truly curb our noise addiction, we need to learn to cancel out not only the noises in our external environment but also the voices of worry, self-doubt, fear, and pessimism rattling around in our own heads. In the next section you'll learn how to actively cancel out the internal noise of negative thinking by using the mental equivalent of those Bose headphones.

STRATEGY 3: CANCEL THE INTERNAL NOISE

Remember, active noise canceling involves not just blocking the noise but emitting more powerful, positive energy waves to counter it. As I mentioned in the first part of this chapter, Bose noise-canceling headphones work because they have microphones that pick up the ambient noise, then emit opposite sound waves. Our brains can do the exact same thing; we can actively create positive thought patterns to counter the negative energy.

This strategy can be used to cancel out not only the noise coming at us from the outside world but also the noise that our own brains create. Negative thinking—whether in the form of fear, anxiety, self-doubt, pessimism, or worry—is the most dangerous type of noise around because it not only impairs our ability to hear the positive signal but undermines all our other efforts at creating positive change.

Pessimism, one of the most common and pervasive forms of internal noise, is a defense mechanism your brain puts up to try to minimize the impact of negative events you experience in life. I encountered a textbook example of this in 2008 when I was talking with a top banking official in China. He told me that he had a simple approach for dealing with the uncertainty of the turbulent market: "I just expect the market to go down each day and [his company's] stock price to drop. That way when I leave work, I've either proven to my team how smart I am, or I go home pleasantly surprised." He had convinced himself that if he just constantly expected bad things to happen, he would always be prepared for the bad and surprised by the good. But notice two problems with this strategy.

First, *pessimism lowers the probability of a good outcome.* In *The Happiness Advantage*, I describe the research about how much of your success is predicted by the belief that your behavior matters. To see how pessimism limits this, imagine that you, like this leader in China, start each day believing that no matter what you do, something bad will happen. You will end up spending no energy or cognitive resources trying to achieve a better outcome. You will spend all day hunkered under cover instead of going on the offensive.

The other dangerous aspect of pessimism rarely gets talked about, so bear with me for a minute. Like many future Harvard men, I spent most of my time in high school traveling with the debate team and spent most of my summers at debate camp. This incredibly geeky pastime had two positive outcomes. First, I had lots of time for studying because I didn't have to worry about dating. Second, I got a letter jacket in debate. (At some point people in my Texas town started rightfully complaining that it was unfair to award letter jackets only to varsity football players and started demanding that other "sports," like the chess team and debate team, should be awarded them as well.)

I received a letter for winning the state championship (twice) because I had a surefire debate strategy: no matter what the other team argued, I countered with at least one argument about how their plan or policy would eventually lead to nuclear war. You want to change our environmental policies? That will anger the Chinese, leading to a trade war, which will eventually result in escalating tensions in the Pacific Rim, leading to nuclear war between Pakistan and India. You want to offer universal health care? That will cause the markets to panic, resulting in a weakened dollar, leading to a global depression, which will inevitably lead to conflict and . . . nuclear war. You want to offer school vouchers? Yep, I would find some explanation for how this would end in nuclear war. How could anyone compete with that? Even if they won all their arguments and convinced the judges of the myriad advantages of their plan, if it also caused nuclear war, there was no way it was worth it. Game over.

That strategy sounds ridiculous (and it was), but I mention it because it is exactly the line of reasoning that a pessimist would use. And it demonstrates the key point I want to make about negative thinking: the more negative and pessimistic the thought, the more it trumps and drowns out any positive argument. By exaggerating the negative outcomes, in other words, I downplayed the likelihood of all the positive ones.

In this section you'll learn how to cancel out the thought patterns that lead to a negative reality by emitting three opposing waves of positive energy:

Wave 1: I will keep my worry in proportion to the likelihood of the event.

Wave 2: I will not ruin ten thousand days to be right on a handful.

Wave 3: I will not equate worrying with being loving or responsible.

Just like those Bose headphones, these waves will cancel out the internal noises of pessimism, fear, anxiety, and worry.

ICING THE KICKER

In the National Football League, coaches often use a strategy called "icing the kicker." Right before the kicker is about to attempt the winning field goal, the opposing coach will call a time-out. The idea is that if you call a time-out at the last second, it disrupts the kicker's rhythm, and then he will miss. The problem is that this hypothesis is false. According to the *Wall Street Journal*, an NFL kicker has a 77.3 percent chance of successfully hitting the field goal in the final two minutes of a game or in overtime. But if you call a time-out to ice the kicker, the likelihood of a successful kick actually *rises* to 79.7 percent, regardless of the distance![16]

So why do some coaches still ice the kicker? Because if at the last second you don't call a time-out when you could have, and the kicker makes the field goal, you feel as if you didn't even try. As New York Giants punter Steve Weatherford explained it to the *New York Times*, "Coaches like to feel like they're doing something, and with field goals, that's what they can do." The fear of being responsible for a loss overwhelms reason; inaction feels worse than making even a last-ditch effort. In other words, icing the kicker is a perfect real-world example of how fear of making a mistake can actually cause us to make a worse mistake!

The fear of being wrong can lead to perpetually skewed decision making.

The one thing all successful people have in common is that they take chances. Every successful executive has taken a chance on an untested new business model, or a questionable new partnership, or an uncertain strategic maneuver. Every successful manager has taken a chance on a dubious new hire or an unverified new initiative or an unconventional new process. Every successful entrepreneur has taken a chance on an innovative product or a foray into an uncharted market or an unplanned pivot. But before you can take the kinds of chances that lead to success, you first have to learn to silence the fear that you will fail.

Of course, fear is a very natural and human emotion. We fear tons of things: people not liking us, our boss skipping over us for a promotion, getting sick from touching the faucet in an airport, not getting asked on a second date, and so on. I cannot list them all here because the sad truth is, most of our daily decision making is fear based. This is a shame, because a *fearful brain that overweighs the negative will continually run from success.*

In *Julius Caesar*, Shakespeare writes, "Cowards die many times before their deaths, / the valiant never taste of death but once." I like Tupac's version better: "A coward dies a thousand deaths, a soldier dies but once." I love that line and have used it multiple times to help me summon the nerve to do something I was scared to do.

The point is, whether it's kicking a field goal or starting a business in your basement or taking on a risky client, if we want to find the courage to take the kinds of chances that success is made of, *we need to make sure that the worry or fear we are feeling is in proportion to the actual likelihood of the feared outcome.* This isn't as hard as it sounds; all it takes is a bit of research. Worried about losing your job? Look up the rates of employment in your industry in your area. Nervous about losing a big account? Check and see how many times that client has switched vendors or suppliers (or whatever your company does for them) in the past. Terrified about catching some awful disease? Find out how many people your age and in similar health condition are actually afflicted. Chances are, these numbers are a lot lower than you initially thought.

Here is one of my favorite examples of how ridiculously irrational our deepest fears can be. Nearly all the parents I know warn their kids to inspect their Halloween candy because of the threat of needles, poison, or razor blades in them. If you don't do this, ask around, most people will tell you the same, and you might even catch warnings on the news about it. There are *no* known or recorded cases of someone poisoning others' kids with Halloween candy. None.[17]

Still, in some cases, where the likelihood of a negative event *is* high, worry can be adaptive—that is, as long as (remember the first criterion of noise) it causes us to take action to prevent that event. So how much should we worry? There's a very simple formula: the amount you should worry should be in direct proportion to the likelihood of the event. Thus if you have a 95 percent chance of getting the job or winning the account or nailing the presentation, you should refuse to spend more than 5 percent of your time worrying about it.

This is why the first wave of positive energy is: "I will keep my worry in proportion to the likelihood of the event."

When I was a house tutor in Harvard's Kirkland House, my students used to come to my office and tell me, with great drama and flair, "I'm going to fail such and such a class." I must have heard that line literally hundreds of times during my eight years of counseling students at Harvard. Of course, the students rarely actually failed. Still, to protect them from the self-fulfilling nature of negative prophecies, I would always have them stop and answer two simple questions:

1. How often has this negative event happened to me in the past?

2. How often does this negative event happen to people in my situation?

Usually, these students had failed zero times in the past—at anything. And as for the second question, fewer than 1 percent of people fail out of Harvard, and usually there are special circumstances. The simple act of reminding themselves that there was virtually zero probability of failure allowed these students' brains to emit positive energy that countered their internal voices of self-doubt and worry.

You can use this same noise-canceling technique at work. Once, during one of my talks about how negative thinking derails success, a nervous Google employee raised his hand and asked, "What about for anxious people? Is there something I could do? I constantly feel like I'm never going to get all this coding done in time so I'll get fired or I'll never get promoted or something."

To be honest, I answered his question inadequately at the time, but now, after doing more research, here's what I wish I had said: You need to engage in some active noise canceling. Ask yourself, how often have you actually failed to get your coding done in the past, or screwed up so badly that you got fired? How often do people around you get fired for not managing an impossibly high workload? I'm guessing almost never. After all, you wouldn't be at Google if you had a bad track record. If you take a deep breath and realize that your brain is just lying to you, you'll emit the positive energy needed to cancel out the noise.

So the next time you are feeling overwhelmed and anxious, take out a sheet of paper. Write out the potential outcomes, both good and bad, of the situation or decision that is distressing you. Then write out your best guess as to the percentage likelihood of each outcome. Let's say you decided to quit your job and get an MBA but are now worried you may have made the wrong decision.

Outcome 1: I get my MBA, then return to my current company at a higher pay grade.

Likelihood: 90 percent, given that my employer promised she would hire me back with a 20 percent raise, and she's not planning on going anywhere. Plus, the data reveal that 90 percent of business school graduates receive at least a small pay bump after receiving their MBAs.

Outcome 2: The economy crashes while I'm in school, and when I get out, there are no jobs to be had.

Likelihood: At most 10 percent, as most MBAs find work, I have an employer already interested, and having an MBA makes me more resilient in a down job market.

Suddenly, your feelings of stress and regret lift. Whether or not your estimations are completely accurate isn't the point; the point is that just the act of assigning probability to both positive and negative outcomes forces your brain to think about them objectively.

Of course, drowning out worry is easier said than done. Emotions, especially negative ones, can register at deafening noise levels. Which is why it's all that much more important to understand the real cost of worry—so that just maybe we can stop paying for it.

THE HIDDEN COST OF WORRY

The belief that worrying will prevent bad things from happening is one of the greatest enemies of positive genius. Yet it is a disturbingly common myth. A senior manager at Morgan Stanley Smith

Barney told me, "Worrying is just being responsible. If I didn't worry that things were going to go badly, can you imagine what would happen to my team? Or my kids?" I have heard comments like this over and over, but if you stop and think for a minute you'll realize how silly this reasoning is. The manager was worrying about not worrying enough!

Perhaps you know people like this at work—people who think worrying is their job. Or worse, perhaps you know family members who equate worrying with love. This worship of worry comes with significant costs. I'm not just talking about the emotional toll. I would gladly suffer an emotional toll if it would actually help my team or my friends or my family, and I'm guessing you would too. I'm talking about how worrying *harms* your team, your friends, and your family by distracting you (remember noise criterion 4?) from the things that are truly productive or meaningful.

Imagine, for example, that you're worried about your child getting injured at school. Chances are, you might be right three or four times over the course of the child's entire educational career. But if you worry about your child getting injured every day, or even every week, of those twelve to fifteen years, you will have mentally experienced the anguish and cost literally thousands of times. Now think about the toll all that worrying can take on a child. Not only is the child sure to internalize your anxiety and emotional stress, but you will be distracted from many other important aspects of parenting, like checking your child's homework or keeping track of who his friends are or making sure the family sits down to dinner together. Worrying does the opposite of helping your child.

This brings me to the second and third waves of active noise canceling: *"I will not ruin ten thousand days to be right on a handful"* and *"I will not equate worrying with being loving or responsible."*

If we want to truly do what's best not only for our loved ones but for our careers, our teams, and our companies, we need to let go of our death grip on fear, anxiety, pessimism, and worry. Not only that, we need to let go of fear and worry because it could be killing us, literally. Researchers from Harvard and a handful of other institutions together found that phobic anxiety and fear destroy the proteins at the end of our chromosomes called *telomeres*, a change that dramatically speeds up the aging process.[18] And there is new research to show that work exhaustion and worry can speed up aging as well.[19]

So try taking a few minutes to write down five things you feel positive about—your children, your sports, your values, your faith. This may sound like a silly exercise, but researchers at the University of Chicago found that when people wrote about their positive feelings for a few minutes, they significantly lowered their levels of worry and pessimism.[20] Not only did it decrease their anxiety, it raised their performance on tests of memory and critical skills by 10 to 15 percent.

When you emit this kind of positive energy, you not only block out the negative noise but improve your concentration, focus, and ability to employ your multiple intelligences. (And while you're at it, you might also want to up your exercise regimen. Researchers in a meta-analysis of forty clinical studies of three thousand subjects found that exercise decreases anxiety and worry by a whopping 20 percent.)[21]

By emitting positive energy and canceling out that internal noise, you can get back the signal that leads to meaning, success, sustained happiness, and even a longer, healthier life.

. . .

Negative noise is everywhere in our society and can drown out the positive signal that points us toward opportunities and information and helps us harness the cognitive, emotional, and social resources that enable us to succeed. To find the signal of success, we need to first learn to differentiate signal from noise; then we need to use both passive and active strategies to reduce and cancel both the noise coming at us from the external world and the noise in our own heads. Every percentage point of noise we decrease increases the strength of the signal and raises the limits of our potential.

In this chapter we've covered the four criteria for determining if external information is noise, provided practical ways of strengthening the signal by reducing just 5 percent of the noise, and finally discussed ways to block out internal noise by actively countering fear, worry, and negative thinking. These skills, combined with those you learned in the previous chapters— perceiving multiple realities, mapping your goals around meaning markers, and accelerating your progress toward success—will help you build a more valuable reality at work and at home.

But to be a true positive genius, it's not enough that you create the most valuable reality for yourself. The final step, which you'll learn in the next chapter, is to bring that reality to other people so that you can harness the exponential power of *all* your combined intelligences and achieve unprecedented levels of success.

MAKING IT PRACTICAL

1. *Noise-check your life.* Check to see if information coming in meets the criteria of noise: unusable, untimely, hypothetical, or distracting. If so, eliminate it.

2. *Do the 5 percent experiment. For two weeks, try to de-crease your information intake by just 5 percent.* And what you should cut isn't just any old 5 percent but information that fits one of the criteria for noise. The key to this experiment is to decrease the total amount of information your brain is trying to process (INFO-total) so that you can free up more energy and re-sources for picking up and processing the important stuff. Remember some of the tricks we talked about above, including keeping the car radio off for the first few minutes of your commute, limiting TV news, and reading fewer articles that report on negative events half a world away.

3. *Create active noise canceling.* Post a sign next to your desk listing the three waves of positive energy:

> "I will keep my worry in proportion to the likelihood of the event."

> "I will not ruin ten thousand days to be right on a handful."

> "I will not equate worrying with being loving or responsible."

4. *Fact-check.* Keep your worry in proportion to the likelihood of the event by asking yourself these two questions:

> *How often has this negative event happened to me in the past?*

> *How often does this negative event occur to people like me normally?*

If you answered these questions objectively, you should find that the percentage will be lower than you feared.

5. *Do a five-minute writing exercise.* Any time you start hearing doubting voices, take just five minutes to write about things you feel passionate and positive about—your children, your sports, your values, your faith. By actively canceling such internal noises, you can increase your performance on intelligence tasks by 10 to 15 percent.

6. *Exercise.* Add exercise to your routine to decrease anxiety by as much as 20 percent. If you are finding it hard to actively decrease the internal noise of worry, hit the gym. Exercise can mute the worry centers in the limbic portion of the brain, lower cortisol levels, and increase levels of optimism.

positive inception

TRANSFERRING YOUR POSITIVE REALITY TO OTHERS

Once you have mastered the first four strategies of positive genius, the most important one still remains—how to transfer that positive reality to your team, colleagues, family members, and others.

In director Christopher Nolan's film *Inception* (2010), Leonardo DiCaprio plays a man named Cobb who uses (never fully explained) futuristic military technology to steal people's corporate secrets by digging into their subconscious while they sleep. Then a secretive entrepreneur named Saito hires Cobb to do something a little different: *plant* an idea—inception—instead of stealing one. The target of inception is the heir of an energy conglomerate whom Cobb's new employers want to persuade to break up an empire he recently inherited from his father. So Cobb's team enters the heir's dreams to plant the idea that the heir's father never wanted his son to go into the family business and is imploring him, from beyond the grave, to go out and build his own business.

For inception to be successful, the idea that Cobb plants in the heir's mind has to be simple, emotional, and positive. So instead of "I must break up my father's empire" or "I hate my father," he plants "My father wants me to build something for myself." As Cobb explains to his team, "The subconscious is motivated by emotion, right? Not reason. We need to find a way to translate this into an emotional concept. . . . Positive emotion trumps negative emotion every time." For Cobb, positive realities are much easier to transfer to others than negative ones because they create lasting change.

Out of the fantasy world and into the world of neuroscience and positive psychology, the research supports Cobb's claim. Over the past several years, researchers have been investigating how perceptions and mindsets can be transferred to others. And as it turns out, the three best strategies for transferring positive genius to others are not that different from the ones Cobb employed. They are: *success franchising* (coming up with a positive behavioral change that is easily replicated), *script writing* (changing a prevailing social script by making it positive), and *creating a shared narrative* (creating value and meaning by appealing to emotion).

While it's true that we cannot *force* others to see the world in a positive way—the ultimate decision rests in their hands—we can plant seeds of positive realities into their brains. The benefits of positive inception are twofold. Not only will we reap the obvious benefits of having other positive geniuses in our companies, on our teams, and in our families, but new positive psychology research covered in this chapter proves that it is easier to sustain *our* own positive reality and build on our own successes when we help others to raise their levels of positive genius as well. *Misery may love company, but positivity cannot live long without it.*

Rest assured that this technique does not rely on some

futuristic mind control method that exists only in the realm of fantasy and science fiction. To the contrary, researchers in the fields of neuroscience and positive psychology are churning out some fascinating findings about how to spread a positive reality that leads to success, both in our personal lives and in the working world. In my last book, *The Happiness Advantage*, I wrote about the ripple effect, which refers to how happiness can be contagious. This chapter goes much deeper to the heart of how ideas spread. Positive inception is not just about spreading happiness but about helping others see the reality in which success (and happiness) is possible. Inception is about better helping others to tap into their multiple intelligences and cognitive resources, and thereby to create happier and more successful teams. That involves the mastery of three key strategies.

Strategy 1: Franchise Success. The first step in creating positive inception is to identify one aspect of a reality—yours or someone else's—that, if replicated, would help other people harness their drive, motivation, and multiple intelligences and become more successful. Research shows that to be contagious, these "success franchises" must be based upon a simple, easy-to-replicate idea. I'll demonstrate how this works in the real world by describing how a hospital was able to effectively improve patient happiness, doctor job satisfaction, and hospital reputation by franchising a positive behavioral change called the 10/5 Way. You'll read how the widespread inception of a simple behavioral change led not only to improved patient outcomes but to a potential $30 million increase in revenue for the hospital. Then I'll show you how to find and create a powerful, simple change in your own life and how to use positive inception to franchise that positive change for others.

Strategy 2: Rewrite the Social Script. Every aspect of our work and home life is guided by hidden social scripts. But certain social scripts wield more influence on our collective behavior than others. Social psychologists have found that the more positive one's *social script*, the greater one's ability to create positive social influence: in fact, a positive social script can increase workplace engagement up to 40 percent. So if you want to wield positive social influence, you often have to rewrite the prevailing social script. Speaking first, or using a "power lead," and utilizing humor are two techniques for writing the kind of social script that leads to positive inception.

Strategy 3: Create a Shared Narrative. Finally, for positive inception to occur, you need to appeal not just to reason but to *emotion*. Fascinating new research shows that when just one person on a team appeals to emotion and highlights meaning in specific, positive ways, it can raise the team's revenue by as much as 700 percent. One of the best ways to plant a positive reality is to construct a narrative around some shared emotional experience, positive *or* negative. Interestingly, my research shows that creating a shared narrative around past adversity or failure is one of the best techniques for creating positive inception. What's more, research from Wharton Business School shows that positive inception works best when it comes from someone other than the team leader: in other words, anyone, with any role or title, can create positive inception if he or she appeals to value and meaning.

The goal of this chapter is to help you transfer your most valuable reality to your teams, colleagues, friends, and family. In doing so, you will create a renewable, sustainable source of positive energy that motivates, energizes, and summons the collective multiple intelligences of those around you. Without inception, our own reality becomes less stable.

An unshared, negative reality is delusional.

A shared, negative reality is disastrous.

An unshared, positive reality is short-lived.

A shared, positive reality is genius.

STRATEGY 1: FRANCHISE SUCCESS (MAKE IT CONTAGIOUS)

WHAT IS A SUCCESS FRANCHISE?

In the introduction to *A Short History of Nearly Everything*, Bill Bryson writes, "Welcome. And congratulations. . . . Why congratulations? Because trillions of particles had to come together in just the right balance for you to even be in existence to hold a book or an eReader, much less read it . . . and for that, every single one of your direct descendants had to overcome dangers, looks, and sickness long enough to be able to have sex."[1] While Bryson is, of course, being humorous, he also makes a good point. The only reason you have survived long enough to read this book is a continued pattern of successful reproduction.

Any success that is not due to blind luck is due to the replication of some effective practice, procedure, or mindset. Only in very rare cases do these successes happen in isolation; the biggest and best accomplishments involve the coordinated efforts of many people replicating an effective behavior or process. "Success franchising" is the technique of getting others to replicate a positive cognitive or behavioral pattern that continually leads to success. The great news when it comes to success franchising is that *any success that can be observed can also be repeated.*

Success franchising is a practice as old as humanity itself. The ability to make fire, one of the most primitive yet monumental human achievements, is an example of success franchising. After all, cavemen didn't keep reinventing fire; once they learned the secret, they replicated what they had learned and then passed that knowledge on to each subsequent generation.

Similarly, in the sixteenth century, the Venetian Arsenal created a success franchise so strong it enabled them to build an entire ship from start to finish in a single day (and that's without any modern machinery)! In the morning they would start with piles and piles of resources and raw materials, and by the end of the evening, thanks to the coordinated efforts of many people following the same pattern of success that they had perfected, an entire oceanworthy ship stood in their place.

In your modern working life, too, you must take the piles of intellectual and emotional resources you and your teams have at your disposal and "build a ship with them" by replicating patterns that have worked well in the past.

Consciously or not, we all have patterns in our professional lives, but the key is to create and repeat patterns or behaviors that continually lead to success, rather than those that produce the same mediocre or negative results. If the manager of a successful restaurant, for example, decided to expand her empire by starting a chain but decided not to replicate any of the elements that had made the previous restaurants successful, you would think that she was insane (and a bad investment). This principle sounds obvious, yet we choose the wrong realities to replicate all the time. Until we learn how to replicate our *positive* reality, we will be forced to waste valuable resources trying to reinvent the wheel each time.

But it doesn't end there. If we want to be successful in our professional lives—whether that success is defined as higher profits or increased market share or the retention of top talent—we need to learn not only how to replicate our own most valuable reality but how to spread it to our teams, colleagues, and even customers or clients. One of the best examples of this came out of some work I was doing at a group of hospitals in New Orleans, and it holds some invaluable lessons for how every one of us can create positive inception in our businesses and lives.

THE FIVE-STAR HOSPITAL: CONTAGIOUS REALITIES

In a 2012 article for the *Harvard Business Review*, I wrote about the extraordinary steps the Louisiana-based company Ochsner Health System made after Katrina to raise positive genius among their eleven thousand health care providers, administrators, salespeople, and staff.[2] I had been invited several times over the course of two years to help their leaders implement my *Happiness Advantage* research. But what I soon realized was that if we really wanted to help them transform their organization, it wasn't enough to just convince a few top leaders that the best way to improve the hospital's bottom line was to raise levels of happiness first. They had to plant the idea that *"happiness is contagious and advantageous"* in the brains of everyone in the organization.

The character Michael Scott from NBC's *The Office* is famous for needlessly and often hilariously pointing out the obvious. In one episode, he declares, "I do not like hospitals. In my mind, they are associated with sickness." This is funny (to me) because *of course* hospitals are associated with sickness. The problem is that, as research shows, when we think about something as being unhealthy, it has an unhealthy effect upon us. That's why people often start to manifest the symptoms of the diseases they most fixate upon, and it's the reason first-year medical students get the infamous "medical school syndrome" in which they start believing that they have each disease they are studying.[3] But this poses a significant problem for hospitals: How can you make people feel healthier in a place associated with sickness and disease?

Simple. You turn your hospital into a Ritz-Carlton.

The Ritz-Carlton hotel brand has become synonymous with "five-star" customer service, and for good reason. Contrary to what you might think, it's not just because of their plush towels or large swimming pools or comfortable beds. It's because the Ritz does business according to a simple code of service: make the guest feel valued, and exceed expectations. I once stayed at a Ritz in D.C., paid for by a client, and when I asked to change rooms because mine smelled of smoke, the hotel immediately found me a better room, then paid for my dinner and drinks and even threw in a free massage to compensate me for the very minor inconvenience. But most people don't know the secret ingredient in Ritz's sensational service: they franchised a policy called the 10/5 Way, which turns out to be the perfect example of how to transform an organization through positive inception.

The 10/5 Way involves just a few simple behavioral rules that all staff are trained to follow. If a guest walks by a Ritz employee within ten feet, the employee should make eye contact and smile. If that guest walks by within five feet, the employee should say, "Hello." This is similar to the policy Sam Walton instituted for his greeters at Walmart, who were supposed to smile whenever they were within ten feet of a customer (now sadly no longer required).[4] It sounds simplistic, but research has shown that these small changes can have a huge impact on customer satisfaction, employee retention, and the bottom line.

After consulting the experts and reviewing the research, the folks at Ochsner Health System figured that if they wanted to improve the performance in the hospitals by creating a reality of happiness and comfort, who better to emulate than one of the best-known luxury franchises on the planet? So they adopted the 10/5 Way.

Some companies "adopt" ideas or policies by sending around a perfunctory e-mail, then forgetting about it. Ochsner *really* adopted the 10/5 Way. They formally trained more than eleven thousand physicians, nurses, managers, and administrators to smile anytime they were within ten feet and say hello anytime they were within five feet of another person—patient *or* fellow employee—and even evaluated them on it as a component of their performance reviews. Of course, a hospital is never going to be as luxurious as the Ritz, but that wasn't the point. The point was to instill a more positive reality among the hospital staff and then franchise that positive mindset and perspective to the patients.

As a researcher, though, it's my job to be skeptical, so I naturally had a lot of questions about how this would work. Would people find the smiling to be inauthentic and forced? Would all this time spent saying hello to everyone distract doctors and nurses from all the other important things they were supposed to be doing? Would negative employees find a loophole and simply walk eleven feet away from everyone in the hospital?

At first, many of the doctors and hospital staff were equally skeptical. Some would say, "Aren't these just cosmetic changes? Smiling couldn't possibly affect the underlying performance of a hospital" or "I don't have time to waste on this silly HR initiative. I'm busy saving lives here." There were some stubborn individuals that were too hard to reach at first. But for the next six months, every time one of those resistant, negative doctors walked down the hallway, something was different. People were saying hello or smiling *at them*. Not just employees, but patients as well. You've probably noticed how when someone says hello or smiles at you, your automatic reaction is to say hello or smile back. Well that's exactly what those doctors started doing. Eventually, they started adopting the 10/5 Way—even if they weren't fully aware they were doing it.

In short, the behavior became contagious. Kara Greer, vice president of organizational development and training at Ochsner, told me that soon the employees who originally didn't follow the 10/5 Way became such anomalies that even they began unconsciously to adopt the new positive patterns, simply so they wouldn't stand out for being unkind.

The 10/5 Way completely transformed the shared reality at the hospital. Some of the doctors had originally had a hard time believing that something so seemingly trivial as saying hello or smiling could possibly have any real impact on health outcomes. But what those skeptics had momentarily forgotten was the scientific and direct correlation between patient satisfaction and successful health outcomes on everything ranging from cardiac recovery to orthodontics work.[5] We sometimes think that the best doctors are the ones who have the most specialized knowledge or the fanciest degrees, but in fact, study upon study, including one published in the *New England Journal of Medicine*, show that the best doctors are the ones who also know how to connect with their patients.[6] It's not just because they make the patient feel warm and fuzzy; patients who feel connected to their doctors are more likely to follow the treatment regimen and return for vital checkups.[7]

Not only did this initiative improve patients' satisfaction with care; it improved outcomes for the hospital. Moreover, patient satisfaction with care is one of the greatest predictors of profit for a hospital; and indeed, within one year, according to Ochsner, the hospitals that franchised the 10/5 Way had a 5 percent increase on Press Ganey's Likelihood to Recommend score (which evaluates whether patients would send their friends to that hospital), a 2.1 percent increase in unique patient visits, and significant improvement in the medical practice provider scores. Ochsner reported $1.8 billion in revenue in 2011. So if they experienced even a 0.1 percent increase in revenue, positive inception saved millions of dollars to help care for more sick people![8] That gives a whole new meaning to the phrase "million-dollar smile."

When we look around at our companies or workplaces, it seems that the employees are all unique individuals with different personalities, thought patterns, beliefs, values, and learning styles. And while this is technically true, it misses an important point. Our *personalities* may be distinct and unique, but our *brains* are highly interconnected; they are linked on a *wireless* mirror neuron network. Mirror neurons, as readers of *The Happiness Advantage* may remember, are those receptors in our brains that cause us to unconsciously mimic the actions of those around us. When we see someone perform an action, like a yawn or a smile, our mirror neurons light up and signal our bodies to perform that same motion. But mirror neurons are so key to positive inception because our *thoughts and perceptions* are what dictate our nonverbal actions. So when you nonverbally express excitement, for example, my mirror neurons pick up on and imitate your expression of excitement. This, in turn, *makes my brain think I'm experiencing the same excitement you are experiencing.* Researcher Paul Marsden at the University of Sussex wrote a great review of this research showing that not only yawns and smiles are contagious but also emotions like stress, anxiety, optimism, confidence, boredom, and engagement.[9] Thanks to our mirror neuron network, in other words, *we are hardwired for inception.*

History offers some dramatic examples of how we are programmed for social contagion. In 1962, in what was known as the June Bug incident, sixty-two factory workers at a textile mill were "bitten" by an insect whose venom apparently caused terrible nausea, vomiting, and numbness of limbs.[10] Many of the dressmakers were hospitalized. Yet after months of investigation, the Communicable Disease Center (CDC) found that the symptoms had been caused not by the venom of a mysterious insect but by sheer, communicable anxiety! As it turned out, the dressmakers had been bitten by mass hysteria.

Perhaps my favorite example of social contagion on record is the Dancing Plague of 1518 (not quite as scary sounding as Ebola or the Black Death, but more interesting). According to reports, it began when a woman in Strasbourg, France, known as Frau Troffea, started dancing in the streets and could not stop.[11] Eventually she collapsed from exhaustion. At first people thought she had had a psychotic episode and that was the end of it. But then she started dancing again. In the next few days, thirty other people also experienced this same uncontrollable need to spastically dance. By the end, the authorities had to get involved because four hundred villagers were compulsively dancing day and night . . . and not out of joy either. This was manic, desperate dancing, resulting in heart attacks and, incredibly, deaths. Frau Troffea's bizarre behavior had become wildly contagious.

A solitary mental breakdown started months of mass hysteria. A single case of false illness created an imaginary epidemic. These stories show how easy it is for us to "catch" the mindset of even a single person. There are tons of stories like this in social psychology. But if you've read the research or taken a class on the subject, you'll know that people rarely talk about the *positive* contagions that have occurred throughout time: mass decisions to abolish slavery, global declines in smoking rates, or widespread nonviolence movements in India or Egypt. *Positive outbreaks can also begin with a single dancer.* If we can create negative franchises, we can equally make positive ones.

The main point I want to highlight here is that you have the power to franchise positive habits in your home or workplace. So try implementing the 10/5 Way in your office or household. Or, if that sounds like too big a task or commitment, try adopting a variation I used in the PBS lecture "The Happiness Advantage for Health" called Flex Your Smile. All you have to do is flex your most powerful muscle three extra times a day. But by this I don't mean smile three times a day. I mean give three *extra* smiles. For example, smile at a colleague you wouldn't normally smile at in the elevator, smile at the barista when you order your morning coffee (yes, I know it can be hard to smile *before* you've had your morning coffee, but try it anyway), and smile at a random stranger on your way home from work. Or smile three extra times during the course of a meeting or a sales pitch and watch how this simple behavior change can transform the environment almost immediately. It might sound silly or implausible, but as we just saw at Ochsner, I doubt that any other one-second behavioral change could create that high a return on investment.

Plus there is scientific proof that you can also raise your social and emotional intelligence simply by smiling. When David Havas and colleagues at the University of Wisconsin had participants flex the facial muscles involved in smiling, he found that merely simulating a smile reduced their ability to get angry at another person.[12] And on the flip side, when people used the muscles associated with frowning, they had a harder time being social. If I told you that you could increase your social intelligence by wearing glasses, you might consider getting some clear glasses for work, right? Well, putting a smile on your face is even easier (and less expensive) and can reap the same benefits. Moreover, researchers have found that when you smile, your brain releases the neurochemical dopamine, which improves *your* mood and your reality as well. Remember, positive realities are contagious in *both* directions.

The point of this research is not to highlight the value of smiling but to show the value of franchising small, simple changes. Another simple franchise adopted by Ochsner was the "no-venting rule." Employees were trained never to vent in the presence of a patient. They could continue to vent about lack of sleep, fatigue, obnoxious patients, and so on to one another, but never in the presence of a patient, even if the patient was not theirs. The no-venting rule applied not only within the confines of the examination room or the doctor's office but in the hallways, the cafeteria, and so on. These days office buildings have specific smoking areas where we cordon off smokers so their smoke doesn't bother others; perhaps we should start implementing "venting areas" to cordon off complainers so they don't poison others with their negativity at the office.

Before you accuse me of suggesting that people be forbidden to voice negative feedback or point out problems that need to be fixed, let me explain. I am not saying that a doctor should be silent if the nurse makes a careless error or if he's forced to work a twenty-four-hour shift. In both scenarios staying silent would be irresponsible and dangerous. What I am suggesting is that a doctor refrain from making comments that only spread negativity and lessen the likelihood of success. Here's the key difference between complaining and pointing out solvable problems. A complaint is an observation about some reality that your comment could not possibly ever change. If you plan on taking positive action, your comment is not a complaint.

Last week I heard a woman in a movie theater whisper loudly to her husband, "It is way too cold in here." I couldn't help but think, either get up and ask the management to turn down the air-conditioning or stop complaining! I don't mean that in a callous way; I'm saying it for her own good. Given what we've learned from positive psychology, we know that by commenting on the cold she's making her brain more conscious of the cold, *which makes her feel colder* (again, what we focus on becomes our reality!). So, out of kindness to yourself, if you find yourself in a similar situation, go ask the manager to change the temperature, get your sweater out of the car, or focus your attention elsewhere, like on enjoying the movie.

Similarly, if you say, "I'm not getting paid enough," but you aren't going to request a raise, highlight your positive behavior in a novel way to your boss, find another job, or take some other action to change the situation (remember the first criterion of noise from the last chapter—if the information is not going to spur positive change, it is noise and should be canceled), then that comment is a complaint and has wasted cognitive energy.

You might try implementing the no-venting rule in your office or household—or at least exile complainers to a cordoned-off "venting area." This is a small, simple change, and that is exactly the point. The smaller the change, the easier it is to spread it to others. Try it. For the next twenty-four hours, smile at everyone who comes within ten feet, and abstain from venting. You'll be amazed to see how quickly and powerfully this can change the tenor of all the interactions you have. And don't be surprised if pretty soon the people around you have picked up these same habits without even being aware of it. Such is the power of positive inception.

Finally, don't forget that positive realities can be contagious in your personal relationships as well. One of my freshmen at Harvard once confided in me that she had been fighting a lot with her parents, who she felt didn't trust her to make good decisions now that she had left the nest. Instead of telling her to write them off as obnoxious parents, which would probably result in the kind of behavior that would only confirm their worst expectations (again, what we focus on becomes our reality), I had her watch for patterns. She came back with an unusual observation. Every time she called them after 9:00 p.m., she and they would fight, but this almost never happened when she called before 9:00. This was usually because she worked really hard on her pre-med studies, and by the time 9:00 p.m. rolled around, she was cognitively depleted and no longer had the mental reserves to be patient, to explain her thoughts clearly, or to let things go. A simple solution: she decided she would "call family before 9:00 p.m. and never after unless there was an emergency." But also observe how this tiny change created positive inception. Her parents soon noticed how much more positive their interactions with their daughter were because of her newfound patience and openness (though they probably didn't know the reason for it). In turn, they became more open and patient on the phone and soon, to her excitement, began to trust more in her decisions. As a result, she found herself wanting to share more about college with them, which created even more trust and goodwill. So you see how positive genius is a continual feedback loop if franchised correctly.

STRATEGY 2: REWRITE THE SOCIAL SCRIPT (MAKE IT POSITIVE)

When I was a teaching fellow for a social psychology course, one of my favorite assignments was to send the students out into Harvard Square to break a social rule and observe what happened. They might get into the elevator in William James Hall and slowly turn around and stare at the people behind them. Or they might lie down in the elevator (which flips people out). They would eat off other people's plates, tip their professors after class for a good lecture, ask someone on a date while they were on a date with someone else, answer a phone call in the middle a lecture, and so on. There are myriad social rules governing our lives, and we all instinctively know what they are. No one has ever had to tell you that you mustn't lie down in elevators or pluck a french fry off a stranger's plate. These unwritten rules that govern our social interactions are known as social scripts.

To be sure, social scripts play a valuable role in our society. The problem arises when these scripts infect us with negative realities that lessen our likelihood of success. That's why the second technique for creating positive inception is finding ways to rewrite the social scripts.

In 2012, a large company, which I will leave unnamed because they were experiencing very low engagement scores, invited me to come speak to a group of managers about the research on praise and recognition and how they could be used to create a more energized work environment. Afterward, the senior HR manager pulled me aside and said that she liked my talk but that it was a little awkward because the managers had recently been encouraged not to be encouraging. I must have looked confused, so she explained, "We are in the midst of our fourth massive restructuring in three years, so we don't feel like it's appropriate to be 'rah-rah' about anything right now. It doesn't seem respectful because we've had to let people go. And we aren't sure when the restructuring will end, so we have toned down praise. Otherwise, people might think, 'Oh, I'm going to get my bonus' or 'I'm definitely going to keep my job,' neither of which is certain right now."

I was stunned. How could this company not see that essentially banning positivity was just about the worst thing you could do in the midst of massive uncertainty? After all, if they weren't going to be motivating people with raises and promotions, they'd better be motivating them with praise and positive leadership! Have you worked for a company or on a team like this? The unwritten rules at the company said, "We can talk about the negatives, frustrations at the leadership, and the stresses, but praise is inappropriate." And they were surprised that they had low engagement scores? Clearly, they needed, and we need, a more positive social script.

THREE MEN MAKE A TIGER

While all social scripts affect our interactions with others, not all have equal influence. According to psychology researcher Bibb Latané from Columbia University, every social script has three components: the strength of the message (S), the immediacy (I), and the number of sources (N).[13] So the degree of social influence a script exerts is determined by the following equation: S + I + N = Social Influence. (I will refrain from the too-obvious theological jokes.)

This equation intuitively makes sense. The stronger and more important the message is, and the more people delivering it, the more influence it will have. At work, you've probably seen this many times. If many members on the team hear a forceful explanation about why they are not receiving more information from senior management, for example, they are more likely to believe that explanation than if they heard it from a single coworker.

When I was in divinity school, I studied some Buddhist and Confucian thinking. One of my favorite Chinese proverbs was "Three men make a tiger." The story behind it went something like this:

On a starless night, three men are sitting quietly and listening to the jungle. All of a sudden, a wild pig runs past, knocks over one of the men, and escapes into the night. The fallen man yells, "Tiger!" Two of the other men, panicked, also yell "Tiger!" As a result, the whole village awakens, and chaos erupts, as the three men tell the harrowing story of the tiger attack. A hunting party is created to rid the village of the terror. The pig, calm now, watches impassively from the trees as the villagers begin to build wooden fences and worried mothers keep their children inside their huts until the "tiger" can be killed. The (false) reality of a tiger on the loose has come to dominate the social rules of the village.

I finished divinity school in 2002. In March of the following year, I watched several senior U.S. politicians repeat a version of this story. Their tiger was weapons of mass destruction.

The whole WMD fiasco demonstrates just how disastrous a negative script can be, especially when it is high in social influence. Clearly, if you want to effectively rewrite a more positive script in your professional life, you're going to have to increase your level of social influence.

Sometimes, depending on the cultural norms at your company, it can be difficult to increase the strength of a positive message without being written off or ostracized. And it is hard to increase the immediacy without sounding hysterical or shrill. So the best approach is to increase the N, the number of people buying into the positive message. Like a politician securing his or her base, focus on the low-hanging fruit—the like-minded, positive people—first. Once you have increased the N, you will have more influence over the middle-of-the-road group. Then once you have planted the seeds of positive change in both those groups, you can work on the most intractably negative coworkers or managers or clients. That seems intuitive, but you'd be surprised how many people get it backward. *Many people identify the most negative people and then throw all of their energy and resources into trying to get them to see more positives. That is a doomed strategy. It's far better to first find people who are more likely to tip to positive; only then, once you have increased your social influence, should you go after the cynics.* There is great strength in numbers when you are planning positive inception.

USE THE POWER LEAD

The more we can spread our positive reality, the better chance we have of making our companies healthier and more positive places. Unfortunately, the script for how we should act and respond to challenges at work is often written by the most vociferously negative people. But contrary to what you might think, if you want your positive message to be heard, the solution is not to be the one who speaks loudest. It's to be the one who speaks *first*.

In 2009, Cameron Anderson and Gavin Kilduff from the University of California, Berkeley, did an interesting experiment demonstrating the power of speaking first.[14] They had one hundred participants split into twenty-five groups of four men or four women to solve a series of GMAT math questions (the test that applicants to business school must take). The researchers videotaped the groups as they worked together to come up with the correct answers. After the tests were finished, they showed the videotapes to a panel of people (who did not know the students in the video) and asked them who they thought the leader in the group might be. In truth, none of the students in the groups had been assigned the role of leader, yet there was full agreement among the naive raters about who the leader was. It was whoever spoke first. Even more incredible, an astonishing 94 percent of the final answers the groups gave were the answers offered by the person who spoke first. Not only did the third-party observers perceive these people as having high social influence, but their own teammates, who knew that no one had been assigned a leadership role, did too. These perceived leaders didn't bully their teammates into picking their answers, and it wasn't that they had more correct answers either. My favorite part of the study was that there was no correlation between math skills and being the first person to speak (which only confirms my long-held suspicion that the first person on a team who speaks up is usually the least qualified person to do so). One person simply held more sway over the group because he or she spoke first.

The point is that simply by being the first to speak, you can set the social script. Michelle Gielan from the University of Pennsylvania describes this as the "power lead."[15] Before getting a master's degree in positive psychology, Gielan was a national news anchor at CBS News in New York. As a journalist, she saw how often newscasts would start with the most sensational, negative story of the day. That lead story would set up the entire program.

Think about how much of an impact the first statement in any dialogue or conversation has on the tenor of the whole exchange. If you are having a conversation with a sick friend, and she leads by talking about a particularly unpleasant doctor's visit, the conversation will revolve around sympathy and disease. But if you take the power lead and start with the positive, perhaps by telling her how much better she looks since you last saw her, you can rewrite the script of the entire interaction.

Whether at work or at home, it's easy to use the power lead to turn your conversations positive. Simply be the first to speak, and start conversations with a positive topic before someone can start the social script with gossip, complaints, or negativity. This idea has inspired me to change the way I start certain types of phone calls. Before, anytime I was slow to get back to someone about something, I used to start the call by saying, "I'm so sorry I didn't get back to you—I've been so incredibly busy" or "Oh, I'm swamped right now." That immediately set the tone of the social script as negative and stressed (or all about me). So now, instead, I start with something great that is going on, or why I'm excited to work with them on a project. It's amazing how people conform to the positive script when I do this. Likewise, when you're put into groups, if you want to set the tone or mood, make sure you get some of the first words in. Think about it, which meeting would you prefer to attend? One that starts with "Let's get going because we have so much to do today and a lot of fires to put out" or one that starts with "I'm happy to see you all today—it's great that we have such a strong team working on these exciting new projects"? Same reality but a very different outlook. Then sit back and watch how people's engagement and motivation improve in response to your power lead. It's one of the most effective tools in this book.

CHANGE YOUR FACE

When it comes to social interactions, many individuals have a blind spot right in front of their faces. Literally. What I mean is that they often forget how big a role facial expressions play in transferring our realities. Worse, they often fail to realize when their faces are communicating the complete opposite of what they actually feel or believe. I cannot tell you how many times I've looked out at a member of an audience who looked as if he were just hating my talk, then had him come up afterward and, with the same sour expression on his face, tell me that the talk was life changing. It's as if we were all walking around talking in a foreign language that no one understood.

A 2010 study by Joshua Davis of Barnard College highlights the impact our facial expressions have on others. In a somewhat shocking procedure, participants were injected with either Botox or Restylane.[16] (I have no idea how in the world he got permission from the institutional review board to do this. It took the IRB at Harvard three months to allow me to videotape freshmen playing charades with Tufts students for a study.) Anyway, both chemicals are substances meant to reduce wrinkles, but Botox works by killing the nerves that control your facial muscles, which limits the range of emotional expression. Restylane, on the other hand, doesn't deaden the nerves that control the muscles, so your face can still produce normal emotional expressions. After injecting the participants, the researchers showed them videos that had previously been determined to be very emotional and asked them to rate the emotional impact. What happened? The people in the Restylane group reported the movie to be much more emotionally charged than did the Botox group. In other words, Botox not only killed their ability to express their emotions facially but muted their emotional reaction. This is a clear indication that failing to show positive emotion on your face can hamper not only your ability to experience positive realities but also your ability to spread positivity to others. It is also a warning to teams and organizations (and definitely the military) that believe that showing no emotion at work has no long-term effects on morale or engagement.

Of course, nonverbal communication includes more than your smile: body language and tone also set the stage for inception. In one study, researchers at the Yale School of Management found that the tone of the leader's voice actually predicted the outcome for the team.[17] Student volunteers were put in teams to collaborate on various business tasks, with the goal of earning money for an imaginary company. Then in came the "manager," who was actually an actor instructed to speak a script in one of four ways: with "cheerful enthusiasm," "serene warmth," "depressed sluggishness," or "hostile irritability." It was the exact same actor with the exact same script (i.e., the words he said were exactly the same), but the *social* script was altered by the nonverbals. Unsurprisingly, the team who experienced the cheerful, enthusiastic leader was more positive. But perhaps more surprisingly, when the "manager" read the script in a positive tone, the teams were also significantly more profitable.

Nonverbals have been found to exert powerful social influence in the military as well. Researchers discovered that in the U.S. Navy annual prizes for efficiency and preparedness—two leadership qualities that, on the surface, should have nothing to do with positivity—are far more frequently awarded to squadrons whose commanding officers are openly encouraging.[18] On the other hand, the teams led by commanders with a negative, controlling, and aloof demeanor generally receive the lowest performance scores. Even in an environment where one would think the harsh "military taskmaster" style of leadership would be most effective, positivity wins out.

At some companies, there is an unwritten social rule that "happiness is weakness": that if you have time to chitchat with a coworker by the water cooler or leave early for a son's baseball game, you're not working hard enough. But as we've seen, these kinds of scripts don't just make for toxic, unpleasant places to work; they undermine productivity, engagement, and ultimately, profitability. The good news is that, given what we have learned about positive inception, we know that you have the power to re-write that script. After all, the social script in every workplace has to be written by somebody—why not you? If, as we saw with the 10/5 Way, something as simple as smiling can change the so-cial script to positive, think about all the other easy ways non-verbal communication can do the same. For one, when you give praise, don't just say it with your words; be sure to make your face and tone fit your words. Nodding encouragingly while co-workers talk not only raises their feelings of being understood but increases connection. Make sure that your tone and nonverbals are not connoting fatigue or boredom. A simple but incredibly powerful way to ensure that your nonverbals are positive is one that I learned from a manager out in Las Vegas who works at Zappos (one of the world's best companies in terms of positive culture). Here's the secret: take a look at the person talking to you. Thanks to our neural network, we unconsciously mirror the people we are with. So if the person you are talking to is not smil-ing, seems fatigued or disengaged, or seems anxious, chances are *your* nonverbals are not as positive as they need to be. If you don't like what you are seeing, change yourself first and see if the other person follows the new script.

CHANGE THE SCRIPT FROM TRAGEDY TO COMEDY

The best script writers are those who write comedies, not tragedies, at work. This is not just because positive people tend to like comedies; it's because humor wields more social influence—and is therefore more effective in creating positive inception. Look at the popularity of shows like *The Daily Show* and *The Colbert Report*, which infuse journalism with humor. They discuss the same stories that conventional news broadcasts discuss, but because they present them in a way that is funny, their ratings are actually higher than those of many conventional news broadcasts. And their popularity doesn't just lie in the fact that they deliver the news with a spoonful of entertainment; as it turns out, funny people are perceived as being smarter and more credible.[19] Humor has been continually found to be a strong predictor of a leader's ability to create profit and performance. In one study, Yung-Tai Tang found a direct and positive correlation between the humor of the leader and the level of innovation in R&D departments.[20]

We are all innately attracted to funny people. But why? From an evolutionary perspective it makes sense that when looking for a romantic partner, we are attracted to those who look fit or strong because they can defend our offspring. It also makes sense that we are attracted to people with good skin, healthy hair, symmetrical bodies, and so on because these are signals that the genes they will pass to our offspring will be high quality and healthy. But why are we attracted to humor? Telling a joke won't improve reproductive success or stop a saber-toothed tiger from attacking your kids. Researchers have actually found the reason. Humor is attractive, not just in romantic partners but in business partners, politicians, journalists, and anyone else writing a social script, because it is a signal of *cognitive fitness.*[21] Your brain must be flexible, quick, and sharp to comprehend or create humor. The funniest people are those who are able to see a version of reality the rest of us might miss. You could say that humor is a marker of an individual's ability to add vantage points.

For three years, I was the head teaching fellow for a class called "Wit and Humor" at Harvard. In that course, designed by Professor Leo Damrosch, we described how everything from leadership to productivity can be dramatically improved by improving your ability to add vantage points through humor. In my writing on the topic, I define humor as "the awareness of an alternative way of viewing the world which shows absurdity or commonalities of life." (Nothing kills humor like scientific definitions.)

But what is it that causes people to find humor in some realities when others find only irritation or embarrassment? Not surprisingly, the answer lies in positive genius. Psychologist Barbara Fredrickson's "broaden and build theory" suggests that experiencing positive emotions expands people's momentary "thought-action repertoires," those paths to using our intellectual resources in the most productive way. That's a fancy way of saying that your perception of reality determines your actions: if you see a path to a positive reality, your brain will be quicker to see humor in the negative events of your external world. Thus, when you have a negative external world at work, you can use humor as a strategic tool to help others see a more positive reality.

The Oxford professor C. S. Lewis said that there are two kinds of people: those who look for miracles and find them, and those who don't look for miracles and see none.[22] The same is true for humor. If you aren't looking for the humor in the external world as you lead meetings, introduce people at a conference, talk to a client on the phone, or create a PowerPoint report, you will miss opportunities to introduce comedy into your social script. Don't worry, you don't have to be a stand-up comedian to use humor for positive inception; you don't even need to be the one to create the jokes. You merely need to share or laugh at them. Keep an e-mail folder with forwards you receive of funny articles or videos, then find ways to work them into the social script during a meeting or a talk. Make a list of the funny stories you tell in your family or embarrassing moments growing up, and share those (when appropriate) with your colleagues or teams. I once did this in college for an English course, and from then on, whenever I needed to insert something funny into a talk, I had a list of options at my fingertips (see the unicorn story at the beginning of my TED talk). You might also make a list of funny lines from your favorite movies, books, or TV shows and "borrow" those as well. How many times in your work life has someone referenced a line from the movie *Office Space* or the TV show *The Office*? Probably a billion, but even then it still "gets a laugh like a quarter of the time" (case in point, Andrew Bernard explaining the humor in saying "Beer me," which probably only a quarter of readers would get). Finally, researchers suggest watching more comedies to improve your comedic timing. We get better at sports by watching good athletes, and the same goes for humor. Humor is one of the most effective—and fun—ways to turn scripts positive at work.

STRATEGY 3: CREATE A SHARED NARRATIVE (MAKE IT MEANINGFUL)

How do you spread positive inception at the world's largest company? The same way you might create a happiness movement for people suffering from a devastating chronic illness: you find champions to create an emotional, meaningful narrative. In this section I'll explain the link. If you can make your message emotional, your chances of creating inception improve dramatically. What's more, you don't need to be a boss or a leader to spread positivity; anyone at any level of the organization can create a shared narrative grounded in emotion and meaning.

There are few projects I've felt more proud of than getting to be the positive psychology expert for the Everyday Matters campaign. The National MS Society's Everyday Matters, supported by Genzyme, a Sanofi company, was a nationwide interactive program to uncover and feature the authentic stories of people who are facing the everday challenges that MS can bring on the path to one's best life. When I got involved with the program, I knew little about MS, but the more I read, the more vicious the currently incurable disease seemed. This illness literally tears apart your brain's ability to communicate effectively with the nerves in your body, resulting in recurring bouts of bone-deep weariness, pain, and paralysis. The more I learned, the more daunting the disease became.

Enter the champions: 1,200 brave individuals dealing with the physical, emotional, and social challenges of MS applied to be part of a program in which they would use some of the techniques from my last book, *The Happiness Advantage*, to improve their coping skills and even reduce their symptoms. Then, from this large group, we chose five individuals who would become our champions of inception. We didn't select these people because they were the happiest, but rather because their stories would show the rest of the MS Society and the world that *happiness is a choice*. I met the five in Denver, where we spent a weekend going through positive psychology findings and laying out a plan for their next few months with their happiness coach, Michelle Clos, who also has MS. From July to November, they were filmed by Kristen Adams, an Emmy Award–winning TV producer (who also has MS), and the film was shown to the rest of the society. I was blown away by their stories. One elementary school teacher in rural Oklahoma named Sallie would wake up every morning, hit with a deluge of fatigue that many of us will never experience, and instead of quitting would get up each day and go to school, bringing hope and inspiration to her students. As a visual reminder of that commitment to her passion, she even made a charm bracelet with one charm for each student in her class, so that she could think about why she was grateful for that student every day.

I learned something very valuable from this experience. We could have spoken to those affected by MS for hours on end about the science of happiness, and it wouldn't have had nearly the effect of those videos on the website (everydayMSmatters .org). That's because to better plant the seeds of a positive reality in a group of people who are confronting a certain challenging experience, you need an emotional narrative delivered by individuals who share that experience. In short, to create positive inception, what we needed were champions. And we found many more than just five of them. I met individuals who got diagnosed with MS and started running marathons, even though they'd never run before. I met people who found love, even though the first-date conversation started with "I have a debilitating, degenerative, incurable disease." These were positive geniuses, and they started a movement. They gave us a narrative that when things are hard, there are very simple ways that we can choose to stay positive, motivated, and focused on overcoming life's great challenges.

Inspired by the Everyday Matters campaign, when Walmart came knocking in 2012, wondering how to create a happiness movement for their 1.5 million associates—many of whom do not have much education, are at the poverty line, have relatives in prison, are single parents, don't have much time away from the floor for training, don't have access to computers, work part time, and are overweight—we knew one of the keys. Positive inception works best when you have an emotional, meaningful, and deeply personal narrative.

With that in mind, my company, Good Think Inc., partnered with Walmart visionary David Hoke and Jamie Brunner at B&B to help design a program where we went into stores to get employees to create sustained positive habits around different domains of their lives: family, fitness, food, and money. At the time of publication this project, called The Zip Challenge, is ongoing, but our plan is that from the thousands of employees' stories we will select champions to go around to stores sharing their stories and inspiring Walmart associates to create a positive habit in their lives. Then, at each of the stores, more and more champions will be selected to keep spreading stories of success, thereby creating positive inception. As the program takes off, and we are testing to see the effects upon health, happiness, and profits, that research should be available on my website, HappinessAdvantage.com, as it comes out.

The key to this program was finding people inside Walmart to lead the movement. So whether the change you want to spread is improved health or better workplace habits, sometimes all it takes is a positive, emotional narrative.

MOVING BEYOND THE LEADER

Most of us assume that you need to be in a leadership role in order to transform the culture or mindset of a team or organization. But some interesting research by a true positive genius, Professor

Adam Grant at Wharton Business School, shows that, in fact, it's more important to connect with people on a deep emotional level as he describes in his fascinating book, *Give and Take*.

Grant's research focused on a class of new hires at a call center who were undergoing a sales and service training. He split the class into four groups and subjected them to slightly different training conditions. At the first group's training, the leader gave a motivational talk in addition to the normal training. At another training, the leader didn't make an appearance, but a fellow employee (called a beneficiary because he was someone who had benefited from the success of the company) gave a short talk on why the call center was so important for the functioning of the company. He talked about how profits from the call center helped the company pay everyone's salary and allowed the company to continue to grow. The third group received just the normal training, with no additional speakers. But at the fourth training, both the leader *and* the grateful employee came to speak.

Even if you guessed that the training with both the leader *and* the beneficiary was most effective in motivating the new hires, I doubt you could guess how positively this affected the performance of the team. When the training was run as usual without any motivating speakers, the group made 46 sales with a total revenue of $3,738. When the leader showed up, sales jumped from 46 to 151, or about 300 percent. But here's where it gets really interesting. In the final group, in which the trainees heard the leader speak about how important the call center was *and* got to meet one of the people positively affected by their future work, the sales jumped from 46 to 271, and the revenue skyrocketed from $3,738 to $21,376. In other words, when a leader shared his positive vision of reality, the revenue increased, but when a fellow employee deepened the emotional connection by showing how that reality affected him, *revenue increased by 700 percent and sales by 500 percent.*[23]

This study shows that people are much more likely to adopt your reality when it is both emotional and real; in this case, the benefited employee lent credibility to the leader's message. If you're a leader, you can talk until you're blue in the face about how your team's hard work benefits the company, but that same message will be perceived as far more credible and powerful if your team also hears it from a fellow rank-and-file employee. This is exactly why politicians invite average people to stump for them on the campaign trail: their message resonates more emotionally with voters when it's delivered by a citizen just like them.

Here's another great example from Grant regarding how much more impact a message can have when it's delivered by someone we connect with. Bob Austin, a manager at Volvo, once wrote a blog post intended to increase engagement and to ripple positive performance in the company. He decided to relate a story in which the son of a Volvo customer got in a terrible car accident but came out alive thanks to the safety features of his Volvo. "Had her son been driving any other car, he would have been killed. . . . The work we do at Volvo genuinely saves lives," Austin said.[24]

His story was powerful, to be sure, but now let's compare it to a speech about a second death that had been avoided thanks to the high safety standards at Volvo. This time, the mother herself got up on stage with him and related the story: "My daughter escaped with minor bruises and scrapes. The police officer's statement to me: 'If it wasn't a Volvo, they probably would not have survived.' "[25] Which version do you think was more effective in implanting the message that Volvo employees were positively changing the world with their work? The point is that positive inception does not have to come from the formal leader; in fact, sometimes it works better if it doesn't.

I once spoke to a salesperson at a large tech company in Austin who was frustrated that he couldn't get his team to be as engaged as he was. He told me that he had spent his last monthly meeting trotting out graph after graph to show how much the company had been growing. But for all his positivity, it didn't seem to have a bit of impact on his employees' reality. So at his next monthly meeting, he invited a client to speak about how pleased he was with the service he had received from the company, as well as one of the salespeople to talk about how much happier he was working here than at his old firm. Suddenly, he said, it was as if he had a whole different team: people were noticeably more engaged, motivated, and productive for weeks following the meeting. Often the best way to raise success rates and increase your bottom line is to use not numbers, but meaning.

The reason this research is so important is that it breaks down the myth about where positive leadership comes from. If you want to convince others of some positive reality at work, find a beneficiary of that reality: a satisfied client, a happy coworker, or perhaps yourself. Then make sure you infuse your message with personal examples showing that the beneficiary's reality is real and valid. For example, if you want to get people to donate to your favorite charity, bring in someone who has benefited from the program. If you want to get your team to feel more motivated, ask a client to record a thirty-second YouTube video describing how pleased they are with something your team has provided. And remember, the more emotional you make it, the more impact it will have.

TURNING ADVERSITY INTO GLUE

Believe it or not, adversity and challenge at work don't have to be the enemies of engagement and motivation; they can actually be the glue. I realize this doesn't sound like something a positive psychology researcher would say, but it's true. Why? The answer lies in Leon Festinger's famous work on a psychological phenomenon called cognitive dissonance.

Cognitive dissonance is a state that occurs when the brain recognizes that it is holding two conflicting beliefs. For example, let's say you have always detested olives. Then one day your wife sneaks them into a pasta sauce, and you find them delightful. Your brain will experience dissonance that you want to dispel. Or let's say you've always considered yourself a conservative. Then an election rolls around, and you find yourself drawn to a liberal. Your brain experiences dissonance. What does this have to do with positive inception? Festinger argues that if you spend a ton of effort on a task, your brain considers that a worthwhile expenditure of cognitive resources. But what if you spend a high effort on something that your brain says is not important, not related to you, not valuable, or not something you enjoy? That leads to cognitive dissonance. Your brain thinks, "Why, oh why, did I pay such a high cognitive cost for something I care so little about?" Your brain hates cognitive dissonance. So it comes up with a justification to explain why you paid such a high cost, usually by deciding that the work actually was of high value. Thus cognitive dissonance can trick your brain into perceiving that you care deeply about a particularly odious task or difficult challenge. Adversity or challenge, in other words, can be used to spur motivation and engagement, and, in turn, it can be used as a tool to spread that mindset to others.

Whereas businesses have been slow to catch on to these ideas, the military has long incorporated them. In fact, there's a lot we could learn about positive inception from the military. I realize I've told a lot of stories about my stint in the navy (and the number of stories I *could* tell could probably take up an entire book), but this one is particularly instructive. When I started my scholarship, I went to a boot camp. Actually, they called it "orientation," which my brain unfortunately assumed would be less akin to armed combat than to summer camp. I was in for a rude awakening—literally. I fell asleep on the bus to "orientation" in Newport, Rhode Island, and awoke to a U.S. Marine drill sergeant yelling at me that I had five seconds to get off the already emptied bus—but not before doing forty pushups. Over the next few hours (though I have no idea how long because they took my watch), they confiscated all our possessions, including any family photos, phones, et cetera, shaved off our hair, and marched us around mercilessly.

Each night we slept at attention fully clothed for our 4:00 a.m. wakeup. We were given just five minutes for meals (as the officers were fond of saying, if the fork goes into your mouth, you're eating too slowly). We were permitted only ten seconds to shave (using government-issued blades, which usually resulted in our getting accused of trying to bleed to death to get out of marching). When I got sunburned after marching in the sun for five hours, I got yelled at: "Achor, why the hell are you destroying government property?" (meaning me).

But there is an underlying reason for all this, and it's not that the officers are secretly sadists (though some of them may have been). Obviously it's crucial for the military not only to retain top talent but to enlist officers with the fiercest commitment and loyalty; after all, they have to be willing to die for their troops and their country. So you might think, why in the world would they want to scare away this talent by putting them through the hell of boot camp? Because when cadets are going through this hellish training, to avoid cognitive dissonance, their brains convince them that they must really value what they are doing. "I am going through hell now *because* I want to be a great officer so badly," the brain thinks. "Why would I go through all this pain if I didn't?" In other words, putting cadets through the wringer instills higher levels of commitment, determination, and loyalty because their brains decide they value it.

When done correctly, introducing collective team stress can have similar benefits in the workplace. In one series of experiments, Elliot Aronson created several initiation scenarios for new hires.[26] Some initiations were mild and easy, like merely introducing oneself or telling a quick story. Others he made embarrassing by forcing the employees to read scripts—aloud—that contained embarrassing words. What happened? The employees who had gone through the mild and easy initiations described their group of fellow employees as having low connection and their group membership as having low value. The employees who had read the scripts with embarrassing words reported that their group was more connected and that they valued their group membership more highly. Just like the ROTC cadets, when these employees paid a high cost to take part in the initiation, they perceived it as more meaningful in order to save their brains from the pain of cognitive dissonance. Think about it: going through rough periods when these are shared with others can create some of the deepest bonds we make. Why can't this happen more with stress at work?

I'm not suggesting that you go around spreading stress and hostility in your workplace. This skill is about *positive* inception, after all. What I am suggesting is that you help people find the *meaning* in the stress and adversity. How? By *focusing on how the team overcame it.* Look again at the military. Sure, they put their cadets through hell, but they also create a shared, positive, meaningful narrative by making their cadets feel a part of something bigger, letting them know what an amazing honor it is to be part of such an amazing history, with such amazing people, fighting for such an amazing country. Adversity, linked with the shared reality that our stress *meant* something, was what bonded us cadets together.

Thus to turn adversity into glue in our teams and in our organizations, we need to plant and spread the message that "the challenges we are experiencing are enhancing." When I'm at conferences speaking, I'll often hear amazing leaders present. For example, after Walmart's 2012 shareholders meeting in Bentonville, Arkansas, rather than ignoring the challenges imposed by budget constraints over the past year, Walmart's global head of HR used those challenges to create positive inception. She planted the idea that "this team has proven its ability to innovate and exceed expectations." Now, instead of getting bogged down in negativity and frustration, the team viewed the challenges as badges of honor, proving that optimism for the future was warranted. Every time your team or company goes through stress, it is an opportunity to show the team why that brought them closer together and made them stronger. Stress is inevitable, but as we have proven before, its effects are not. *Stress can tear a team apart if ignored or feared, but if used as a positive, it can be the glue. The key is to find the right narrative.*

For example, when I was working with Adobe in 2011, Maria Yap, the product management director, sent me a fantastic video the company had made to create a shared narrative around a past challenge. The video, *Behind the Splash Screen: The Making of CS5*, tells the story behind the release of Creative Suite 5, one of Adobe's flagship products: it narrates how the team failed at first, then banded together, then eventually succeeded. Importantly, the video features not just the leader of the team but also many other members of the team talking about their pride in overcoming the challenges in making CS5: how they had to revise the entire code and how they were given six months to accomplish what was normally a yearlong task.

The positive genius of this video lies in the fact that it uses the narrative of a triumph over adversity to create an emotional connection (much as the military does in their recruitment videos).[27] The message is clear: "We can band together through thick and thin to create and innovate successfully." I could hear the pride in Yap's e-mail, and you can hear it in the voices of the team members in the video. It's the pride you hear in people who deeply value the work they are doing.

Most teams and leaders forget that there is a moment for incredible positive inception after a success had been achieved. Too often, we finish a project or hit a sales target or meet a deadline and immediately are on to the next task or challenge. But in doing so we miss out on creating a narrative of meaning. So when you achieve a major success at work, don't move on without taking a moment to use the adversity you overcame as glue for your team. You don't have to have a professional team to create a video like Adobe's. You can do it with your words. Better yet, a few smartphones and an hour on a moviemaker program on your computer will do the trick just as well. Create a narrative of your success, including any missteps, failures, and challenges you encountered along the way. If you don't have the time to make a video, pictures of past successes work as well. At Adobe, they have a whole wall covered with reproductions of the company's patents to remind the employees of all the innovation that goes on there. How else can you do this at your own work, or in your personal life, to create an emotional narrative that people can embrace and share?

We need to make positive inception a conscious part of our leadership at work and our ownership of our environments. How much of your work time is devoted to talking about how amazing being part of this team is? Are group successes celebrated as much as individual ones? Is there a shared emotional narrative about the past challenges the group has overcome? Or are challenges seen as the enemy of the team, rather than the glue? As with the Walmart project and the Everyday Matters campaign for the MS Society, another great way to create inception is to find champions or become one yourself. The companies I've worked with who have best spread positive realities through their ranks have had an internal champion beating the drum of how positive change mattered in his or her life.

In the fall of 2012, my company Good Think Inc. partnered with Delivering Happiness at Work, the Zappos consulting arm based on Tony Hsieh's book, to help create positive inception at companies. We loved their approach because Zappos is a prime example of a culture founded upon positive inception. It takes a lot of social capital to get everyone on a team to buy into an idea. Literally all the people who work there identify themselves as part of Zappos' culture; Zappos even publishes an annual "culture book" with pictures of all their employees and unedited descriptions of why they like working there. And this is due, in large part, to the shared narratives that are created within the teams. For example, each department in the call center has its own theme. One might have a pirate theme, and when people come by on the VIP tour, they all yell, "Arrghh!" (of course, covering the phones with their hands so as not to freak out their customers on the phones). You might think this behavior is unprofessional, and in many organizations it might not fit in with company culture. But in this case it creates a shared experience, however silly, that binds team members. But let me flip the question: Is your current team engaged and connected enough that they would be willing to yell like a pirate in front of a crowd of VIPs? Or is the only thing connecting your team their titles and desk proximity?

I spoke at the company-wide Zappos All Hands Meeting in 2012, where Tony Hsieh, instead of focusing on last year's revenue and sales numbers, devoted a huge amount of time to *why* people love working at Zappos. Some love working there because they are obsessed with shoes. Some love it because they find deep meaning in delivering great customer service, and some because they love working for an innovative company that lets them dress up and scream like a pirate. What are you doing to help people at work fall in love with your company? Even if you aren't a boss or manager, it's your responsibility/opportunity as a positive genius to help others see the valuable reality that you do. Find what makes work meaningful for you, and then create a simple narrative to help others see what you see.

If you are successful at creating a positive reality but incapable of sharing it with others, then that reality will be limited and short-lived. But by utilizing the techniques of positive inception, you can create a renewable source of positive energy for you and the people around you. In this chapter, we have discussed the three big keys to positive inception: franchising, script writing, and creating a shared narrative. The key to mastering them, though, is to let go of the myth that you cannot change other people. We *can* change people, but only by planting the seeds of a more positive reality. So remember, if you want to successfully transfer your positive reality, you must make that reality contagious, influential, and meaningful. Once you have done that, you have become a master mental architect, capable not only of creating positive genius but of spreading it on a massive scale.

The farther and wider you spread positive genius, the more potential you'll be able to unleash. Once you have amplified the collective intelligences of your teams, companies, families, and communities, there is truly no limit to what you can achieve.

MAKING IT PRACTICAL

1. *Use numbers to your advantage.* We know that social influence is defined by S + I + N, strength of the message plus the immediacy of the message plus the number of people delivering it. The easiest variable to increase in this equation is N, the number of sources of the positive message. So go after the low-hanging fruit first. Like a politician securing his or her base, start by spreading your reality to like-minded, positive people before trying to persuade the negative Nellies. Raising your numbers will help you build the influence you need to plant seeds of positive change among the cynics.

2. *Create a franchise.* Find simple, emotional, and positive patterns you can replicate and franchise to others around you. One such pattern might be a no-venting rule in your office or household. Or look for patterns

that lead to negative interactions—and change them, as the college student did when she improved her relationship with her family by adopting a rule to call them only before 9:00 p.m.

3. *Use the power lead.* The first person to speak in a conversation often sets the direction of the entire social script. Thus, if we want to create meaningful and productive interaction, we need to lead with something positive. Remember Michelle Gielan's idea of starting each conversation with a compliment or encouraging comment or even just by mentioning something good that is going on in your life. The very beginning of a conversation or meeting is the prime time to create positive inception.

4. *Add three smiles.* Try implementing the 10/5 Way in your office or household. Or, if that sounds like too big a commitment, simply flex your most powerful muscle three extra times a day. Three *extra* smiles.

5. *Use humor.* You don't have to be a stand-up comedian yourself to turn your social script into a comedy. When you hear a hilarious line in a comedy sketch or sitcom, write it in a notepad function on your phone, then find a way to use it over the next twenty-four hours. Keep an e-mail folder of funny articles or videos you receive from other people, then find ways to work them into the social script during a meeting or a talk (just don't become *that guy* who over-forwards). Make a list of the funny stories you tell in your family or embarrassing moments growing up and share these (when appropriate) with your colleagues or teams.

6. *Create a narrative.* This one is more time intensive but can be a source of renewable positivity for years to come. Develop a shared positive narrative about a time your team or company overcame an obstacle or challenge, and share it, either in digital or in written form. Write out a real story, with conflict, climax, and a resolving action. Include pictures or even video. Turn a triumph over adversity into the glue that binds your team together, while raising levels of loyalty, drive, and engagement.

positive inspiration

A CASE FOR CHANGE

{ *It is by experience that we discover and by science that we prove.*

Scientific discoveries often happen by accident and experience, not logic. For me, one such discovery occurred in the desert of the United Arab Emirates. If you have read my first book, you know about my signature mirror neuron experiment, which I have now done in fifty-one countries. I merely partner people up and have one person try to control his or her face to show no emotion for seven full seconds. Then I have the other person "smile warmly and genuinely directly into the eyes of the [first] person." It is much more difficult than it sounds. In fifty of the fifty-one countries, 80 to 85 percent of the people in the room broke down and smiled before the seven seconds was over. But it was in that fifty-first country that I had a eureka experience that helped me understand positive genius much more fully.

In May of 2012, I was invited by the royal family in Abu Dhabi to give a talk. I was so excited about the opportunity to go dune bashing in all-terrain vehicles and ride camels across the desert that when it came time for my lecture I wasn't thinking. Sheikha (a royal wife in Abu Dhabi) Salama Bint Hamdan Al Nahyan asked me to speak at her foundation about how to change realities for women in the Middle East. As was my habit, I kicked off the talk with my smiling experiment. It wasn't until midway through that I realized my mistake: half the room was veiled.

If I had thought about this, I might not have tried the experiment. Who would think to try a smiling experiment with veiled women? But I'm so glad that I made that error because, incredibly, *the experiment still worked.* The women in the audience told me that they could see smiles in their partner's eyes. Even behind the veil, these unseen smiles were contagious. None of these women could see their partner's face, yet they still became infected by her smile.

The point here is that no matter what seemingly insurmountable barrier is in our lives, we can build and transfer our positive reality to others. And in fact, sometimes the greatest opportunities to do this are the ones that are slightly hidden. Thus a positive genius is someone who sees solutions, possibilities, and connections that are unseen by the average person. *Positive geniuses know that to see the things others miss we must step back and take a departure from the way we have lived life up to this moment.*

In the early 1900s, Henri Poincaré, a famous French mathematician, came up with the concept of "relativity," a discovery that is, of course, most commonly attributed to Albert Einstein.[1] Not many people know this (I had not heard of Poincaré myself before taking a class on him), but Poincaré and Einstein revolutionized modern physics at the exact same time. Whereas

Einstein felt that the flaws in Newton's thinking could be solved with physics, Poincaré felt that the problem was mostly mathematical. They saw the same problem through different lenses and came up with similar answers—but that is not why I'm highlighting these two geniuses. By looking at their writings, I want to highlight *why* they were geniuses.

In 1908, in *Science and Method*, Poincaré wrote: "Then I turned my attention to the study of some arithmetical questions apparently without much success . . . Disgusted with my failure, I went to spend a few days at the seaside, and *thought of something else* [italics mine]. One morning, walking on the bluff, the idea came to me, with just the same characteristics of brevity, suddenness and immediate certainty."[2]

In the same work he also wrote about how he had solved a different problem: "For fifteen days I strove to prove that there could not be any functions like those I have since called Fuchsian functions. I was then very ignorant; every day I seated myself at my work table, stayed an hour or two, tried a great number of combinations and reached no results. One evening, contrary to my custom, I drank black coffee and could not sleep. *Ideas rose in crowds; I felt them collide until pairs interlocked, so to speak, making a stable combination.* By the next morning I had established the existence of a class of Fuchsian functions."[3] (How many times have we beaten our heads against a problem, trying to prove that there is no solution, only to later discover we were wrong?)

And regarding yet another instance of creative activity, he wrote: "Thereupon I left for Mont-Valerian, where I was to go through my military service; so I was very differently occupied. *One day, going along the street, the solution of the difficulty which had stopped me suddenly appeared to me* [italics mine]. . . . So I wrote out my final memoir at a single stroke and without difficulty."[4]

Three solutions, all by surprise. As a psychology researcher interested in innovation and intelligent creativity, I love his phrasing. He was walking down the street and the solution "appeared" to him.

In each of these moments of positive genius, Poincaré came to these conclusions while *not* thinking about the problems. Actually, let me qualify this: he was very much thinking about these work problems, just not using his conscious brain. He was allowing his unconscious brain to help. According to another brilliant scientist, Yale psychologist Scott Kaufman, the unconscious portion of your brain works on problems using *different* processes than your conscious brain.[5]

What problems and obstacles are you trying to solve in your life? How are you going about it? As Adam Galinsky from the Kellogg School of Management explains, "Conscious thought is better at making linear, analytic decisions, but unconscious thought is especially effective at solving complex problems. Unconscious activation may provide inspirational sparks underlying the 'Aha!' moment that eventually leads to important discoveries."[6]

But the key to unlocking these unconscious processes is taking time to *not think* about your challenge or problem. In other words, to engage all of your brain and achieve those "aha moments," you sometimes need to shut a portion of your brain off. The greatest "aha!" moments in our lives occur not when we are working without stop, but when we stop working.

Einstein reported the same phenomenon of positive genius. In 1905, after a frustrating conversation with his friend Michele Besso in which he tried to reconcile all the problems he saw with Newtonian physics, he conceded defeat and gave up.[7] While bouncing in a streetcar in Bern, Switzerland, the impoverished and defeated Einstein looked back over his shoulder and saw the

Bern clock tower. He casually wondered what would happen if his streetcar suddenly zoomed away from the clock at the speed of light. Perhaps Einstein just wanted to get home faster. Maybe the great Einstein needed to go to the bathroom. But as he would put it, "A storm broke loose in my mind." This was his unconscious brain offering his conscious brain a novel idea that would soon upend everything we thought we knew about the universe: that time was not the same everywhere in the universe. Einstein was not squiggling incomprehensible mathematical formulations on the board when he made his discovery. He was not in a physics lab. He was just on his way home.

In other words, the two greatest geniuses of modern physics made their most groundbreaking discoveries when they stopped thinking and just let their unconscious brains take over. That's because once you have fully built and embraced a positive reality, that reality becomes embedded deep in your unconscious brain processes. Thus the skills of positive intelligence can become second nature, allowing you to harness all your intelligences without consciously trying, or even being consciously aware of it.

Think about the biggest challenge you are currently facing, the one that has been most plaguing you. How do you take your current business and scale it? How can you pivot into another job in your industry? How can you find a way to manage your far-flung team while not being in the same location? How can you get your beloved child or spouse to stop feeling depressed and making poor decisions? Instead of beating your head against a wall, spending eighty hours a week solving this problem, just stop. Take a few moments from your daily stream of life and let your unconscious take over.

The greater the complexity of your problem—and I think we

can all agree that Einstein and Poincaré were attempting to solve problems much bigger and more challenging than the ones we face in our daily working lives—the greater the need for a positive reality that transcends consciousness. Success on a massive scale, in other words, requires a reality in which, even if our conscious minds can't see a solution, our unconscious minds know that one is possible.

In all my research, and all my work with some of the most brilliant business leaders around the globe, one conclusion has remained constant: there is a big difference between being smart and being *inspired*. Many brilliant people never feel the kind of inspiration that leads to life-changing discoveries or achievements. That's because to be inspired you need to stop seeing the world through the same old lens. No matter how high your IQ, your emotional intelligence, or your ability to relate to others, if you can't learn to change your reality, you'll never be truly inspired. So take time after this book to reflect upon all that you've learned. Think about how these skills have changed your mindset, your habits, your everyday life. Let your new reality seep into your subconscious. Once you do you'll find yourself capable of the kind of inspiration necessary for true greatness.

I am hoping, with your help, that this book and the research within will contribute to leading us toward a much-needed renaissance in our companies and schools, akin to the Renaissance in Europe, which heralded a golden age of discovery and growth as people became aware that they could know more about their world than they ever imagined.

But of course, research is useless unless it is lived. Now that you have made it this far in the book, you have over thirty practical takeaways and have read about over fifty scientific discoveries.

But information alone does not cause transformation. The key now is to incorporate just a few of these strategies, maybe just one at a time, into your life.

The costs of changing nothing are stagnation and resignation to the status quo. But the benefits of changing your reality—and sharing that positive reality with others—are the kinds of successes, discoveries, and breakthroughs that can transform not only your own life but the world.

We need more positive geniuses in our companies, our families, and our communities. We need you.

notes

THE POWER OF POSITIVE GENIUS

1. Manfred Zimmermann, "Neurophysiology of Sensory Systems," in *Fundamentals of Sensory Physiology*, 3rd, rev. ed., ed. Robert F. Schmidt (New York: Springer, 1986), 116.

2. A. R. Jensen, *Clocking the Mind: Mental Chronometry and Individual Differences* (Amsterdam: Elsevier, 2006).

3. Daniel Goleman, *Emotional Intelligence* (New York: Bantam Books, 1995), 36.

4. Glenn Elert, *The SAT: Aptitude or Demographics?*, E-World, May 11, 1992, http://hypertextbook.com/eworld/sat.shtml.

5. Thomas J. Stanley, *The Millionaire Mind* (Kansas City: Andrews McMeel, 2001).

6. Peter Salovey and J. D. Mayer, "Emotional Intelligence," *Imagination, Cognition, and Personality* 9 (1990): 185–211.

7. Hilaire Fernandes, "Designing Interactive Contents: Thales and Pyramid Height Calculus," using Dr. Geo II interactive geometry software, n.d., http://people.ofset.org/hilaire/drgeo2/demos/2-thales/index.html.

8. This research is summarized from my previous book, *The Happiness Advantage* (New York: Crown, 2010).

9. Shawn Achor, "Positive Intelligence," *Harvard Business Review*, January-February 2012, http://hbr.org/2012/01/positive-intelligence/ar/1.

10. A. Crum, P. Salovey, and S. Achor, "Re-thinking Stress: The Role of

Mindsets in Determining the Stress Response," *Journal of Personality and Social Psychology,* forthcoming, June 2013.

11. D. R. Proffitt, "Embodied Perception and the Economy of Action," *Perspectives on Psychological Science* 1, no. 2 (2006): 110–22; J. K. Witt, D. R. Proffitt, and W. Epstein, "Perceiving Distance: A Role of Effort and Intent," *Perception* 33 (2004): 570–90.

12. If you are interested in seeing the metrics we used in coming up with this research, you can take the tests on the University of Pennsylvania's website, authentichappiness.org. You can also take the Success Scale used in my research, developed in the spring of 2010 at the Institute for Applied Positive Research, positiveresearch.com. We created a series of three ten-question metrics, which are now some of the fastest and most powerful predictors of long-term success and engagement. You can read more about them at positiveresearch.com.

SKILL 1: REALITY ARCHITECTURE: CHOOSING THE MOST VALUABLE REALITY

1. I'm told the navy understandably doesn't allow untrained individuals to do this anymore after a fisherman's boat was destroyed when a sub dropped down on it and crushed it.

2. Manfred Zimmermann, "Neurophysiology of Sensory Systems," in *Fundamentals of Sensory Physiology,* 3rd, rev. ed., ed. Robert F. Schmidt (New York: Springer, 1986), 116.

3. Shawn Achor, "Make Stress Work for You," February 15, 2011, HBR Blog Network, http://blogs.hbr.org/cs/2011/02/make_stress_work_for _you.html.

4. N. Schneiderman, G. Ironson, and S. D. Siegel, "Stress and Health: Psychological, Behavioral, and Biological Determinants," *Annual Review of Clinical Psychology* 1, no. 1 (2005): 607–28; American Psychological Association, "Stress in America: Our Health at Risk," press release, January 2012, www.apa.org/news/press/releases/stress/2011/final-2011 .pdf.

5. Ibid.

6. According to an *Archives of Internal Medicine* study cited in Krista Mahr, "Achy Breaky Heart," *Time,* November 1, 2007, www.time.com/time/ magazine/article/0,9171,1678678,00.html.

7. Jane Eisinger, "High Anxiety," *Association Management,* August 2001, www.asaecenter.org/Resources/AMMagArticleDetail.cfm?Item Number=5252.

8. George Chrousos, "Stress and Disorders of the Stress System," *Nature Reviews Endocrinology* 5 (July 2009): 374–81, doi:10.1038/ nrendo.2009.106.

9. L. Cahill, L. Gorski, and K. Le, "Enhanced Human Memory Consolida-

tion with Post-learning Stress: Interaction with the Degree of Arousal at Encoding," *Learning and Memory* 10, no. 4 (2003): 270–74.

10. P. A. Hancock and J. L. Weaver, "On Time Distortion under Stress," *Theoretical Issues in Ergonomics Science* 6, no. 2 (2005): 193–211.

11. E. S. Epel, B. S. McEwen, and J. R. Ickovics, "Embodying Psychological Thriving: Physical Thriving in Response to Stress," *Journal of Social Issues* 54, no. 2 (1998): 301–22.

12. C. L. Park, L. H. Cohen, and R. L. Murch, "Assessment and Prediction of Stress-Related Growth," *Journal of Personality* 64, no. 1 (1996): 71–105; R. G. Tedeschi and L. G. Calhoun, "Posttraumatic Growth: Conceptual Foundations and Empirical Evidence," *Psychological Inquiry* 15, no. 1 (2004): 1–18.

13. Bruce Goldman, "Study Explains How Stress Can Boost Immune System," *Inside Stanford Medicine*, June 22, 2012, http://med.stanford.edu/ism/2012/june/stress.html.

14. S. E. Palmer, E. Rosch, and P. Chase, "Canonical Perspective and the Perception of Objects," in *Attention and Performance IX*, ed. John B. Long and Alan D. Baddeley (Hillsdale, NJ: Lawrence Erlbaum, 1981), 135–51.

15. Daniel P. Jones and Karen Peart, "Class Helping Future Doctors Learn the Art of Observation," *Yale News*, April 10, 2009, http://news.yale.edu/2009/04/10/class-helping-future-doctors-learn-art-observation.

16. Ibid.

17. Ibid.

18. Richard Wiseman, "The Luck Factor," *Skeptical Inquirer*, May–June 2003, www.richardwiseman.com/resources/The_Luck_Factor.pdf.

19. S. Glazer, "Social Support across Cultures," *International Journal of Intercultural Relations* 30 (2006): 605–22.

20. M. P. Walker, "The Role of Sleep in Cognition and Emotion," *Annals of the New York Academy of Sciences* 1156 (2009): 168–97; Els van der Helm and Matthew P. Walker, "Overnight Therapy: The Role of Sleep in Emotional Brain Processing," PubMed Central, June 23, 2010, www.ncbi.nlm.nih.gov/pmc/articles/PMC2890316/.

21. Shai Danziger, Jonathan Levav, and Liora Avnaim-Pesso, "Extraneous Factors in Judicial Decisions," *Proceedings of the National Academy of Sciences* 108, no. 17 (2011), www.pnas.org/content/108/17/6889.full.

22. M. Losada, "Work Teams and the Losada Line: New Results," *Positive Psychology News Daily*, December 9, 2008, http://positivepsychologynews.com/news/guest-author/200812091298.

23. Barbara Fredrickson, *Positivity: Groundbreaking Research Reveals How to Embrace the Hidden Strength of Positive Emotions, Overcome Negativity, and Thrive* (New York: Crown, 2009).

24. Ibid.

25. Tom Rath, "The Impact of Positive Leadership," *Gallup Business Journal*, May 13, 2004, http://gmj.gallup.com/content/11458/impact-positive-leadership.aspx.

26. Loretta Malandro, "Discover Your Leadership Blind Spots," *Businessweek*, September 1, 2009, www.businessweek.com/managing/content/sep2009/ca2009091_828190.htm.

27. Trina C. Kershaw and Stellan Ohlsson, "Training for Insight: The Case of the Nine-Dot Problem," in *Proceedings of the Twenty-third Annual Conference of the Cognitive Science Society*, ed. Johanna D. Moore and Keith Stenning (Mahwah, NJ: Lawrence Erlbaum, 2001), 489–93, http://conferences.inf.ed.ac.uk/cogsci2001/pdf-files/0489.pdf.

28. A. M. Isen and J. Reeve, "The Influence of Positive Affect on Intrinsic and Extrinsic Motivation: Facilitating Enjoyment of Play, Responsible Work Behavior, and Self-Control," *Motivation and Emotion* 29, no. 4 (December 2005): 297–325.

29. Richard Nisbett, *The Geography of Thought* (New York: Free Press, 2003).

30. Sharon K. Parker and Carolyn M. Axtell, "Seeing Another Viewpoint: Antecedents and Outcomes of Employee Perspective Taking," *Academy of Management Journal* 44, no. 6 (December 2001): 1085–1100.

31. Bill Clinton, "Clinton on Clinton," interview by Diane Salvatore, *Independent*, December 20, 2005, www.independent.co.uk/news/people/profiles/clinton-on-clinton-8051116.html.

SKILL 2: MENTAL CARTOGRAPHY: MAPPING YOUR SUCCESS ROUTE

1. Ebonie D. Hazel, "Survey Finds Depression Pervasive in College," *Harvard Crimson*, March 31, 2003, www.thecrimson.com/article/2003/3/31/survey-finds-depression-pervasive-in-college/.

2. S. Agrawal and J. K. Harter, *Wellbeing as a Predictor of New Disease Burden: A Two-Year Examination of 11,306 Survey Panel Members' Health and Wellbeing* (Omaha, NE: Gallup, 2011).

3. L. Hermer and E. Spelke, "A Geometric Process for Spatial Reorientation in Young Children," *Nature* 370 (1994): 57–59.

4. Alex Edmans, "The Link Between Job Satisfaction and Firm Value, with Implications for Corporate Social Responsibility," *Academy of Management Perspectives* 26, no. 4 (November 2012): 1–19; Tom Rath and Jim Harter, T*he Economics of WellBeing* (Washington, DC: Gallup Press, 2010), www.ofyp.umn.edu/ofypmedia/focusfy/The_Economics _of_Wellbeing.pdf.

5. S. T. Innstrand, E. M. Langballe, and E. Falkum, "A Longitudinal Study of the Relationship between Work Engagement and Symptoms of Anxiety and Depression," *Stress and Health: Journal of the International So-*

ciety for the Investigation of Stress 28, no. 1 (2012): 1–10, doi: 10.1002/ smi.1395.

6. Bill Barnett, "Make Your Job More Meaningful," HBR Blog Network, April 25, 2012, http://blogs.hbr.org/cs/2012/04/make_your_job_more _meaningful.html.

7. Tom Rath and Jim Harter, "Wellbeing: What You Need to Thrive," interview by Jennifer Robison, *Gallup Business Journal*, May 12, 2010, http://businessjournal.gallup.com/content/127643/wellbeing-need -thrive.aspx.

8. Michael Corbin, "On the Tracks of Addiction," *Urbanite*, March 1, 2011, www.urbanitebaltimore.com/baltimore/on-the-tracks-of-addiction/ Content?oid=1378874.

9. Amy L. Shelton and Timothy P. McNamara, "Systems of Spatial Reference in Human Memory," *Cognitive Psychology* 43 (2001): 274–310, www.psy.vanderbilt.edu/faculty/mcnamara/lab/visual/CogPsyc2001 .pdf.

10. Judy Sargent, Reg Arthur Williams, Bonnie Hagerty, Judith Lynch-Sauer, and Kenneth Hoyle, "Sense of Belonging as a Buffer against Depressive Symptoms," *Journal of the American Psychiatric Nurses Association* 8, no. 4 (August 2002): 120–29; Carolyn Schwartz, "Teaching Coping Skills Enhances Quality of Life More Than Peer Support: Results of a Randomized Clinical Trial with Multiple Sclerosis Patients," *Health Psychology* 18, no. 3 (1999): 211–20. A great summary is Stephen G. Post's "It's Good to Be Good: Science Says It's So," *Health Progress*, July-August 2009, 18–25, www.stonybrook.edu/bioethics/ goodtobegood.pdf.

11. Mihaly Csikszentmihalyi, *Finding Flow: The Psychology of Engagement with Everyday Life* (New York: Basic Books, 1997).

12. Shawn Achor, "The Happiness Dividend," HBR Blog Network, June 23, 2011, http://blogs.hbr.org/cs/2011/06/the_happiness_dividend.html.

13. Shawn Achor, "Why a Happy Brain Performs Better," HBR IdeaCast, November 25, 2010, http://blogs.hbr.org/ideacast/2010/11/why-a -happy-brain-performs-bet.html.

14. Peter Bregman, "Too Much to Do? Take on More," HBR Blog Network, May 10, 2011, http://blogs.hbr.org/bregman/2011/05/i-know-how-to -handle.html.

15. "Prayer of Saint Francis of Assisi," www.catholic-forum.com/saints/ pray0027.htm.

16. Shawn Achor, "The Happiness Dividend," HBR Blog Network, June 23, 2011, http://blogs.hbr.org/cs/2011/06/the_happiness_dividend.html.

17. Barbara Fredrickson, *Positivity: Groundbreaking Research Reveals How to Embrace the Hidden Strength of Positive Emotions, Overcome Negativity, and Thrive* (New York: Crown, 2009), 58–60.

18. This is one of the most interesting and convoluted stories in recent his-

tory. See Steven Lee Myers, "Chinese Embassy Bombing: A Wide Net of Blame," *New York Times*, April 17, 2000.

19. Lisa Getter, "U.S. Military Accidents Linked to Flawed Maps," *Los Angeles Times*, May 16, 1999, http://articles.latimes.com/1999/may/16/news/mn-37866.

20. Frank Jacobs, "The First Google Maps War," *New York Times*, February 28, 2012, http://opinionator.blogs.nytimes.com/2012/02/28/the-first-google-maps-war/.

SKILL 3: THE X-SPOT: FINDING SUCCESS ACCELERANTS

1. Jane E. Allen, "Adrenaline-Fueled Sprint Makes Some Marathons Deadly," ABC News, November 21, 2011, http://abcnews.go.com/Health/HeartDisease/marathon-deaths/story?id=15000378#.UAwJoY5alvY.

2. Robert Rosenthal and Lenore Jacobson, *Pygmalion in the Classroom* (New York: Holt, Rinehart and Winston, 1968).

3. Ellen Langer, *Counterclockwise: Mindful Health and the Power of Possibility* (New York: Ballantine, 2009).

4. Ran Kivetz, Oleg Urminsky, and Yuhuang Zheng, "The Goal-Gradient Hypothesis Resurrected: Purchase Acceleration, Illusionary Goal Progress, and Customer Retention," *Journal of Marketing Research* 43 (February 2006): 39–58.

5. Duane P. Schultz and Ellen Sydney Schultz, *A History of Modern Psychology*, 10th ed. (Mason, OH: Cengage, 2011), 239–42.

6. Kivetz, Urminsky, and Zheng, "Goal-Gradient Hypothesis."

7. Ibid.

8. Minjung Koo and Ayelet Fishbach, "Dynamics of Self-Regulation: How (Un)accomplished Goal Actions Affect Motivation," *Journal of Personality and Social Psychology* 94, no. 2 (2008): 183–95.

9. J. K. Witt, S. A. Linkenauger, and D. R. Proffitt, "Get Me Out of This Slump! Visual Illusions Improve Sports Performance," *Psychological Science* 23 (2012): 397–99.

10. Witt, Linkenauger, and Proffitt, "Get Me Out of This Slump!"

11. J. K. Witt and M. Sugovic, "Performance and Ease Influence Perceived Speed," *Perception* 39 (2010): 1341–53.

12. Stephen Garcia and Avishalom Tor, "The N-Effect: More Competitors, Less Competition," *Psychological Science* 20, no. 7 (2009): 871–77.

13. Ibid.

14. "MLB Park Factors—2012," 2013, http://espn.go.com/mlb/stats/parkfactor.

15. See "Park Factors," www.parkfactors.com/, for examples.

16. Bill Petti, "The Impact on Hitters Who Change Parks," March 14, 2012, www.fangraphs.com/blogs/index.php/the-actual-impact-of-hitters -changing-parks/.

17. C. R. Riener, J. K. Stefanucci, D. R. Proffitt, and G. Clore, "An Effect of Mood on the Perception of Geographical Slant," *Cognition and Emotion* 25, no. 1 (2011): 174–82; J. K. Witt, D. R. Proffitt, and W. Epstein, "Perceiving Distance: A Role of Effort and Intent," *Perception* 33 (2004): 570–90; S. Schnall, J. R. Zadra, and D. R. Proffitt, "Direct Evidence for the Economy of Action: Glucose and the Perception of Geographical Slant," *Perception* 39, no. 4 (2010), 464–82, doi: 10.1068/p6445; J. R. Zadra and G. L. Clore, "Emotion and Perception: The Role of Affective Information," *Wiley Interdisciplinary Reviews: Cognitive Science* 2, no. 6 (2011): 676–85.

18. Susan Weinschenk, "100 Things You Should Know about People: #60—Cognitive 'Loads' Are the Most 'Expensive,'" W Blog, February 17, 2011, www.theteamw.com/2011/02/17/100-things-you-should -know-about-people-60-cognitive-loads-are-the-most-expensive/.

19. K. D. Vohs, R. F. Baumeister, B. J. Schmeichel, J. M. Twenge, N. M. Nelson, and D. M. Tice, "Making Choices Impairs Subsequent Self-Control: A Limited-Resource Account of Decision Making, Self-Regulation, and Active Initiative," *Journal of Personality and Social Psychology* 94 (2008): 883–98.

20. David Daniels, "Top 100 Pregame Pump Up Songs of All Time," Bleacher Report, April 20, 2011, http://bleacherreport.com/articles/ 672617-top-100-pregame-pump-up-songs-of-all-time.

21. Bob Holmes, "Why Time Flies in Old Age," *New Scientist,* November 23, 1996, www.newscientist.com/article/mg16422180.900-look -how-time-flies.

22. Sandra Blakeslee, "Running Late? Researchers Blame Aging Brain," *New York Times*, March 24, 1998, www.nytimes.com/1998/03/24/ science/running-late-researchers-blame-aging-brain.html?pagewanted =all&src=pm.

23. Mihaly Csikszentmihalyi, *Finding Flow: The Psychology of Engagement with Everyday Life* (New York: Basic Books, 1997).

24. J. A. Taylor and D. F. Shaw, "The Effects of Outcome Imagery on Golf-Putting Performance," *Journal of Sports Sciences* 20, no. 8 (2002): 607–13.

25. Gabriele Oettingen, Hyeon-ju Pak, and Karoline Schnetter, "Self-Regulation of Goal-Setting: Turning Free Fantasies about the Future into Binding Goals," *Journal of Personality and Social Psychology* 80, no. 5 (May 2001): 736–53.

26. V. K. Ranganathan, V. Siemionow, J. Z. Liu, V. Sahgal, and G. H. Yue,

"From Mental Power to Muscle Power: Gaining Strength by Using the Mind," *Neuropsychologia* 42, no. 7 (2004): 944–56.

27. "How to Make a Screen Saver with Pictures," n.d., www.ehow.com/how_2386316_make-screen-saver-pictures.html.

SKILL 4: NOISE CANCELING: BOOSTING YOUR POSITIVE SIGNAL BY ELIMINATING THE NEGATIVE NOISE

1. William James, *The Principles of Psychology* (New York: Cosimo, 2007), 2:103, quoted in Patricia A. Knowles, Stephen J. Grove, and Kay Keck, "Signal Detection Theory and Sales Effectiveness," *Journal of Personal Selling and Sales Management* 14, no. 2 (Spring 1994): 1.

2. Daniel Bukszpan, "14 Spectacularly Wrong Predictions," CNBC.com, May 19, 2011, www.cnbc.com/id/43094187/14_Spectacularly_Wrong_Predictions?slide=15.

3. Manfred Zimmermann, "Neurophysiology of Sensory Systems," in *Fundamentals of Sensory Physiology*, 3rd, rev. ed., ed. Robert F. Schmidt (New York: Springer, 1986), 116.

4. Susan Weinschenk, "100 Things You Should Know about People:#98— Attention Is Selective," W Blog, April 3, 2011, www.theteamw.com/2011/04/03/100-things-you-should-know-about-people-98-attention-is-selective/.

5. Kevin R. Foster and Hannah Kokko, "The Evolution of Superstitious and Superstition-like Behaviour," *Proceedings of the Royal Society of London, B: Biological Sciences* 276 (2009): 31–37, doi 10.1098/rspb.2008.0981.

6. "How Good Are the Weather Forecasts?," April 7, 2003, http://weather.slimyhorror.com/.

7. Stephen J. Dubner, "How Valid Are TV Weather Forecasts?," Freakonomics, April 21, 2008, www.freakonomics.com/2008/04/21/how-valid-are-tv-weather-forecasts/.

8. Laura Helmuth, "Fear and Trembling in the Amygdala," *Science*, April 25, 2003, 568–69, http://labnic.unige.ch/papers/PV_cns2003_science.pdf.

9. M. Losada and E. Heaphy, "The Role of Positivity and Connectivity in the Performance of Business Teams: A Nonlinear Dynamics Model," *American Behavioral Scientist* 47, no. 6 (2004): 740–65.

10. B. L. Fredrickson and M. Losada, "Positive Affect and the Complex Dynamics of Human Flourishing," *American Psychologist* 60, no. 7 (2005): 678–86.

11. Michael Zhuang, "Tracking Jim Cramer's Performance: January 2007 Stock Picks," *Seeking Alpha*, March 14, 2008, http://seekingalpha.com/article/68536-tracking-jim-cramer-s-performance-january-2007-stock-picks.

12. Sheena S. Iyengar and Mark R. Lepper, "When Choice Is Demotivat-

ing: Can One Desire Too Much of a Good Thing?," *Journal of Personality and Social Psychology* 79, no. 6 (December 2000): 995–1006; Susan Weinschenk, "100 Things You Should Know about People: #10—You Want More Choices and Information Than You Can Actually Process," November 13, 2009, www.theteamw.com/2009/11/13/100-things -you-should-know-about-people-10-your-want-more-choices-and -information-than-you-can-actually-process/.

13. Roger E. Bohn and James E. Short, "How Much Information? 2009 Report on American Consumers," *Consumer Reports*, December 9, 2009, last updated January 2010, http://hmi.ucsd.edu/pdf/HMI_2009 _ConsumerReport_Dec9_2009.pdf.

14. U.S. Bureau of Labor Statistics, "Labor Force Statistics from the Current Population Survey, 2008 Annual Averages—Household Data— Tables from Employment and Earnings," www.bls.gov/cps/cps_aa2008 .htm.

15. See W. Russell Neuman, Yong Jin Park, and Elliot Panek, "Tracking the Flow of Information into the Home: An Empirical Assessment of the Digital Revolution in the U.S. from 1960–2005," paper presented at the International Communications Association Annual Conference, Chicago, 2009, www.wrneuman.com/Flow_of_Information.pdf.

16. "When Icing the Kicker Can Backfire," Wall Street Journal Online, September 22, 2010, http://online.wsj.com/article/SB1000142405274 87041292045755061121940986 70.html.

17. "Halloween Poisonings," Snopes.com, n.d., www.snopes.com/horrors/ poison/halloween.asp.

18. O. I. Kereke, J. Prescott, J. Y. Y. Wong, et al., "High Phobic Anxiety Is Related to Lower Leukocyte Telomere Length in Women," PLOS ONE 7, no. 7 (2012): e40516, doi:10.1371/journal.pone.0040516.

19. K. Ahola, I. Sirén, M. Kivimäki, et al., "Work-Related Exhaustion and Telomere Length: A Population-Based Study," PLOS ONE 7, no. 7 (2012): e40186, doi:10.1371/journal.pone.0040186.

20. Gerardo Ramirez and Sian L. Beilock, "Writing about Testing Worries Boosts Exam Performance in the Classroom," abstract, *Science*, January 14, 2011, www.sciencemag.org/content/331/6014/211.abstract.

21. Matthew P. Herring, Patrick J. O'Connor, and Rodney K. Dishman, "The Effect of Exercise Training on Anxiety Symptoms among Patients: A Systematic Review," *Archives of Internal Medicine* 170, no. 4 (2010): 321–31.

SKILL 5: POSITIVE INCEPTION: TRANSFERRING YOUR POSITIVE REALITY TO OTHERS

1. Bill Bryson, *A Short History of Nearly Everything* (New York: Broadway Books, 2003), 9.

2. Shawn Achor, "Positive Intelligence," *Harvard Business Review*, January–February 2012, http://hbr.org/2012/01/positive-intelligence/ar/1.

3. Roger Collier, "Imagined Illnesses Can Cause Real Problems for Medical Students," PubMed Central, March 25, 2008, www.ncbi.nlm.nih .gov/pmc/articles/PMC2267854/.

4. Sheila Radatz, "What Happened to the Face of Walmart?," TribLocal, Plainfield [IL], February 25, 2012, http://triblocal.com/plainfield/ community/stories/2012/02/where-is-the-face-of-walmart/.

5. Shelly Reese, "Patient Experience Correlates with Clinical Quality," *Managed Healthcare Executive*, May 1, 2009, http://managedhealth careexecutive.modernmedicine.com/mhe/article/articleDetail.jsp?id =595838.

6. A. K. Jha, E. J. Orav, J. Zheng, and A. M. Epstein, "Patients' Perception of Hospital Care in the United States," *New England Journal of Medicine* 359 (2008): 1921–31.

7. W. Boulding, S. W. Glickman, M. P. Manary, K. A. Schulman, and R. Staelin, "Relationship between Patient Satisfaction with Inpatient Care and Hospital Readmission within 30 Days," *American Journal of Managed Care* 17 (2011): 41–48.

8. Ochsner Health System, "Annual Financial Information Disclosure for the Twelve Months ended December 31, 2011," http://media.nola.com/ business_impact/other/12%2011%20OHS%20Financial%20Info%20 final.pdf.

9. Paul Marsden, "Memetics and Social Contagion: Two Sides of the Same Coin?," *Journal of Memetics* 2 (1998), http://jom-emit.cfpm.org/1998/ vol2/marsden_p.html.

10. A. C. Kerckhoff and K. W. Back, *The June Bug: A Study in Hysterical Contagion* (New York: Appleton-Century-Crofts, 1968).

11. "The Dancing Plague of 1518," Cogitz, September 2, 2009, http://cogitz .wordpress.com/2009/09/02/the-dancing-plague-of-1518/.

12. D. A. Havas, A. M. Glenberg, K. A. Gutowski, M. J. Lucarelli, and R. J. Davidson, "Cosmetic Use of Botulinum Toxin-A Affects Processing of Emotional Language," *Psychological Science* 21, no. 7 (2010): 895–900.

13. Bibb Latané, "The Psychology of Social Impact," *American Psychologist* 36 (1981): 343–56.

14. Cameron Anderson and Gavin J. Kilduff, "Why Do Dominant Personalities Attain Influence in Face-to-Face Groups? The Competence-Signaling Effects of Trait Dominance," *Journal of Personality and Social Psychology* 96, no. 2, (2009): 491–503, http://web-docs.stern.nyu.edu/ pa/traitdominance_kilduff.pdf.

15. Allan Pulga, "Michelle Gielan: The Power of Positive Communication," iQmetrix, October 17, 2011, www.iqmetrix.com/article/2011/10/ michelle-gielan-power-positive-communication.

16. Joshua Ian Davis, A. Senghas, F. Brandt, and K. Ochsner, "The Effects of BOTOX Injections on Emotional Experience," *Emotion* 10, no. 3 (2010): 433–40.

17. W. Bachman, "Nice Guys Finish First: A SYMLOG Analysis of U.S. Naval Commands," in *The SYMLOG Practitioner: Applications of Small Group Research*, ed. Richard B. Polley, A. Paul Hare, and Philip J. Stone (New York: Praeger, 1988), cited in Daniel Goleman, *Working with Emotional Intelligence* (New York: Bantam Books, 1998), 188.

18. Ibid.

19. Daniel Howrigan and Kevin MacDonald, "Humor as a Mental Fitness Indicator," *Evolutionary Psychology* 6, no. 4 (2008): 652–66.

20. Yung-Tai Tang, "The Relationship between Use of Humor by Leaders and R&D Employee Innovative Behavior: Evidence from Taiwan," *Asia Pacific Management Review* 13, no. 3 (2008): 635–53, http://apmr .management.ncku.edu.tw/comm/updown/DW0810021530.pdf.

21. Matthew Gervais and David Sloan Wilson, "The Evolution and Functions of Laughter and Humor: A Synthetic Approach," *Quarterly Review of Biology* 80, no. 4 (December 2005): 395–430.

22. C. S. Lewis, *Miracles* (London: Collins/Fontana, 1947).

23. Adam Grant, "Leading with Meaning: Beneficiary Contact, Prosocial Impact, and the Performance Effects of Transformational Leadership," *Academy of Management Journal* 55, no. 2 (2012): 458–76.

24. Adam Grant and David Hoffman, "Outsourcing Inspiration: The Performance Effects of Ideological Messages from Leaders and Beneficiaries," *Organizational Behavior and Human Decision Processes* 116 (November 2011): 173–87.

25. Ibid.

26. Elliot Aronson and J. Mills, "The Effect of Severity of Initiation on Liking for a Group," *Journal of Abnormal and Social Psychology* 59 (1959): 177–81.

27. Julieanne Kost, *Julieanne's 5 Favorite Features in Photoshop 13.1*, video, www.youtube.com/photoshop#p/c/6B0B55A0B9EF5D93/1/yUQsPwj TsqQ.

POSITIVE INSPIRATION: A CASE FOR CHANGE

1. Henri Poincaré, "The Principles of Mathematical Physics," translated in *Congress of Arts and Science, Universal Exposition, St. Louis, 1904* (Boston: Houghton Mifflin, 1905), 1:604, and chs. 7–9 of *The Value of Science*, in *The Foundations of Science*, trans. George Bruce Halsted (1913; repr., New York: Science Press, 1921), 297–320.

2. Henri Poincaré, *Science and Method*, in *Foundations of Science*, 388, http://books.google.com/books?id=qgkeAAAAMAAJ&printsec

=frontcover&source=gbs_ge_summary_r&cad=0#v=onepage&q&f
=false.

4. Ibid., 388.

5. Scott Barry Kaufman and Jerome L. Singer, "The Creativity of 'Dual Process' System 1 Thinking," Scientific American Guest Blog, January 17, 2012, http://blogs.scientificamerican.com/guest-blog/2012/01/17/the-creativity-of-dual-process-system-1-thinking/.

6. Chen-Bo Zhong, Ap Dijksterhuis, and Adam D. Galinsky, "The Merits of Unconscious Thought in Creativity," *Psychological Science* 19, no. 9 (September 2008): 912–18.

7. Michio Kaku, "The Theory behind the Equation," NOVA beta, October 11, 2005, www.pbs.org/wgbh/nova/physics/theory-behind-equation.html.

index

Achor, Amy, 68–70
Achor, Joe, 1–2, 34, 68–70
Achor, Sharon, 1, 35, 68–70
Adams, Kristen, 210
Adobe, 20, 219–221
Aegis missile system, 109–111, 121
Alternative realities, recognizing, 25–36
Altruism, 62, 90
Amygdala, 60, 83
Anderson, Cameron, 201–202
Angles and Dangles drill, 23–24
Anxiety and worry, 169, 171–181
Aronson, Elliot, 218
Art Institute of Chicago, 36
Austin, Bob, 214
Axtell, Carolyn, 60

Backaches, 26, 33
Baltimore, Maryland, 81–82
Bank of America, 20
Barnard College, 204

Baumeister, Roy, 133
Baylor University, 1, 2
BeforeHappiness.com, 20, 63
Behind the Splash Screen: The Making of CS5 (Adobe video), 220
Belichick, Bill, 34
Besso, Michele, 229
Black Thursday, 151
Blind spots, overcoming, 26, 53–56
Body language, 205
Bohn, Roger, 164, 165
Botox, 204
Brain, 2–4, (*see also* Mental cartography; Noise canceling; Positive inception; Reality architecture; X-spot theory)
amygdala, 60, 83
glucose levels in, 44–45, 131
limbic centers, 60, 181
overload, 153–155

Brain, (*continued*)
  prefrontal cortex, 60, 82
  time perception and, 137
Brandeis University, 100
Braverman, Irwin, 38
Broaden and build theory, 208
Brock, Jordan, 92
Brunner, Jamie, 212
Bryson, Bill, 186
Buffett, Warren, 151
Bureau of Labor Statistics, 165
Bush, George W., 146
Businessweek, 53

Cerebral cortex, 137
Champion moments, 17, 123, 125,
  144
Chinchilla, Laura, 102
Chinese compass, 57–58
Chinese Embassy, Kosovo, 101–102
CIA (Central Intelligence Agency),
  101–102
Cleveland Clinic Foundation, 142
Clinton, Bill, 62–63
Clos, Michelle, 210
Coffee cup experiment, 34–36
Coffee shop experiment, 116–117
Cognitive dissonance, 216–217
Cognitive fitness, 207–208
Collective team stress, 217–218
Collins, Jim, 167
Columbia University, 162, 199
  Graduate School of Business, 44,
    116
Commitment, escalation of, 120
Communicable Disease Center
  (CDC), 193
Cortisol, 181
Costa Rica, 102
Craig, Ian, 81

Cramer, Jim, 161
Crum, Ali, 13, 31, 33, 34
Csikszentmihalyi, Mihaly, 91, 137
Cultural differences, 56–60

Daily cycle, 44–45, 133
Damrosch, Leo, 208
Dancing Plague of 1518, 193
Davis, Joshua, 204
Defensive pessimism, 99
Delivering Happiness at Work, 221
Dell Computers, 92
Depression, xiv, 65, 66, 72, 90
DiCaprio, Leonardo, 182
Diversity, 59–60, 63
Divorce, 52
Dopamine, 195
Dymaxion map, 88–89

Eating habits, 44–45, 62
Ebbinghaus illusion, 122–123
Ecological momentary assessment
  (EMA), 82
Economic crisis and recession
  (2008-11), 27–29, 41, 97, 102
EEG (electroencephalogram), 3, 4
Eggleston, J. D., 158
Einstein, Albert, 227–231
Emotional intelligence, 5–6, 8–10,
  16, 27, 55, 231
  EQ (emotional intelligence
    quotient), 6, 8, 39, 65
  Emotional Intelligence (Goleman), 6
Emotions, concealing, 54
Endorphins, 107
Epstein, David, 81
Escalation of commitment, 120
Escape routes, mapping success
    routes before, 67–68, 96–101,
    106

Everyday Matters campaign, xiv, 210–211, 221

EverydayMSmatters.org, 211

Evoked potential, 2–6

"Evolution of Superstitious and Superstition-like Behaviour, The" (Foster and Kokko), 156

Exercise, 107–109, 144, 178, 181

Eye movement experiments, 58–59, 100

Eye-tracking machines, 3

Facebook, xv, 167

Facial expressions, 204–205

Fatique, 26, 33, 43, 132

Fear, 169, 172–174, 179

Festinger, Leon, 216

Fielder, Prince, 128

50 percent mark, 14, 111

Fight-or-flight response, 33, 100

Finding Flow: The Psychology of Engagement with Everyday Life (Csikszentmihalyi), 91, 137

Fishbach, Ayelet, 120

Fisher, Irving, 151, 152

5 percent experiment, 164–168, 179, 180

Flex Your Smile exercise, 194

fMRI (functional magnetic resonance imaging), 3

Focal point, 90

Foster, Kevin R., 156

Francis of Assisi, St., 95

Freddie Mac, xiv, 167

Frederickson, Barbara, 51, 99–100, 208

Friedlaender, Linda, 38

Friedman, Milton, 151

Fundamental attribution error (FAE), 91–92

Furr-Holden, Debra, 81

Galinsky, Adam, 229

Gallup, George, 73

Galton, Sir Arthur, 4

Garcia, Stephen, 126

Gardner, Howard, 5, 6

Gates, Bill, 151

Genzyme, 210

Geography of Thought, The (Nisbett), 58

Gielan, Michelle, 202, 224

Give and Take (Grant), 213

Glucose levels, 44–45, 131

Goal gradient theory, 113, 115–116

Goal theory (see X-spot theory)

Goleman, Daniel, 6

Golf experiment, 122–123, 127

Gomes, Bob, 155

Good Think Inc., 212, 221

Good to Great: Why Some Companies Make the Leap . . . and Others Don't (Collins), 167

Google, xv, 9, 20, 99, 135, 167, 175

Gottman, John, 52

Grades, performance prediction and, 5

Grant, Adam, 213, 214

Greatest Trade Ever, The (Zuckerman), 150

Great Pyramid, 7–8

Greer, Kara, 191

Growth hormones, 32

Happiness Advantage, The (Achor), xiii, 53, 65, 80, 82, 95, 135, 164, 167, 170, 184, 192, 210, 226

HappinessAdvantage.com, 88, 212

Happiness Advantage for Health
   lecture (PBS), 87, 194

"Happiness Dividend, The"
   (Achor), 97

Harvard Business Review, 12, 29,
   97, 188

Harvard University, xiii, 38, 56, 65,
   67, 74–75, 93, 146–147, 161,
   174–175, 178, 197, 208

Havas, David, 194

Headaches, 26, 33

Health and Human Services, U.S.
   Department of, xvi

Heuristics, 24

Hoke, David, 212

Hospitals, 188–192, 195

HSBC, 47

Hsieh, Tony, 221, 222

Hugo Boss, 20

Hull, Clark, 113–116

Humana, 49

Humor, 185, 207–209, 224

Icing the kicker, 172

Impact awareness, 54

Inception (film), 182–183

INFOtotal, 167–168, 180

Institute for Applied Positive
   Research, 66, 156

Intelligence, 4–11, 36
   IQ (intelligence quotient), 4–6,
   8–10, 27, 39, 55, 65, 152, 231

Internal noise, canceling, 148,
   169–180

Iraq War, 146

Irrational optimism, 13

IRS (Internal Revenue Service),
   96

Iyengar, Sheena, 162

Jacobson, Lenore, 113

James, William, 148

Jerk, the (amygdala), 83

Jobs, Steve, 151

Johns Hopkins University, 81, 83

Johnson & Johnson, 20

Journaling, 87

Journal of Marketing Research, 116

*Journal of the American Medical
   Association*, 39

Julius Caesar (Shakespeare), 173

June Bug incident, 193

Kanizsa, Gaetano, 45

Kanizsa triangle, 45–46

Kaufman, Scott, 229

Kellogg School of Management,
   229

Kershaw, Trina, 55

Kilduff, Gavin, 201–202

Kimball Electronics, 46–47

Knox, Frank, 151, 152

Kokko, Hanna, 156

Koo, Minjung, 120

Langer, Ellen, 113

Latané, Bibb, 199

Learned Optimism (Seligman), 88

Lepper, Mark, 162

Lewis, C. S., 208

Likelihood to Recommend score,
   192

Limbic centers, 60, 181

Little, Brian, 74

Losada, Marcial, 51

Losada Line, 51

"Luck Factor, The" (Wiseman), 42

Mad Money (television show), 161

Maharam, Lewis, 108

Malandro, Loretta, 53, 54
Mangan, Peter, 136
Map hijackers, 79–85, 105–106
Mapping (*see* Mental cartography)
Marsden, Paul, 192
Mayer, John D., 5
McNamara, Timothy, 86
Mealtimes, 44–45, 62
Meaning markers, xvii, 64–85,
   104–105
Meaning portfolio, diversifying,
   78–79, 104–105
Medical school syndrome, 188–189
Mental cartography, 16, 17,
   64–106
   checking and updating map,
      101–104, 106
   diversifying meaning portfolio,
      78–79, 104–105
   map hijackers, 79–85, 105–106
   map success routes before escape
      routes, 67–68, 96–101, 106
   meaning markers, xvii, 64–85,
      104–105
   reorienting mental map for
      success, 67, 85–95, 105
Microsoft, 119
Military, 21–24, 109–111, 217–219
Millionaire Mind, The (Stanley), 5
Mindshare Technologies, 66
Mirror neurons, 192, 226
Mood and Anxiety Symptom
   Questionnaire (MASQ), 32
Morgan Stanley Smith Barney, 35,
   78, 177
Most valuable reality, pursuing, 27,
   46–60
Multiple realities (*see* Reality
   architecture)
Multiple sclerosis (MS), 210–211

National Association of Safety
   Professionals, 98
National Football League, 172
National Institute on Drug Abuse,
   Johns Hopkins University,
   81
National MS Society, xiv, 130, 210,
   221
Nature, 70
N-effect, 125–127
Negative reality (*see* Mental
   cartography; Noise canceling;
   Positive inception; Reality
   architecture; X-spot theory)
New England Journal of Medicine,
   191
Newton, Isaac, 228
New York Times, 102, 172
New York University, 141
Nicaragua, 102
Nine Dots Test, 54–55
Nisbett, Richard, 58–59
Noise
   defined, 149
   four criteria of, 18, 156–158
Noise canceling, xvii, 16, 18,
   146–181
   canceling internal noise, 148,
      169–180
   recognizing signal, 148–159
   stopping addiction to noise, 148,
      159–169
Nolan, Christopher, 182
Nonverbal communication, 205,
   206
No-venting rule, 195, 196

Obama, Barack, 62
Ochsner Health System, 188–192,
   194, 195

Office, The (television show), 188, 209

Office Space (film), 209

Ohlsson, Stellan, 55

Optimism, 13, 14, 181

Parker, Sharon, 60

Pastora, Edén, 102

Paulson, John, 150–151

Pearl Harbor, 151–152

Perspective, 36–46, 57

Pessimism, 98–99, 152, 169–172

Pfizer study, 76–77

Philadelphia Marathon, 108

Poincaré, Henri, 227–231

Pong video game, 123–124

Pool, Ithiel de Sola, 165

Positive genius, (*see also* Mental cartography; Noise canceling; Positive inception; Reality architecture; X-spot theory)

defined, xvii

Positive habits, 87–88

Positive inception, xvii, 11, 16, 18–19, 182–225

shared narrative creation, 183, 185–186, 209–222, 225

social script rewriting, 183, 184–185, 198–209, 222

success franchising, 18, 183, 184, 186–197, 222, 223–224

Positive reality (*see* Mental cartography; Noise canceling; Positive inception; Reality architecture; X-spot theory)

Positivity (Frederickson), 99–100

Positivity ratio, 17, 50–53, 63

Post-traumatic growth, 32

Power lead, 19, 185, 202–203, 224

Prefrontal cortex, 60, 82

Press Ganey, 192

Preston, Kenzie, 81

Proceedings of the Royal Society of London, 156

Procrastination, 82–83, 132

Proffitt, Dennis, 15, 130

Pygmalion effect, 113

Quality of Life Inventory, 32

Reality architecture, xvii, 16–17, 21–63

adding vantage points, 26–27, 36–46

pursuing most valuable reality, 27, 46–60

recognizing alternative realities, 25–36

Renaissance, 231

Renew Data Corporation, 155

Restylane, 204

Reward programs, 116–119

Ripple effect, happiness and, 184

Ritz-Carlton hotels, 189

Romantic relationships, positivity ratio and, 52

Rosenthal, Robert, 113

Rowling, J. K., 150

Salovey, Peter, 5, 6, 13, 31

SAT scores, 5, 126

Science and Method (Poincaré), 228

Seligman, Martin, 88

70 percent mark, 112, 119, 143, 145

Shakespeare, William, 173

Shared narrative creation, 183, 185–186, 209–222, 225

Shaw, David, 141

Sheldon, Amy, 86

Short, James, 164, 165
Short History of Nearly Everything, A (Bryson), 186
Signal
  defined, 149
  recognizing, 148–159
  -to-noise ratio, 155, 159–162
Sleep, 43–44, 45, 62–63
Smiling, 189–191, 194–196, 206, 224, 227
Social contagion, 186–197
Social intelligence, 6, 8–10, 16, 27, 55, 152
Social Intelligence (Gardner), 6
Social script rewriting, 183, 184–185, 198–209, 222
Social support, 42, 53, 93–95, 97
Sports, 107–108, 125, 128–129, 172
Stanford University, 32, 86, 162
Stanley, Thomas J., 5
Stock market crash (1929), 151
Stress
  negative effects of, 26
  perception of, 13
  performance enhancement and, 31–34
  research on, 31–33
  rethinking, 29–34, 46, 61, 97
  side effects of, 30–31
Stress Mindset Measure (SMM), 32
Success
  prediction of, 4–5, 9–11
  prism of, 7–11, 35, 61, 255
  reorienting mental map for, 67, 85–95, 105
Success accelerants, 15–17 (*see also* X-spot theory)

Success franchising, 18, 183, 184, 186–197, 222, 223–224
Sugovic, Mila, 124
Suicide, 65

Tang, Yung-Tai, 207
Target (proximity), zooming in on, 112, 113–121, 143
Target size (likelihood of success), magnifying, 112, 121–130, 143
Taylor, Jamie, 141
Telomeres, 178
10/5 Way, 184, 189–191, 194, 206, 224
Test takers, number in room of, 126–127
Thales of Miletus, 7–8
Thinker, the (prefrontal cortex), 82
"Three men make a tiger" (Chinese proverb), 200
Thrust (energy required), recalculating, 112–113, 130–143
Time, perceptions of, 134–138
Time Paradox, The (Zimbardo), 134
Tone of voice, 205
Tor, Avishalom, 126
Troffea, Frau, 193
Tupac, 173
Twenty-Second Rule, 135

UBS, 13, 26, 28, 31, 167
  Rethinking Stress study, 46
University of California, Berkeley, 201–202
University of Chicago, 178
University of Denver, 93
University of Illinois, 55
University of New Hampshire, 5
University of New South Wales, 60

University of North Carolina, 51
University of Pennsylvania, 202
University of San Diego, 164
University of Sheffield, 60
University of Sussex, 192
University of Virginia, 15, 130
University of Wisconsin, 194
User Experience Network, 131–132

Vanderbilt University, 86
Vantage points, 26–27, 36–46, 48,
    60, 63
Venetian Arsenal, 187
Vision boarding, 141–142
Visualization, 142, 145
Vohs, Kathleen, 132
Voice, tone of, 205
Volvo, 214

W Blog, 154
Wall Street Journal, 172
Walmart, xiv–xv, 189, 211–212,
    219, 221
Walton, Sam, 189
Weatherford, Steve, 172
Weather predictions, 157–158
Weinschenk, Susan, 131–132
Weisbuch, Max, 93
Wharton Business School, 72, 185,
    213
Winfrey, Oprah, 150
Wire, The (HBO series), 80–81

Wiseman, Richard, 42
Witt, Jessica, 124
WMD fiasco, 200
Woods, Tiger, 150
Work altruists and isolators, 94–95
Work Performance Scale, 32
World War II, 151–152
Worry and anxiety, 169, 171–181
Worst-case scenarios, 97–98
Wrzesniewski, Amy, 72

X-spot theory, xvii, 16, 17, 107–145
    magnifying target size (likelihood
        of success), 112, 121–130, 143
    recalculating thrust (energy
        required), 112–113, 130–143
    zooming in on target (proximity),
        112, 113–121, 143

Yale Center for British Arts, 38
Yale School of Management, 205
Yale School of Medicine, 38–40
Yale University, 5, 13, 26, 31, 72
Yap, Mari, 219, 220
Young Presidents' Organization
    (YPO), 54, 59

Zappos, 206, 221–222
Zhaung, Michael, 161
Zimbardo, Philip, 134
Zorro Circle, 164
Zuckerman, Gregory, 150

International bestseller!

A must-read for everyone trying to excel in a world of increasing workloads, stress, and negativity. Happiness is not the belief that we don't need to change; it is the realization that we can.

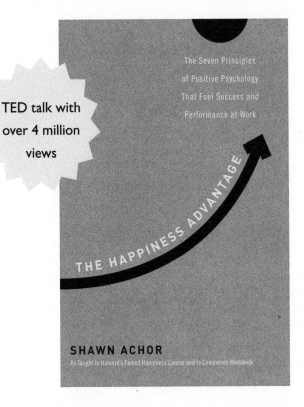

TED talk with over 4 million views

The Seven Principles of Positive Psychology That Fuel Success and Performance at Work

THE HAPPINESS ADVANTAGE

SHAWN ACHOR

As Taught in Harvard's Famed Happiness Course and to Companies Worldwide

"Shawn Achor is funny, self-deprecating, and devastating to my notions of what his field is all about."
—*Boston Globe*

"*The Happiness Advantage* reveals the most important discoveries coming out of modern psychology."
—Ram Brafman, bestselling coauthor of *Sway* and *Click*